BMOL 10030

BMOL 10030

Compiled from:

Pharmacology for Nurses: A Pathophysiologic Approach
Fourth Edition
Adams, Holland and Urban

Microbiology: An Introduction
Eleventh Edition
Tortora, Funke and Case

Introductory Pathophysiology: For Nursing and Healthcare Professionals
First Edition
Mark Zelman, Elaine Tompary, Jill Raymond, Paul Holdaway, Mary Lou Mulvihill,
Martin Steggall and Maria Dingle

Biology: Science for Life with Physiology
Fourth Edition
C. Belk and V. Borden Maier

Harlow, England • London • New York • Boston • San Francisco • Toronto • Sydney • Auckland • Singapore • Hong Kong
Tokyo • Seoul • Taipei • New Delhi • Cape Town • Sao Paulo • Mexico City • Madrid • Amsterdam • Munich • Paris • Milan

Pearson Education Limited
Edinburgh Gate
Harlow
Essex CM20 2JE

And associated companies throughout the world

Visit us on the World Wide Web at:
www.pearson.com/uk

© Pearson Education Limited 2014

Compiled from:

Pharmacology for Nurses: A Pathophysiologic Approach
Fourth Edition
Adams, Holland and Urban
ISBN 978-1-292-02787-6
© Pearson Education Limited 2014

Microbiology: An Introduction
Eleventh Edition
Tortora, Funke and Case
ISBN 978-1-292-02630-5
© Pearson Education Limited 2014

Introductory Pathophysiology: For Nursing and Healthcare Professionals
First Edition
Mark Zelman, Elaine Tompary, Jill Raymond, Paul Holdaway, Mary Lou Mulvihill,
Martin Steggall and Maria Dingle
ISBN 978-0-273-72386-8
© Pearson Education Limited 2011

Biology: Science for Life with Physiology
Fourth Edition
C. Belk and V. Borden Maier
ISBN 978-1-292-02327-4
© Pearson Education Limited 2014

ISBN 978-1-78434-665-2

Printed and bound in Great Britain by Bell and Bain Ltd, Glasgow

Contents

Pharmacokinetics

Pharmacokinetics

Learning Outcomes

After reading this chapter, the student should be able to:

1. Explain the applications of pharmacokinetics to clinical practice.
2. Identify the four components of pharmacokinetics.
3. Explain how substances travel across plasma membranes.
4. Discuss factors affecting drug absorption.
5. Explain the metabolism of drugs and its applications to pharmacotherapy.
6. Discuss how drugs are distributed throughout the body.
7. Describe how plasma proteins affect drug distribution.
8. Identify major processes by which drugs are excreted.
9. Explain how enterohepatic recirculation might affect drug activity.
10. Explain the applications of a drug's onset, peak, and plasma half-life ($t_{1/2}$) to duration of pharmacotherapy.
11. Explain how a drug reaches and maintains its therapeutic range in the plasma.
12. Differentiate between loading and maintenance doses.

Key Terms

absorption
affinity
blood–brain barrier
conjugates
dissolution
distribution
drug–protein complex
duration of drug action
enterohepatic recirculation

enzyme induction
excretion
fetal–placental barrier
first-pass effect
hepatic microsomal enzyme system
loading dose
maintenance dose
metabolism
minimum effective concentration

onset of drug action
peak plasma level
pharmacokinetics
plasma half-life ($t_{1/2}$)
prodrugs
therapeutic range
toxic concentration

Weblink: Nursing Times.Net Article: Pharmacokinetics

Medications are given to achieve a desirable effect. To produce this effect, the drug must reach its target cells. For some medications, such as topical agents used to treat superficial skin conditions, this is a relatively simple task. For others, however, the process of reaching target cells in sufficient quantities to produce a physiological change may be challenging. Drugs are exposed to a myriad of different barriers and destructive processes after they enter the body. The purpose of this chapter is to examine factors that act on the drug as it travels to reach its target cells.

1 Pharmacokinetics: How the Body Handles Medications

The term **pharmacokinetics** is derived from the root words *pharmaco,* which means "medicine," and *kinetics,* which means "movement or motion." Pharmacokinetics is thus the study of drug movement throughout the body. In practical terms, it describes how the body deals with medications. Pharmacokinetics is a core subject in pharmacology, and a firm grasp of this topic allows the nurse to better understand and predict the actions and side effects of medications in patients.

Drugs face numerous obstacles in reaching their target cells. For most medications, the greatest barrier is crossing the many membranes that separate the drug from its target cells. A drug taken by mouth, for example, must cross the plasma membranes of the mucosal cells of the gastrointestinal tract and the capillary endothelial cells to enter the bloodstream. To leave the bloodstream, the drug must again cross capillary cells, travel through the interstitial fluid, and depending on the mechanism of action, the drug may also need to enter target cells and cellular organelles such as the nucleus, which are surrounded by additional membranes. These are examples of just some of the barriers that a drug must successfully penetrate before it can produce a response.

While moving toward target cells and passing through the various membranes, drugs are subjected to numerous physiological processes. For medications given by the enteral route, stomach acid and digestive enzymes often act to break down the drug molecules. Enzymes in the liver and other organs may chemically change the drug molecule to make it less active. If the drug is seen as foreign by the body, phagocytes may attempt to remove it, or an immune response may be triggered. The kidneys, large intestine, and other organs attempt to excrete the medication from the body.

These examples illustrate pharmacokinetic processes: *how the body handles medications.* The many processes of pharmacokinetics are grouped into four categories:

absorption, distribution, metabolism, and excretion, as illustrated in ▲ Figure 1.

2 The Passage of Drugs Through Plasma Membranes

Pharmacokinetic variables depend on the ability of a drug to cross plasma membranes. With few exceptions, drugs must penetrate these membranes to produce their effects. Like other chemicals, drugs primarily use two processes to cross body membranes:

1. *Active transport.* This is movement of a chemical against a concentration or electrochemical gradient; *cotransport* involves the movement of two or more chemicals across the membrane.

2. *Diffusion or passive transport.* This is movement of a chemical from an area of higher concentration to an area of lower concentration.

Plasma membranes consist of a lipid bilayer, with proteins and other molecules interspersed in the membrane. This lipophilic membrane is relatively impermeable to large molecules, ions, and polar molecules. These physical characteristics have direct application to pharmacokinetics. For example, drug molecules that are small, nonionized, and lipid soluble will usually pass through plasma membranes by simple diffusion and more easily reach their target cells. Small water-soluble agents such as urea, alcohol, and water can enter through pores in the plasma membrane. Large molecules, ionized drugs, and water-soluble agents, however, will have more difficulty crossing plasma membranes. These agents may use other means to gain entry, such as protein carriers or active transport.

3 Absorption of Medications

Absorption is a process involving the movement of a substance from its site of administration, across body membranes, to circulating fluids. Drugs may be absorbed across the skin and associated mucous membranes, or they may move across membranes that line the gastrointestinal (GI) or respiratory tract. Most drugs, with the exception of a few topical medications, intestinal anti-infectives, and some radiologic contrast agents, must be absorbed to produce an effect.

Absorption is the primary pharmacokinetic factor determining the length of time it takes a drug to produce its effect. In order for a drug to be absorbed it must dissolve. The rate of **dissolution** determines how quickly the drug disintegrates and disperses into simpler forms; therefore, drug formulation is an important factor of bioavailability. In general, the more rapid the dissolution, the faster the drug absorption and the faster the onset of drug action. For example, famotidine (Pepcid RPD) administered as an orally disintegrating tablet dissolves within seconds and after being swallowed is delivered to the stomach where it blocks acid secretion from the stomach, thereby treating

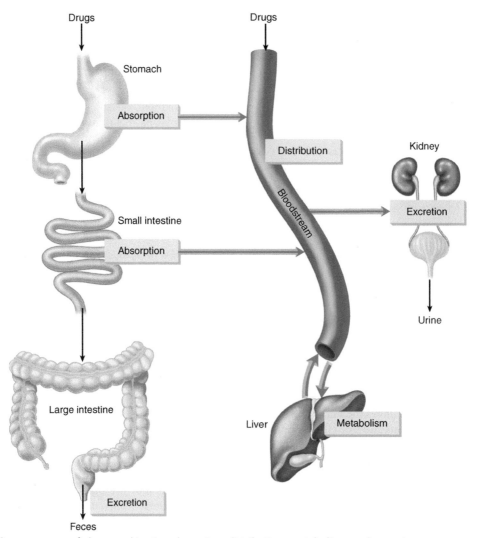

▲ *Figure 1* The four processes of pharmacokinetics: absorption, distribution, metabolism, and excretion

conditions of excessive acid secretion. At the other extreme some drugs have shown good clinical response as slowly dissolving drugs such as liothyronine sodium (T3) and thyroxine (T4) administered for resolution of hypothyroid symptoms. In some instances it is advantageous for a drug to disperse rapidly. In other cases, it is better for the drug to be released slowly where the effects are more prolonged for positive therapeutic benefit.

Absorption is conditional on many factors. Drugs in elixir or syrup formulations are absorbed faster than tablets or capsules. Drugs administered in high doses are generally absorbed more quickly and have a more rapid onset of action than those given in low concentrations. The speed of digestive motility, surface area, pH, lipid solubility, exposure to enzymes in the digestive tract, and blood flow to the site of drug administration also affect absorption. Because drugs administered IV directly enter the bloodstream, absorption to the tissues after the infusion is very rapid. IM medications take longer to absorb. Other factors

that influence the absorption of medications include the following:

- Drug formulation and dose.
- Size of the drug molecule.
- Surface area of the absorptive site.
- Digestive motility or blood flow.
- Lipid solubility.
- Degree of ionization.
- Acidity or alkalinity (pH).
- Interactions with food and other medications.

The degree of ionization of a drug also affects its absorption. A drug's ability to become ionized depends on the surrounding pH. Aspirin provides an excellent example of the effects of ionization on absorption, as depicted in ▲ Figure 2. In the acid environment of the stomach, aspirin is in its *nonionized* form and thus readily absorbed

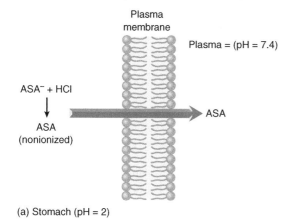

(a) Stomach (pH = 2)

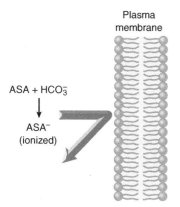

(b) Small intestine (pH = 8)

▲ *Figure 2* Effect of pH on drug absorption: (a) a weak acid such as aspirin (ASA) is in a nonionized form in an acidic environment and absorption occurs; (b) in a basic environment, aspirin is mostly in an ionized form and absorption is prevented

and distributed by the bloodstream. As aspirin enters the alkaline environment of the small intestine, however, it becomes *ionized*. In its ionized form, aspirin is not as likely to be absorbed and distributed to target cells. Unlike acidic drugs, medications that are weakly basic are in their nonionized form in an alkaline environment; therefore, basic drugs are absorbed and distributed better in alkaline environments such as in the small intestine. The pH of the local environment directly influences drug absorption through its ability to ionize the drug. In simplest terms, it may help the nurse to remember that acids are absorbed in acids, and bases are absorbed in bases.

Drug–drug or food–drug interactions may influence absorption. Many examples of these interactions have been discovered. For example, administering tetracyclines with food or drugs containing calcium, iron, or magnesium can significantly delay absorption of the antibiotic. High-fat meals can slow stomach motility significantly and delay the absorption of oral medications taken with the meal. Dietary supplements may also affect absorption. Common ingredients in herbal weight-loss products such as aloe leaf, guar gum, senna, and yellow dock exert a laxative effect that may decrease intestinal transit time and reduce drug

absorption. Nurses must be aware of drug interactions and advise patients to avoid known combinations of foods and medications that significantly affect drug action.

4 Distribution of Medications

Distribution involves the transport of drugs throughout the body. The simplest factor determining distribution is the amount of blood flow to body tissues. The heart, liver, kidneys, and brain receive the most blood supply. Skin, bone, and adipose tissue receive a lower blood supply; therefore, it is more difficult to deliver high concentrations of drugs to these areas.

The physical properties of the drug greatly influence how it moves throughout the body after administration. Lipid solubility is an important characteristic, because it determines how quickly a drug is absorbed, mixes within the bloodstream, crosses membranes, and becomes localized in body tissues. Lipid-soluble agents are not limited by the barriers that normally stop water-soluble drugs; thus, they are more completely distributed to body tissues.

Some tissues have the ability to accumulate and store drugs after absorption. The bone marrow, teeth, eyes, and adipose tissue have an especially high **affinity,** or attraction, for certain medications. Examples of agents that are attracted to adipose tissue are thiopental (Pentothal), diazepam (Valium), and lipid-soluble vitamins. Tetracycline binds to calcium salts and accumulates in the bones and teeth. Once stored in tissues, drugs may remain in the body for many months and are released very slowly back to the circulation.

Not all drug molecules in the plasma will reach their target cells, because many drugs bind reversibly to plasma proteins, particularly albumin, to form **drug–protein complexes.** Drug–protein complexes are too large to cross capillary membranes; thus, the drug is not available for distribution to body tissues. Drugs bound to proteins circulate in the plasma until they are released or displaced from the drug–protein complex. Only unbound (free) drugs can reach their target cells or be excreted by the kidneys. This concept is illustrated in ▲ Figure 3. Some drugs, such as the anticoagulant warfarin (Coumadin), are highly bound; 99% of the drug in the plasma is bound in drug–protein complexes and is unavailable to reach target cells.

Drugs and other chemicals compete with one another for plasma protein–binding sites, and some agents have a greater affinity for these binding sites than other agents. Drug–drug and drug–food interactions may occur when one drug displaces another from plasma proteins. The displaced medication can immediately reach high levels in the bloodstream and produce adverse effects. Drugs such as aspirin or valproates, for example, displace Coumadin from the drug–protein complex, thus raising blood levels of free Coumadin and dramatically enhancing the risk of hemorrhage. Most drug guides give the percentage of medication bound to plasma proteins; when giving multiple drugs that are highly bound, the nurse should monitor the patient closely for adverse effects.

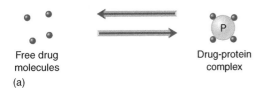

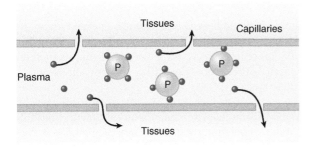

▲ *Figure 3* Plasma protein binding and drug availability: (a) drug exists in a free state or bound to plasma protein; (b) drug–protein complexes are too large to cross membranes

There are several types of drug–drug interactions. These include the following:

- *Addition.* The action of drugs taken together as a *total.*
- *Synergism.* The action of drugs resulting in a *potentiated* (more than total) effect.
- *Antagonism.* Drugs taken together with *blocked* or *opposite* effects.
- *Displacement.* When drugs are taken together, one drug may shift another drug at a nonspecific protein-binding site (e.g., plasma albumin), thereby altering the desired effect.

The brain and placenta possess special anatomic barriers that prevent many chemicals and medications from entering. These barriers are referred to as the **blood–brain barrier** and **fetal–placental barrier.** Some medications such as sedatives, antianxiety agents, and anticonvulsants readily cross the blood–brain barrier to produce actions in the central nervous system. In contrast, most antitumor medications do not easily cross this barrier, making brain cancers difficult to treat.

The fetal–placental barrier serves an important protective function, because it prevents potentially harmful substances from passing from the mother's bloodstream to the fetus. Substances such as alcohol, cocaine, caffeine, and certain prescription medications, however, easily cross the placental barrier and can potentially harm the fetus. Consequently, a patient who is pregnant should not take any prescription medication, over-the-counter (OTC) drug, or herbal therapy without first consulting with a health care provider. The health care provider should always question female patients in the childbearing years regarding their pregnancy status before prescribing a drug.

5 Metabolism of Medications

Metabolism, also called *biotransformation,* is the process of chemically converting a drug to a form that is usually more easily removed from the body. Metabolism involves complex biochemical pathways and reactions that alter drugs, nutrients, vitamins, and minerals. The liver is the primary site of drug metabolism, although the kidneys and cells of the intestinal tract also have high metabolic rates.

Medications undergo many types of biochemical reactions as they pass through the liver, including hydrolysis, oxidation, and reduction. During metabolism, the addition of side chains, known as **conjugates,** makes drugs more water soluble and more easily excreted by the kidneys.

Most metabolism in the liver is accomplished by the **hepatic microsomal enzyme system.** This enzyme complex is sometimes called the P-450 system, named after cytochrome P-450 (CYP-450), which is a key component of the system. As they relate to pharmacotherapy, the primary actions of the hepatic microsomal enzymes are to inactivate drugs and accelerate their excretion. In some cases, however, metabolism can produce a chemical alteration that makes the resulting molecule *more* active than the original. For example, the narcotic analgesic codeine undergoes biotransformation to morphine, which has significantly greater ability to relieve pain. In fact, some agents, known as **prodrugs,** have no pharmacologic activity unless they are first metabolized to their active form by the body. Examples of prodrugs include benazepril (Lotensin) and losartan (Cozaar).

Changes in the function of the hepatic microsomal enzymes can significantly affect drug metabolism. A few drugs have the ability to increase metabolic activity in the liver, a process called **enzyme induction.** For example, phenobarbital causes the liver to synthesize more microsomal enzymes. By doing so, phenobarbital increases the rate of its own metabolism as well as that of other drugs metabolized in the liver. In these patients, higher doses of medication may be required to achieve the optimum therapeutic effect.

Certain patients have decreased hepatic metabolic activity, which may alter drug action. Hepatic enzyme activity is generally reduced in infants and elderly patients; therefore, pediatric and geriatric patients are more sensitive to drug therapy than middle-age patients. Patients with severe liver damage, such as that caused by cirrhosis, will require reductions in drug dosage because of the decreased metabolic activity. Certain genetic disorders have been recognized in which patients lack specific metabolic enzymes; drug dosages in these patients must be adjusted accordingly. The nurse should pay careful attention to laboratory values that may indicate liver disease so that doses may be adjusted.

Metabolism has a number of additional therapeutic consequences. As illustrated in ▲ Figure 4, drugs absorbed after oral administration cross directly into the hepatic portal circulation, which carries blood to the liver before it is distributed to other body tissues. Thus, as blood passes through the liver circulation, some drugs can be completely metabolized to an inactive form before they ever reach the

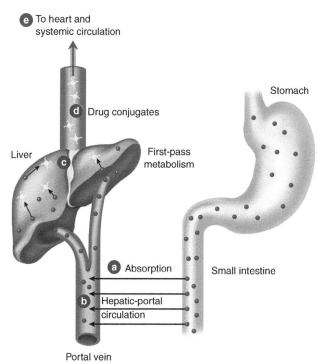

e To heart and systemic circulation

d Drug conjugates

Liver

c

First-pass metabolism

Stomach

a Absorption

b Hepatic-portal circulation

Small intestine

Portal vein

▲ *Figure 4* First-pass effect: (a) drugs are absorbed; (b) drugs enter hepatic portal circulation and go directly to liver; (c) hepatic microsomal enzymes metabolize drugs to inactive forms; (d) drug conjugates, leaving liver; (e) drug is distributed to general circulation

general circulation. This **first-pass effect** is an important mechanism, since a large number of oral drugs are rendered inactive by hepatic metabolic reactions. Alternative routes of delivery that bypass the first-pass effect (e.g., sublingual, rectal, or parenteral routes) may need consideration for these drugs.

6 Excretion of Medications

Drugs are removed from the body by the process of **excretion.** The rate at which medications are excreted determines the concentration of the drugs in the bloodstream and tissues. This is important because the concentration of drugs in the bloodstream determines their duration of action. Pathologic states, such as liver disease or renal failure, often increase the duration of drug action in the body because they interfere with natural excretion mechanisms. Dosing regimens must be carefully adjusted in these patients.

Although drugs are eliminated from the body by numerous organs and tissues, the primary site of excretion is the kidney. In an average-size person, approximately 180 L of blood is filtered by the kidneys each day. Free drugs, water-soluble agents, electrolytes, and small molecules are easily filtered at the glomerulus. Proteins, blood cells, conjugates, and drug–protein complexes are not filtered because of their large size.

After filtration at the renal corpuscle, chemicals and drugs are subjected to the process of reabsorption in the

renal tubule. Mechanisms of reabsorption are the same as absorption elsewhere in the body. Nonionized and lipid-soluble drugs cross renal tubular membranes easily and return to the circulation; ionized and water-soluble drugs generally remain in the filtrate for excretion.

There are many factors that can affect drug excretion. These include the following:

- Liver or kidney impairment.
- Blood flow.
- Degree of ionization.
- Lipid solubility.
- Drug–protein complexes.
- Metabolic activity.
- Acidity or alkalinity (pH).
- Respiratory, glandular or biliary activity.

Drug–protein complexes and substances too large to be filtered at the glomerulus are sometimes secreted into the distal tubule of the nephron. For example, only 10% of a dose of penicillin G is filtered at the glomerulus; 90% is secreted into the renal tubule. As with metabolic enzyme activity, secretion mechanisms are less active in infants and older adults.

Certain drugs may be excreted more quickly if the pH of the filtrate changes. Weak acids such as aspirin are excreted faster when the filtrate is slightly alkaline, because aspirin is ionized in an alkaline environment, and the drug will remain in the filtrate and be excreted in the urine. Weakly basic drugs such as diazepam (Valium) are excreted faster with a slightly acidic filtrate, because they are ionized in this environment. This relationship between pH and drug excretion can be used to advantage in critical care situations. To speed the renal excretion of acidic drugs such as aspirin in an overdosed patient, an order may be written to administer sodium bicarbonate. Sodium bicarbonate will make the urine more basic, which ionizes more aspirin, causing it to be excreted more readily. The excretion of diazepam, on the other hand, can be enhanced by giving ammonium chloride. This will acidify the filtrate and increase the excretion of diazepam.

Impairment of kidney function can dramatically affect pharmacokinetics. Patients with renal failure will have diminished ability to excrete medications and may retain drugs for an extended time. Doses for these patients must be reduced to avoid drug toxicity. Because small to moderate changes in renal status can cause rapid increases in serum drug levels, the nurse must constantly monitor kidney function in patients receiving drugs that may be nephrotoxic (low margin of safety).

Drugs that can easily be changed into a gaseous form are especially suited for excretion by the respiratory system. The rate of respiratory excretion is dependent on factors that affect gas exchange, including diffusion, gas solubility, and pulmonary blood flow. The elimination of volatile anesthetics following surgery is primarily dependent on respiratory activity—the faster the respiratory rate, the

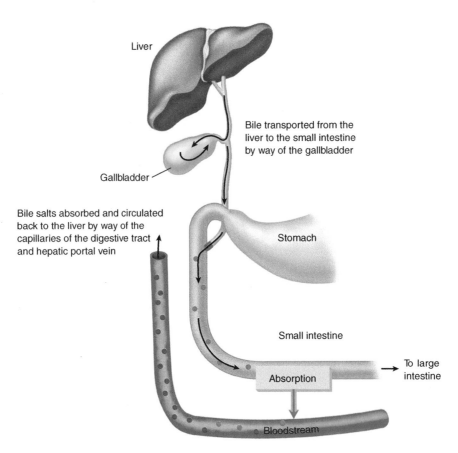

Liver

Bile transported from the liver to the small intestine by way of the gallbladder

Gallbladder

Bile salts absorbed and circulated back to the liver by way of the capillaries of the digestive tract and hepatic portal vein

Stomach

Small intestine

Absorption

To large intestine

Bloodstream

▲ *Figure 5* Enterohepatic recirculation

greater the excretion. Conversely, the respiratory removal of water-soluble agents such as alcohol is more dependent on blood flow to the lungs—the greater the blood flow into lung capillaries, the greater the excretion. In contrast with other methods of excretion, the lungs excrete most drugs in their original nonmetabolized form.

Glandular activity is another elimination mechanism. Water-soluble drugs may be secreted into the saliva, sweat, or breast milk. The odd taste that patients sometimes experience when given IV drugs is an example of the secretion of agents into the saliva. Another example of glandular excretion is the garlic smell that can be detected when standing next to a perspiring person who has recently eaten garlic. Excretion into breast milk is of considerable importance for basic drugs such as morphine or codeine, because these can achieve high concentrations and potentially affect the nursing infant. Nursing mothers should always check with their health care provider before taking any prescription medication, OTC drug, or herbal supplement.

Some drugs are secreted in the bile, a process known as *biliary excretion*. In many cases, drugs secreted into bile will enter the duodenum and eventually leave the body in the feces. However, most bile is circulated back to the liver by **enterohepatic recirculation,** as illustrated in ▲ Figure 5. A

percentage of the drug may be recirculated numerous times with the bile. Biliary reabsorption is extremely influential in prolonging the activity of cardiac glycosides, some antibiotics, and phenothiazines. Recirculated drugs are ultimately metabolized by the liver and excreted by the kidneys. Recirculation and elimination of drugs through biliary excretion may continue for several weeks after therapy has been discontinued.

7 Drug Plasma Concentration and Therapeutic Response

The therapeutic response of most drugs is directly related to their level in the plasma. Although the concentration of the medication at its *target tissue* is more predictive of drug action, this quantity is impossible to measure in most cases. For example, it is possible to conduct a laboratory test that measures the serum level of the drug lithium carbonate (Eskalith) by taking a blood sample; it is a far different matter to measure the quantity of this drug in neurons within the central nervous system (CNS). Indeed, it is common practice for nurses to monitor the plasma levels of certain drugs that have a low safety profile.

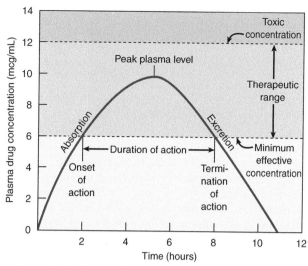

▲ *Figure 6* Single-dose drug administration: pharmacokinetic values for this drug are as follows: onset of action = 2 hours; duration of action = 6 hours; termination of action = 8 hours after administration; peak plasma concentration = 10 mcg/mL; time to peak drug effect = 5 hours; $t_{1/2}$ = 4 hours

Several important pharmacokinetic principles can be illustrated by measuring the serum level of a drug following a single-dose administration. These pharmacokinetic values are shown graphically in ▲ Figure 6. This figure demonstrates two plasma drug levels. First is the **minimum effective concentration,** the amount of drug required to produce a therapeutic effect. Second is the **toxic concentration,** the level of drug that will result in serious adverse effects. The plasma drug concentration *between* the minimum effective concentration and the toxic concentration is called the **therapeutic range** of the drug. These values have great clinical significance. For example, if the patient has a severe headache and is given half of an aspirin tablet, the plasma level will remain below the minimum effective concentration, and the patient will not experience pain relief. Two or three tablets will increase the plasma level of aspirin into the therapeutic range, and the pain will subside. Taking six or more tablets may result in adverse effects, such as GI bleeding or tinnitus. For each drug administered, the nurse's goal is to keep its plasma concentration in the therapeutic range. For some drugs, the therapeutic range is quite wide; for other medications, the difference between a minimum effective dose and a toxic dose may be dangerously narrow.

8 Onset, Peak Levels, and Duration of Drug Action

Onset of drug action represents the amount of time it takes to produce a therapeutic effect after drug administration. Factors that affect drug onset may be many, depending on numerous pharmacokinetic variables. As the drug is absorbed and then begins to circulate throughout the body, the level of medication reaches its peak. Thus, the **peak plasma level** occurs when the medication has reached its highest concentration in the bloodstream. It should be mentioned that depending on accessibility of medications

to their targets, peak drug levels are not necessarily associated with optimal therapeutic effect. In addition, multiple doses of medication may be necessary to reach therapeutic drug levels. **Duration of drug action** is the amount of time it takes for a drug to maintain its desired effect until *termination* of action. Many variables can affect the duration of drug action. These include the following:

- Drug concentration (amount of drug given).
- Dosage (how often a drug is given or scheduled).
- Route of drug administration (oral, parenteral, or topical).
- Drug–food interactions.
- Drug–supplement interactions.
- Drug–herbal interactions.
- Drug–drug interactions.

The most common description of a drug's duration of action is its **plasma half-life** $(t_{1/2})$, defined as the length of time required for the plasma concentration of a medication to decrease by one-half after administration. Some drugs have a half-life of only a few minutes, whereas others have a half-life of several hours or days. The longer it takes a medication to be excreted, the greater the half-life. For example, a drug with a $t_{1/2}$ of 10 hours would take longer to be excreted and thus produce a longer effect in the body than a drug with a $t_{1/2}$ of 5 hours.

The plasma half-life of a drug is an essential pharmacokinetic variable with important clinical applications. Drugs with relatively short half-lives, such as aspirin ($t_{1/2}$ = 15 to 20 minutes), must be given every 3 to 4 hours. Drugs with longer half-lives, such as felodipine (Plendil) ($t_{1/2}$ = 10 hours), need to be given only once a day. If a patient has extensive renal or hepatic disease, the plasma half-life of a drug will increase, and the drug concentration may reach toxic levels. In these patients, medications must be given less frequently, or the dosages must be reduced.

9 Loading Doses and Maintenance Doses

Few drugs are administered as a single dose. Repeated doses result in an accumulation of drug in the bloodstream, as shown in ▲ Figure 7. Eventually, a plateau will be reached where the level of drug in the plasma is maintained continuously within the therapeutic range. At this level, the amount administered has reached equilibrium with the amount of drug being eliminated, resulting in the distribution of a continuous therapeutic level of drug to body tissues. Theoretically, it takes approximately four half-lives to reach this equilibrium. If the medication is given as a continuous infusion, the plateau can be reached quickly and be maintained with little or no fluctuation in drug plasma levels.

The plateau may be reached faster by administration of loading doses followed by regular maintenance doses. A **loading dose** is a higher amount of drug, often given only once or twice to "prime" the bloodstream with a sufficient level of drug. Before plasma levels can drop back toward zero, intermittent **maintenance doses** are given to keep the plasma drug concentration in the therapeutic range. Although blood levels of the drug fluctuate with this approach, the equilibrium state can be reached almost as

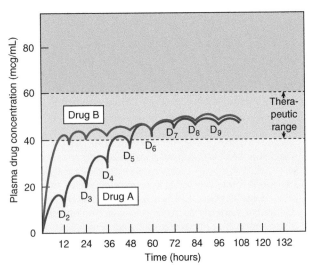

▲ *Figure 7* Multiple-dose drug administration: drug A and drug B are administered every 12 hours; drug B reaches the therapeutic range faster, because the first dose is a loading dose

rapidly as with a continuous infusion. Loading doses are particularly important for drugs with prolonged half-lives and for situations in which it is critical to raise drug plasma levels quickly, as might be the case when administering an antibiotic for a severe infection. In Figure 7, notice that it takes almost five doses (48 hours) before a therapeutic level is reached using a routine dosing schedule. With a loading dose, a therapeutic level is reached within 12 hours.

Chapter Review

KEY CONCEPTS

The numbered key concepts provide a succinct summary of the important points from the corresponding numbered section within the chapter. If any of these points are not clear, refer to the numbered section within the chapter for review.

1 Pharmacokinetics focuses on the movement of drugs throughout the body after they are administered.

2 The physiological properties of plasma membranes determine movement of drugs throughout the body. The four components of pharmacokinetics are absorption, metabolism, distribution, and excretion.

3 Absorption is the process by which a drug moves from the site of administration to the bloodstream. Absorption depends on the size of the drug molecule, its lipid solubility, its degree of ionization, and interactions with food or other medications.

4 Distribution comprises the methods by which drugs are transported throughout the body. Distribution depends on the formation of drug–protein complexes and special barriers such as the placenta or brain barriers.

5 Metabolism is a process that changes a drug's activity and makes it more likely to be excreted. Changes in hepatic metabolism can significantly affect drug action.

6 Excretion processes eliminate drugs from the body. Drugs are primarily excreted by the kidneys but may be excreted into bile, by the lung, or by glandular secretions.

7 The therapeutic response of most drugs depends on their concentration in the plasma. The difference between the minimum effective concentration and the toxic concentration is called the therapeutic range.

8 Onset, peak plasma level, and plasma half-life represent the duration of action for most drugs.

9 Repeated dosing allows a plateau drug plasma level to be reached. Loading doses allow a therapeutic drug level to be reached rapidly.

NCLEX-RN® REVIEW QUESTIONS

1. A patient has an order for a tetracycline antibiotic and has been instructed to avoid taking the medication with foods, beverages, or drugs that contain calcium, iron, or magnesium. The patient takes the antibiotic along with a daily multivitamin, not realizing that the vitamin contains iron. What effect may this have on the tetracycline?
   1. Impaired absorption
   2. Increased distribution
   3. Decreased metabolism
   4. Impaired excretion

2. A patient has a malignant brain tumor. What pharmacokinetic phase may be affected by the presence of the tumor?
   1. Absorption
   2. Distribution
   3. Metabolism
   4. Excretion

3. A patient with cirrhosis of the liver exhibits decreased metabolic activity. This will require what possible changes? (Select all that apply.)
   1. A reduction in the dosage of the drugs
   2. A change in the timing of medication administration
   3. An increased dose of prescribed drugs
   4. Giving all prescribed drugs by intramuscular injection
   5. More frequent monitoring for adverse drug effects.

4. The patient requires a drug that is known to be completely metabolized by the first-pass effect. What change will be needed when this drug is administered?
   1. The drug must be given more frequently.
   2. The drug must be given in higher doses.
   3. The drug must be given in a lipid-soluble form.
   4. The drug must be given by a nonoral route such as parenterally.

5. A patient who is in renal failure may have a diminished capacity to excrete medications. The nurse must assess the patient more frequently for what development?
   1. Increased risk of allergy
   2. Decreased therapeutic drug effects
   3. Increased risk for drug toxicity
   4. Increased absorption of the drug from the intestines

6. What is the rationale for the administration of a loading dose of a drug?
   1. It decreases the number of doses that must be given.
   2. It results in lower dosages being required to achieve therapeutic effects.
   3. It decreases the risk of drug toxicity.
   4. It more rapidly builds plasma drug levels to a plateau level.

CRITICAL THINKING QUESTIONS

1. Describe the types of barriers drugs encounter from the time they are administered until they reach their target cells.

2. Why is the drug's plasma half-life important to nurses?

3. Describe how the excretion process of pharmacokinetics may place patients at risk for adverse drug effects.

4. Explain why drugs metabolized through the first-pass effect might need to be administered by the parenteral route.

Pearson Nursing Student Resources
Find additional review materials at
nursing.pearsonhighered.com
Prepare for success with additional NCLEX®-style practice questions, interactive assignments and activities, Web links, animations and videos, and more!

GLOSSARY

Absorption the process of moving a drug across body membranes

Affinity chemical attraction that impels certain molecules to unite with others to form complexes

Blood–brain barrier anatomical structure that prevents certain substances from gaining access to the brain

Conjugates side chains that, during metabolism, make drugs more water soluble and more easily excreted by the kidney

Dissolution dissolving of a tablet or capsule form of a drug

Distribution the process of transporting drugs through the body

Drug–protein complex drug that has bound reversibly to a plasma protein, particularly albumin, that makes the drug unavailable for distribution to body tissues

Duration of drug action length of time that therapeutic drug actions last

Enterohepatic recirculation recycling of drugs and other substances by the circulation of bile through the intestine and liver

Enzyme induction process in which a drug changes the function of the hepatic microsomal enzymes and increases metabolic activity in the liver

Excretion the process of removing substances from the body

Fetal–placental barrier special anatomical structure that inhibits entry of many chemicals and drugs to the fetus

First-pass effect mechanism whereby drugs are absorbed across the intestinal wall and enter into the hepatic portal circulation

Hepatic microsomal enzyme system as it relates to pharmacotherapy, liver enzymes that inactivate drugs and accelerate their excretion; sometimes called the P-450 system

Loading dose comparatively large dose given at the beginning of treatment to rapidly obtain the therapeutic effect of a drug

Maintenance dose dose that keeps the plasma drug concentration continuously in the therapeutic range

Metabolism total of all biochemical reactions in the body

Minimum effective concentration amount of drug required to produce a therapeutic effect

Onset of drug action time it takes for a therapeutic effect of a drug to appear

Peak plasma level highest amount of drug in the bloodstream

Pharmacokinetics study of how drugs are handled by the body

Plasma half-life ($t_{1/2}$) the length of time required for the plasma concentration of a drug to decrease by half after administration

Prodrug drug that becomes more active after it is metabolized

Therapeutic range the dosage range or serum concentration that achieves the desired drug effects

Toxic concentration level of drug that will result in serious adverse effects

BIBLIOGRAPHY AND REFERENCES

Brunton, L. L., Lazo, J. S., & Parker, K. L. (Eds.). (2006). *Goodman & Gilman's The pharmacological basis of therapeutics* (11th ed.). New York, NY: McGraw-Hill.

Cass, R. T., Brooks, C. D., Havrilla, N. A., Tack, K. J., Borin, M. T., Young, D., & Bruss, J. B. (2011, September 12). Pharmacokinetics and safety of single and multiple doses of ACHN-490 injection administered intravenously in healthy subjects. *Antimicrobial Agents and Chemotherapy.*

Corsonello, A., Pedone, C., & Incalzi, R. A. (2010). Age-related pharmacokinetic and pharmacodynamic changes and related risk of adverse drug reactions. *Current Medicinal Chemistry, 17*(6), 571–584.

Geppetti, P., & Benemei, S. (2009). Pain treatment with opioids: Achieving the minimal effective and the minimal interacting dose. *Clinical Drug Investigation, 29*(Suppl. 1), 3–16.

Jain, R., Chung, S. M., Jain, L., Khurana, M., Lau, S. W., Lee, J. E., . . . Sahajwalla, C. G. (2011, July). Implications of obesity for drug therapy: Limitations and challenges. *Clinical Pharmacology and Therapeutics, 90*(1), 77–89.

Knadler, M. P., Lobo, E., Chappell, J., & Bergstrom, R. (2011, May 1). Duloxetine: Clinical pharmacokinetics and drug interactions. *Clinical Pharmacokinetics, 50*(5), 281–294.

Lampela, P., Hartikainen, S., Sulkava, R., & Huupponen, R. (2007). Adverse drug effects in elderly people—a disparity between clinical examination and adverse effects self-reported by the patient. *European Journal of Clinical Pharmacology, 63,* 979–980.

Liles, A. M. (2011, May–June). Medication considerations for patients with chronic kidney disease who are not yet on dialysis [Review]. *Nephrology Nursing Journal, 38*(3), 263–270.

Parle, J., Roberts, L., Wilson, S., Pattison, H., Roalfe, A., Haque, M. S., . . . Hobbs, F. D. (2010, August). A randomized controlled trial of the effect of thyroxine replacement on cognitive function in community-living elderly subjects with subclinical hypothyroidism: The Birmingham Elderly Thyroid study. *Journal of Clinical Endocrinology and Metabolism, 95*(8), 3623–3632.

Smith, D. A., Obach, R. S., Williams, D. P., & Park, B. K. (2009, April 15). Clearing the MIST (metabolites in safety testing) of time: The impact of duration of administration on drug metabolite toxicity. *Chemico-Biological Interactions, 179*(1), 60–67.

ANSWERS

Answers to NCLEX-RN® Review Questions

1. *Answer: 1*

Rationale: Taking the tetracycline along with an iron-containing drug such as a multivitamin may impair absorption of the tetracycline. Options 2, 3, and 4 are incorrect. Taking the tetracycline along with an iron-containing drug would not decrease, increase, or impair distribution, metabolism, or excretion of the drug. These pharmacokinetic processes occur after absorption has taken place. *Cognitive Level:* Applying. *Nursing Process:* Implementation. *Client Need:* Physiological Integrity.

2. *Answer: 2*

Rationale: To be effective in treating the tumor, the drug must reach its site of action in the brain, the process known as distribution. The blood–brain barrier may be a physical barrier to the distribution of the drug and cause difficulty in treating the tumor. Options 1, 3, and 4 are incorrect. The presence of a tumor in the brain would not affect a drug's absorption, metabolism, or excretion. Other organ systems are involved in these pharmacokinetic processes. *Cognitive Level:* Analyzing. *Nursing Process:* Assessment. *Client Need:* Physiological Integrity.

3. *Answers: 1, 5*

Rationale: The liver is the primary site of drug metabolism. Clients with severe liver damage, such as that caused by cirrhosis, will require reductions in drug dosage because of the decreased metabolic activity. Even with decreased dosage, more frequent monitoring is required to detect adverse drug effects that may be related to impaired metabolism. Options 2, 3, and 4 are incorrect. A change in the timing of administration may still include a drug dosage that is too great for the liver to metabolize and the dosage should not be increased. Giving all drugs by a parenteral route would not change the drug's dosage. *Cognitive Level:* Analyzing. *Nursing Process:* Implementation. *Client Need:* Physiological Integrity.

4. *Answer: 4*

Rationale: Some oral drugs are rendered inactive by hepatic metabolic reactions, during the process known as the first-pass effect. An alternative route, such as parenteral, may need to be used. Options 1, 2, and 3 are incorrect. Giving the drug more frequently, in higher dosages, or in a lipid-soluble form would not alter the complete first-pass effect of metabolism as the drug passes through the liver. *Cognitive Level:* Applying. *Nursing Process:* Implementation. *Client Need:* Physiological Integrity.

5. *Answer: 3*

Rationale: The kidneys are the primary site of excretion. Renal failure increases the duration of the drug's action because of decreased excretion. The client must be assessed for drug toxicity. Options 1, 2, and 4 are incorrect. Decreased excretion of the drug will not increase the risk of allergies, decrease therapeutic drug effects, or increase the absorption of the drug. *Cognitive Level:* Analyzing. *Nursing Process:* Assessment. *Client Need:* Physiological Integrity.

6. *Answer: 4*

Rationale: Giving a loading dose of a drug more rapidly achieves a plateau level in the therapeutic range that may then be continued by maintenance doses. Option 1, 2, and 3 are incorrect. A loading dose will not decrease the number of doses required, decrease the amount of dosage required, or lower the risk of drug toxicity. *Cognitive Level:* Applying. *Nursing Process:* Implementation. *Client Need:* Physiological Integrity.

Answers to Critical Thinking Questions

1. For most medications, the greatest barrier is crossing the many membranes that separate the drug from its target cells. A drug taken by mouth must cross the plasma membranes of the mucosal cells of the gastrointestinal tract and the capillary endothelial cells to enter the bloodstream. To leave the bloodstream, it must again cross capillary cells, travel through interstitial fluid, and enter target cells by passing through their plasma membranes. Depending on the mechanism of action, the drug may also need to enter cellular organelles, such as the nucleus, which are surrounded by additional membranes. While seeking their target cells and attempting to pass through the various membranes, drugs are subjected to numerous physiological substances such as stomach acids and digestive enzymes.

2. The plasma half-life is the time required for the concentration of the medication in the plasma to decrease to half its initial value after administration. This value is important to the nurse because the longer the half-life, the longer it takes the medication to be excreted. The medication will then produce a longer effect in the body. The half-life determines how often a medication will be administered. Renal and hepatic diseases will prolong the half-life of drugs, increasing the potential for toxicity.

3. The process of eliminating drugs from the body most often occurs by excretion through the kidneys. Renal impairment will alter this excretion, placing the patient at risk for adverse drug effects, often drug toxicity. Gaseous forms of drugs are eliminated through respiration; patients with impaired respiratory effort or those with respiratory disease may also experience adverse drug effects. Because water-soluble forms of drugs may be eliminated through breast milk, infants of breast-feeding mothers may be at risk for adverse drug effects if the drug crosses through the milk in large enough quantities.

4. Many oral drugs are rendered inactive by hepatic metabolism as the drug first passes through that system. Alternative routes of delivery that bypass the first-pass effect (sublingual, rectal, or parenteral routes) may need to be considered for these drugs.

Pharmacodynamics

From Chapter 5 of *Pharmacology for Nurses: A Pathophysiologic Approach,* 4th Edition. Michael Adams, Norman Holland, Carol Urban.

Pharmacodynamics

Learning Outcomes

After reading this chapter, the student should be able to:

1. Explain the applications of pharmacodynamics to nursing practice.
2. Discuss how frequency distribution curves may be used to explain how patients respond differently to medications.
3. Explain the importance of the median effective dose (ED_{50}) to nursing practice.
4. Compare and contrast median lethal dose (LD_{50}) and median toxicity dose (TD_{50}).
5. Discuss how a drug's therapeutic index is related to its margin of safety.
6. Explain the significance of the graded dose–response relationship to nursing practice.
7. Compare and contrast the terms *potency* and *efficacy*.
8. Distinguish among an agonist, a partial agonist, and an antagonist.
9. Explain the relationship between receptors and drug action.
10. Explain possible future developments in the field of pharmacogenetics.

Key Terms

agonist
antagonist
efficacy
frequency distribution curve
graded dose–response
idiosyncratic response
median effective dose (ED_{50})

median lethal dose (LD_{50})
median toxicity dose (TD_{50})
nonspecific cellular responses
partial agonist (agonist-antagonist drug)

pharmacodynamics
pharmacogenetics

pharmacogenomics
potency
receptor
second messenger
therapeutic index

In clinical practice, nurses quickly learn that medications do not affect all patients in the same way: A dose that produces a dramatic response in one patient may have no effect on another. In other cases, the differences in response are not easily explained. Despite this patient variability, health care providers must choose optimal doses while avoiding unnecessary adverse effects. This is not an easy task given the wide variation of patient responses within a population. This chapter examines the mechanisms by which drugs affect patients, and how nurses can apply these principles to clinical practice.

1 Pharmacodynamics and Interpatient Variability

The term **pharmacodynamics** comes from the root words *pharmaco*, which means "medicine," and *dynamics*, which means "change." In simplest terms, pharmacodynamics refers to how a medicine *changes* the body. A more complete definition explains pharmacodynamics as the branch of pharmacology concerned with the mechanisms of drug action and the relationships between drug concentration and responses in the body.

Pharmacodynamics has important nursing applications. Health care providers must be able to predict whether a drug will produce a significant change in patients. Although clinicians often begin therapy with average doses taken from a drug guide, intuitive experience often becomes the practical method for determining which doses of medications will be effective in a given patient. Knowledge of therapeutic indexes, dose–response relationships, and drug–receptor interactions will help nurses provide safe and effective treatment.

Interpatient variability in responses to drugs can best be understood by examining a frequency distribution curve. A **frequency distribution curve,** shown in ▲ Figure 1, is a graphical representation of the number of patients responding to a drug action at different doses. Notice the wide range in doses that produced the patient responses shown on the curve. A few patients responded to the drug at very low doses. As the dose was increased, more and more patients responded. Some patients required very high doses to elicit the desired response. The peak of the curve indicates the largest number of patients responding to the drug. The curve does not show the *magnitude* of response, only whether a measurable response occurred among the patients. As an example, think of the given response to an antihypertensive drug as being a reduction of 20 mmHg in systolic blood pressure. A few patients experienced the desired 20-mm reduction at a dose of only 10 mg of drug. A 50-mg dose gave the largest number of patients a 20-mmHg reduction in blood pressure; however, a few

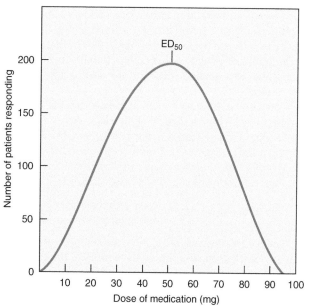

▲ *Figure 1* Frequency distribution curve: interpatient variability in drug response

patients needed as much as 90 mg of drug to produce the same 20-mmHg reduction.

The dose in the middle of the frequency distribution curve represents the drug's **median effective dose (ED$_{50}$).** The ED$_{50}$ is the dose required to produce a specific therapeutic response in 50% of a group of patients. Drug guides sometimes report the ED$_{50}$ as the average or standard dose.

The interpatient variability shown in Figure 1 has important nursing implications. First, nurses should realize that the standard or average dose predicts a satisfactory therapeutic response for only *half* the population. In other words, many patients will require more or less than the average dose for optimum pharmacotherapy. Using the systolic blood pressure example, assume that a large group of patients is given the average dose of 50 mg. Some of these patients will experience toxicity at this level because they needed only 10 mg to achieve blood pressure reduction. Other patients in this group will probably have no reduction in blood pressure. By observing the patient, taking vital signs, and monitoring associated laboratory data, the nurse uses skills that are critical in determining whether the average dose is effective for the patient. It is not enough to simply memorize an average dose for a drug; the nurse must know when and how to request whether doses should be adjusted to obtain the optimum therapeutic response.

2 Therapeutic Index and Drug Safety

Administering a dose that produces an optimum therapeutic response for each individual patient is only one component of effective pharmacotherapy. Nurses must also be able to predict whether the dose is safe for the patient.

Frequency distribution curves can also be used to represent the safety of a drug. The LD_{50} is the dose of drug that will be lethal in 50% of a group of animals. As with ED_{50}, a group of animals will exhibit considerable variability in lethal dose; what may be a nontoxic dose for one animal may be lethal for another.

To examine the safety of a particular drug, the LD_{50} can be compared with the ED_{50}, as shown in ▲ Figure 2a. In this example, 10 mg of drug X is the average *effective* dose, and 40 mg is the average *lethal* dose. The ED_{50} and LD_{50} are used to calculate an important value in pharmacology, a drug's **therapeutic index,** the ratio of a drug's LD_{50} to its ED_{50}.

$$\text{Therapeutic index} = \frac{\text{median lethal dose } LD_{50}}{\text{median effective dose } ED_{50}}$$

The larger the difference between the two doses, the greater the therapeutic index. In Figure 2a, the therapeutic index is 4 (40 mg ÷ 10 mg). Essentially, this means that it would take an error in magnitude of *approximately* 4 times the average dose to be lethal to a patient. Thus, the

therapeutic index is a measure of a drug's safety margin: The higher the value, the safer the medication.

As another example, the therapeutic index of a second drug is shown in ▲ Figure 2b. Drug Z has the same ED_{50} as drug X but shows a different LD_{50}. The therapeutic index for drug Z is only 2 (20 mg ÷ 10 mg). The difference between an effective dose and a lethal dose is very small for drug Z; thus, the drug has a narrow safety margin. The therapeutic index offers the nurse practical information on the safety of a drug and a means to compare one drug with another.

Because the LD_{50} cannot be experimentally determined in humans, the **median toxicity dose (TD_{50})** is a more practical value in a clinical setting. The TD_{50} is the dose that will produce a given toxicity in 50% of a group of patients. The TD_{50} value may be extrapolated from animal data or based on adverse effects recorded in patient clinical trials.

3 The Graded Dose–Response Relationship and Therapeutic Response

In the previous examples, frequency distribution curves were used to graphically visualize patient differences in responses to medications in a *population*. It is also useful to visualize the variability in responses observed within a *single patient*.

The **graded dose–response** relationship is a fundamental concept in pharmacology. The graphical representation of this relationship is called a dose–response curve, as illustrated in ▲ Figure 3. By observing and measuring the patient's response obtained at different doses of the drug, one can explain several important clinical relationships.

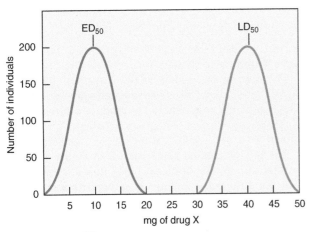

(a) Drug X : TI = $\frac{LD_{50}}{ED_{50}} = \frac{40}{10} = 4$

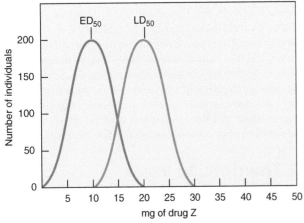

(b) Drug Z : TI = $\frac{LD_{50}}{ED_{50}} = \frac{20}{10} = 2$

▲ *Figure 2* Therapeutic index: (a) drug X has a therapeutic index of 4; (b) drug Z has a therapeutic index of 2

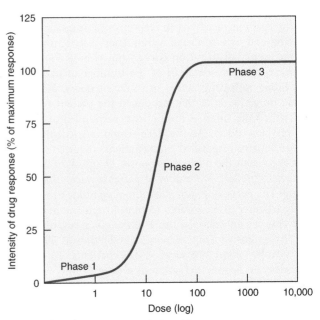

▲ *Figure 3* Dose–response relationship

The three distinct phases of a dose–response curve indicate essential pharmacodynamic principles that have relevance to nursing practice. Phase 1 occurs at the lowest doses. The flatness of this portion of the curve indicates that few target cells have yet been affected by the drug. Phase 2 is the straight-line portion of the curve. This portion often shows a linear relationship between the amount of drug administered and the degree of response obtained from the patient. For example, if the dose is doubled, twice as much response is obtained. This is the most desirable range of doses for pharmacotherapeutics, since giving more drug results in proportionately more effect; a lower drug dose gives less effect. In phase 3, a plateau is reached in which increasing the drug dose produces no additional therapeutic response. This may occur for a number of reasons. One explanation is that all the receptors for the drug are occupied. Practically it means that the drug has brought 100% relief, such as when a migraine headache has been terminated; giving higher doses produces no additional relief. In phase 3, although increasing the dose does not result in more therapeutic effect, nurses should be mindful that increasing the dose may produce toxic effects.

4 Potency and Efficacy

Within a pharmacologic class, not all drugs are equally effective at treating a disorder. For example, some antineoplastic drugs kill more cancer cells than others; some antihypertensive agents lower blood pressure to a greater degree than others; and some analgesics are more effective at relieving severe pain than others in the same class. Furthermore, drugs in the same class are effective at different doses; one antibiotic may be effective at a dose of 1 mg/kg, whereas another is most effective at 100 mg/kg. Nurses need a method to compare one drug with another in order to administer treatment effectively.

There are two fundamental ways to compare medications within therapeutic and pharmacologic classes. First is the concept of **potency.** A drug that is more potent will produce a therapeutic effect at a lower dose, compared with another drug in the same class. For example, consider two agents, drug X and drug Y, that both produce a 20-mm drop in blood pressure. If drug X produces this effect at a dose of 10 mg and drug Y produces it at 60 mg, then drug X is said to be more potent. Thus, potency is one way to compare the doses of two independently administered drugs in terms of how much is needed to produce a particular response. A useful way to visualize the concept of potency is by examining dose–response curves. Compare the two drugs shown in ▲ Figure 4a. In this example, drug A is more potent because it requires a lower dose to produce the same effect.

The second method used to compare drugs is called **efficacy,** which is the magnitude of maximal response that can be produced from a particular drug. In the example in ▲ Figure 4b, drug A is more efficacious because it produces a higher maximal response.

Which is more important to the success of pharmacotherapy, potency or efficacy? Perhaps the best way to understand these concepts is to use the specific example of headache pain. Two common over-the-counter (OTC) analgesics are ibuprofen (200 mg) and aspirin (650 mg). The fact that ibuprofen relieves pain at a lower dose indicates that this agent is *more potent* than aspirin. At recommended doses, however, both are equally effective at relieving headache pain; thus, they have the *same efficacy*. If the patient is experiencing severe pain, however, neither aspirin nor ibuprofen has sufficient efficacy to bring relief. Narcotic analgesics such as morphine have a greater efficacy than aspirin or ibuprofen and can effectively treat this type of pain. From a pharmacotherapeutic perspective, efficacy is almost always more important than potency. In the previous example, the average dose is unimportant to the patient, but headache relief is essential. As another comparison, the patient with cancer is much more concerned about how many cancer cells have been killed (efficacy) than what dose the nurse administered (potency). Although the nurse will often hear claims that one drug is more potent than another, a more compelling concern is whether the drug is more efficacious.

5 Cellular Receptors and Drug Action

Drugs act by modulating or changing existing physiological and biochemical processes. To exert such changes requires that drugs interact with specific molecules and chemicals normally found in the body. A cellular macromolecule to which a medication binds in order to initiate its effects is called a **receptor.** The concept that a drug binds to a receptor to cause a change in body chemistry or physiology is a fundamental theory in pharmacology. *Receptor theory* explains the mechanisms by which most drugs produce their effects. It is important to understand, however, that these receptors do not exist in the body solely to bind drugs. Their normal function is to bind endogenous molecules such as hormones, neurotransmitters, and growth factors.

Although a drug receptor can be any type of macromolecule, the vast majority are proteins. As shown in ▲ Figure 5, a receptor is depicted as a three-dimensional protein associated with the cellular plasma membrane. The extracellular structural component of the receptor usually consists of several protein subunits arranged around a central canal or channel. Other protein segments as a part of the receptor macromolecule are inserted into the plasma membrane. Channels may be opened by changes in voltage across the membrane as when voltage-gated calcium channels are opened when electrical signals arrive at nerve endings. In this instance, an electrical signal will open channels and calcium will rush into the nerve terminal to release vesicles containing endogenous neurotransmitters. Chemical gated channels, a second type of receptor, will be activated by neurotransmitters after they are released into the synapse. Both channels are ways that drugs produce a response by modulating receptors in the body.

A drug attaches to its receptor in a specific manner, in much the way that a thumb drive docks to a USB port in a

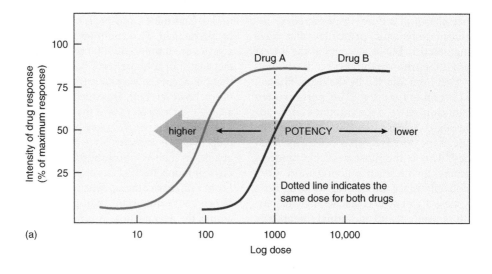

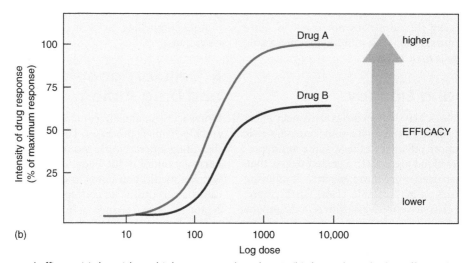

▲ *Figure 4* Potency and efficacy: (a) drug A has a higher potency than drug B; (b) drug A has a higher efficacy than drug B

computer. Small changes to the structure of a drug, or its receptor, may weaken or even eliminate binding (docking) between the two molecules. Once bound, drugs may trigger a series of **second messenger** events within the cell, such as the conversion of adenosine triphosphate (ATP) to cyclic adenosine monophosphate (cyclic AMP), the release of intracellular calcium, or the activation of specific G proteins and associated enzymes. This is very much like the internal actions that go on within a computer. Biochemical cascades initiate the drug's action by either stimulating or inhibiting normal activity of the cell.

Not all receptors are bound to plasma membranes; some are intracellular molecules such as DNA or enzymes in the cytoplasm. By interacting with these types of receptors, medications are able to inhibit protein synthesis or regulate cellular events such as replication and metabolism. Examples of agents that bind intracellular components include steroid medications, vitamins, and hormones.

Receptors and their associated drug mechanisms are extremely important in therapeutics. Receptor *subtypes* are

being discovered and new medications are being developed at a faster rate than at any other time in history. These subtypes permit the "fine-tuning" of pharmacology. For example, the first medications affecting the autonomic nervous system affected all autonomic receptors. It was discovered that two basic receptor types existed in the body, *alpha* and *beta,* and drugs were then developed that affected only one type. The result was more specific drug action, with fewer adverse effects. Still later, several subtypes of alpha and beta receptors, including alpha$_1$, alpha$_2$, beta$_1$, and beta$_2$, were discovered that allowed even more specificity in pharmacotherapy. In recent years, researchers have further divided and refined these receptor subtypes. It is likely that receptor research will continue to result in the development of new medications that activate very specific receptors and thus direct drug action to avoid unnecessary adverse effects.

Some drugs act independently of cellular receptors. These agents are associated with other mechanisms, such as changing the permeability of cellular membranes, depressing membrane excitability, or altering the activity of cellular

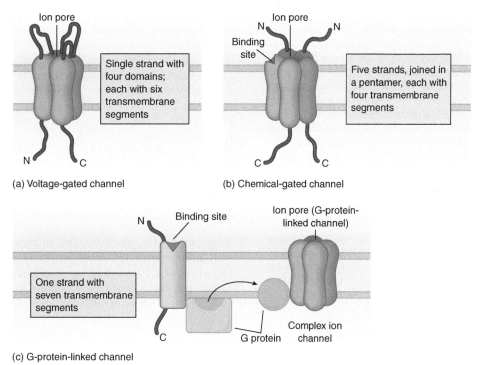

▲ *Figure 5* Cellular receptors

pumps. Actions such as these are described as **nonspecific cellular responses.** Ethyl alcohol, general anesthetics, and osmotic diuretics are examples of agents that act by nonspecific mechanisms.

6 Types of Drug–Receptor Interactions

When a drug binds to a receptor, several therapeutic consequences can result. In simplest terms, a specific activity of the cell is either enhanced or inhibited. The actual biochemical mechanism underlying the therapeutic effect, however, may be extremely complex. In some cases, the mechanism of action is not known.

When a drug binds to its receptor, it may produce a response that *mimics* the effect of the endogenous regulatory molecule. For example, when the drug bethanechol (Urecholine) is administered, it binds to acetylcholine receptors in the autonomic nervous system and produces the same actions as acetylcholine. A drug that produces the same type of response as the endogenous substance is called an **agonist.** Agonists sometimes produce a greater maximal response than the endogenous chemical. The term **partial agonist** or **agonist-antagonist drug** describes a medication that produces a weaker, or less efficacious, response than an agonist.

A second possibility is that a drug will occupy a receptor and *prevent* the endogenous chemical from acting. This drug is called an **antagonist.** Antagonists often compete with agonists for the receptor binding sites. For example, the drug atropine competes with acetylcholine for specific receptors associated with the autonomic nervous system. If the dose

is high enough, atropine will inhibit the effects of acetylcholine, because acetylcholine cannot bind to its receptors.

Not all antagonism is associated with receptors. *Functional* antagonists inhibit the effects of an agonist not by competing for a receptor but by changing pharmacokinetic factors. For example, antagonists may slow the absorption of a drug. By speeding up metabolism or excretion, an antagonist may enhance the removal of a drug from the body. The relationships that occur between agonists and antagonists explain many of the drug–drug and drug–food interactions that occur in the body.

7 Pharmacology of the Future: Customizing Drug Therapy

Until recently, it was thought that single drugs should provide safe and effective treatment to every patient in the same way. Unfortunately, a significant portion of the population either develops unacceptable side effects to certain drugs or is unresponsive to them. Many scientists and clinicians are now discarding the one-size-fits-all approach to drug therapy, which was designed to treat an entire population without addressing important interpatient variation.

With the advent of the Human Genome Project and other advances in medicine, pharmacologists began with the hope that future drugs might be customized for patients with specific genetic similarities. In the past, unpredictable and unexplained drug reactions had been labeled as **idiosyncratic responses.** It is hoped that performing a DNA test before administering a drug may someday address idiosyncratic differences.

Pharmacogenetics is the area of pharmacology that examines the role of heredity in drug response. The greatest advances in pharmacogenetics have been the identification of the human genome and subtle genetic differences in drug-metabolizing enzymes among patients. **Pharmacogenomics** deals with the influence of genetic variation on drug response in patients by correlating gene expression or actual variants of the human genome. Genetic differences in enzymes are responsible for a significant portion of drug-induced toxicity. Other examples have been genetic differences in cholesterol management, arrhythmias, heart failure, hypertension, warfarin anticoagulation, and responsiveness with antiplatelet agents. Further characterization of the human genome and subsequent application of pharmacogenetic information may someday allow for customized drug therapy. Imagine being able to prevent drug toxicity with a single gene test or to predict in advance whether placement of a stent will be successful. Although therapies based on a patient's genetic variability have not been cost effective, strides in both fields may radically change the way pharmacotherapy will be practiced in the future.

Chapter Review

KEY CONCEPTS

The numbered key concepts provide a succinct summary of the important points from the corresponding numbered section within the chapter. If any of these points are not clear, refer to the numbered section within the chapter for review.

1 Pharmacodynamics is the area of pharmacology concerned with how drugs produce *change* in patients and the differences in patient responses to medications.

2 The therapeutic index, expressed mathematically as $TD_{50} \div ED_{50}$, is a value representing the margin of safety of a drug. The higher the therapeutic index, the safer is the drug.

3 The graded dose–response relationship describes how the therapeutic response to a drug changes as the medication dose is increased.

4 Potency, the dose of medication required to produce a particular response, and efficacy, the magnitude of maximal response to a drug, are means of comparing medications.

5 Drug–receptor theory is used to explain the mechanism of action of many medications.

6 Agonists, partial agonists, and antagonists are substances that compete with drugs for receptor binding and can cause drug–drug and drug–food interactions.

7 In the future, pharmacotherapy will likely be customized to match the genetic makeup of each patient.

NCLEX-RN® REVIEW QUESTIONS

1. A patient experiences profound drowsiness when a stimulant drug is given. This is an unusual reaction for this drug, a reaction that has not been associated with that particular drug. What is the term for this type of drug reaction?
   1. Allergic reaction
   2. Idiosyncratic reaction
   3. Enzyme-specific reaction
   4. Unaltered reaction

2. The provider has ordered atropine, a drug that will prevent the patient's own chemical, acetylcholine, from causing parasympathetic effects. What type of drug would atropine be considered?
   1. An antagonist
   2. A partial agonist
   3. An agonist
   4. A protagonist

3. A nursing student reads in a pharmacology textbook that 10 mg of morphine is considered to provide the same pain relief as 200 mg of codeine. This indicates that the morphine would be considered more _____ than codeine. (Fill in the blank.)

4. What is the term used to describe the magnitude of maximal response that can be produced from a particular drug?
   1. Efficacy
   2. Toxicity
   3. Potency
   4. Comparability

5. The nurse looks up butorphanol (Stadol) in a drug reference guide prior to administering the drug and notes that it is a partial agonist. What does this term tell the nurse about the drug?
   1. It is a drug that produces the same type of response as the endogenous substance.
   2. It is a drug that will occupy a receptor and prevent the endogenous chemical from acting.
   3. It is a drug that causes unpredictable and unexplained drug reactions.
   4. It is a drug that produces a weaker, or less efficacious, response than an agonist drug.

6. The nurse reads that the drug to be given to the patient, has a "narrow therapeutic index." The nurse knows that this means that the drug has what properties?
   1. It has a narrow range of effectiveness and may not give this patient the desired therapeutic results.
   2. It has a narrow safety margin and even a small increase in dose may produce adverse or toxic effects.
   3. It has a narrow range of conditions or diseases that the drug will be expected to treat successfully.
   4. It has a narrow segment of the population for whom the drug will work as desired.

CRITICAL THINKING QUESTIONS

1. If the ED_{50} is the dose required to produce an effective response in 50% of a group of patients, what happens in the other 50% of the patients after a dose has been administered?

2. Great strides are being made in pharmacogenomics and personalized medicine. What are some of the advantages that pharmacogenomics may have for the pharmacologic treatment of patients?

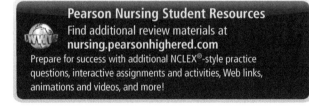

GLOSSARY

Agonist drug that is capable of binding with receptors to induce a cellular response

Antagonist drug that blocks the response of another drug

Efficacy the ability of a drug to produce a desired response

Frequency distribution curve graphic depiction of drug response in a population

Graded dose-response relationship between and measurement of the patient's response obtained at different doses of a drug

Idiosyncratic response unpredictable and unexplained drug reaction

Median effective dose (ED$_{50}$) dose required to produce a specific therapeutic response in 50% of a group of patients

Median lethal dose (LD$_{50}$) often determined in preclinical trials, the dose of drug that will be lethal in 50% of a group of animals

Median toxicity dose (TD$_{50}$) dose that will produce a given toxicity in 50% of a group of patients

Nonspecific cellular response drug action that is independent of cellular receptors and is not associated with other mechanisms, such as changing the permeability of cellular membranes, depressing membrane excitability, or altering the activity of cellular pumps

Partial agonist (agonist-antagonist drug) medication that produces a weaker, or less efficacious, response than an agonist

Pharmacodynamics study of how the body responds to drugs

Pharmacogenetics area of pharmacology that examines the role of genetics in drug response

Pharmacogenomics influence of genetic variation on drug response in patients by correlating gene expression or actual variants of the human genome

Potency the strength of a drug at a specified concentration or dose

Receptor the structural component of a cell to which a drug binds in a dose-related manner to produce a response

Second messenger cascade of biochemical events that initiates a drug's action by either stimulating or inhibiting the normal activity of the cell

Therapeutic index the ratio of a drug's LD$_{50}$ to its ED$_{50}$

BIBLIOGRAPHY AND REFERENCES

Buxton, I. L. O. (2006). Pharmacokinetics and pharmacodynamics: The dynamics of drug absorption, distribution, action, and elimination. In L. L. Brunton, J. S. Lazo, & K. L. Parker (Eds.), *Goodman & Gilman's The pharmacological basis of therapeutics* (11th ed., pp. 1–40). New York, NY: McGraw-Hill.

Corbett, R. W., & Owens, L. W. (2011, May–June). Introductory pharmacology for clinical practice. *Journal of Midwifery & Women's Health, 56*(3), 190–197.

Hoshino-Yoshino, A., Kato, M., Nakano, K., Ishigai, M., Kudo, T., & Ito, K. (2011, September 6). Bridging from preclinical to clinical studies for tyrosine kinase inhibitors based on pharmacokinetics/pharmacodynamics and toxicokinetics/toxicodynamics. *Drug Metabolism and Pharmacokinetics.*

Meechan, R., Jones, H., & Valler-Jones, T. (2011, July 15–28). Do medicines OSCEs improve drug administration ability? *British Journal of Nursing, 20*(13), 817–822.

Mieko, T. (2009). Perspectives on the current state of pharmacogenomics in drug development. Yakuga Kuzasshi—*Journal of the Pharmaceutical Society of Japan, 129*(1), 135–145.

Oates, J. A. (2006). The science of drug therapy. In L. L. Brunton, J. S. Lazo, & K. L. Parker (Eds.), *Goodman & Gilman's The pharmacological basis of therapeutics* (11th ed., pp. 117–136). New York, NY: McGraw-Hill.

Philip, A. K., & Philip, B. (2011). Chronopharmaceuticals: Hype or future of pharmaceutics. *Current Pharmaceutical Design, 17*(15), 1512–1516.

Roden, D. M., Johnson, J. A., Kimmel, S. E., Krauss, R. M., Medina, M. W., Shuldiner, A., & Wilke, R. A. (2011, September 16). Cardiovascular pharmacogenomics. *Circulation Research, 109*(7), 807–820.

Van den Anker, J. N., Schwab, M., & Kearns, G. L. (2011). Developmental pharmacokinetics. *Handbook of Experimental Pharmacology, 205*, 51–75.

Weiss, M. (2011, October). Functional characterization of drug uptake and metabolism in the heart. *Expert Opinion on Drug Metabolism and Toxicology, 7*(10), 1295–1306.

Weiss, M., Krejcie, T. C., & Avram, M. J. (2011, August 26). A physiologically based model of hepatic ICG clearance: Interplay between sinusoidal uptake and biliary excretion. *European Journal of Pharmaceutical Sciences.*

Zuern, C. S., Schwab, M., Gawaz, M., & Geisler, T. (2010, June). Platelet pharmacogenomics. *Journal of Thrombosis and Haemostasis, 8*(6), 1147–1158.

ANSWERS

Answers to NCLEX-RN® Review Questions

1. *Answer: 2*

Rationale: An unpredictable and unexplained drug reaction is known as an *idiosyncratic* reaction. Individual genetic differences may be the foundation for some idiosyncratic reactions. Options 1, 3, and 4 are incorrect. Allergic reactions may be unpredictable and unexplained but they are characterized by well-known symptoms related to stimulating the immune system. Enzyme-specific and unaltered responses are not terms that are used to describe drug reactions. *Cognitive Level:* Applying. *Nursing Process:* Implementation. *Client Need:* Physiological Integrity.

2. *Answer: 1*

Rationale: An antagonist occupies a receptor site and prevents endogenous chemicals or other drugs from acting. Options 2, 3, and 4 are incorrect. An agonist produces the same type of response as the endogenous substance. A partial agonist is a medication that produces a weaker response than an agonist. A protagonist is not a term used in pharmacology. *Cognitive Level:* Applying. *Nursing Process:* Implementation. *Client Need:* Physiological Integrity.

3. *Answer:*

Rationale: This indicates that the morphine would be considered more **potent** than codeine. *Rationale:* A drug that is more potent will produce a therapeutic effect at a lower dose. *Cognitive Level:* Applying. *Nursing Process:* Implementation. *Client Need:* Physiological Integrity.

4. *Answer: 1*

Rationale: The term *efficacy* refers to the maximal response that can be produced from a particular drug. Options 2, 3, and 4 are incorrect. *Toxicity* is a term used to describe serious or life-threatening adverse effects. *Potency* refers to the amount of the drug that is needed to produce a particular response. *Comparability* is not a term used in pharmacology and drugs may be compared in many different ways, including efficacy and potency. *Cognitive Level:* Applying. *Nursing Process:* Implementation. *Client Need:* Physiological Integrity.

5. *Answer: 4*

Rationale: A drug that produces a weaker, or less efficacious, response than an agonist drug is known as a partial agonist or sometimes as an agonist-antagonist. Options 1, 2, and 3 are incorrect. A drug that produces the same type of response as the endogenous substance is an *agonist*. A drug that will occupy a receptor and prevent the endogenous chemical from acting is an *antagonist*. A drug that causes an unpredictable and unexplained drug reaction is said to cause an *idiosyncratic* reaction. *Cognitive Level:* Applying. *Nursing Process:* Implementation. *Client Need:* Physiological Integrity.

6. *Answer: 2*

Rationale: A narrow therapeutic index indicates that there is only a small amount of difference between the dosage needed to be effective (ED_{50}) and the dosage that will be toxic (LD_{50}). Extra caution should be taken with drugs with a narrow therapeutic index to avoid giving an excessive dose and to ensure patient safety. Options 1, 3, and 4 are incorrect. A narrow therapeutic index does not refer to the effectiveness, disease conditions, or client populations that the drug may treat. *Cognitive Level:* Applying. *Nursing Process:* Implementation. *Client Need:* Physiological Integrity.

Answers to Critical Thinking Questions

1. The other 50% of the patients did not experience the desired effect from the dose.

2. By understanding how a drug works with the unique genetic sequencing in a patient, drugs may be selected to produce more targeted effects and cause less adverse effects. For example, if a patient is known to have a genetic variant that would cause a serious adverse effect if drug "X" was given, another drug could be chosen to effectively treat the condition without the harmful effect.

Juergen Berger/Photo Researchers

The Microbial World and You

Visualize microbiology and check your understanding with a pre-test at www.masteringmicrobiology.com.

The overall theme of this text is the relationship between microbes (very small organisms that usually require a microscope to be seen) and our lives. This relationship involves not only the familiar harmful effects of certain microorganisms, such as disease and food spoilage, but also their many beneficial effects. In this chapter we introduce you to some of the many ways microbes affect our lives. Microbes have been fruitful subjects of study for many years. We begin by introducing you to how organisms are named and classified, followed by a short history of microbiology that reveals how much we have learned in just a few hundred years. We then discuss the incredible diversity of microorganisms and their ecological importance, noting how they maintain balance in the environment by recycling chemical elements such as carbon and nitrogen among the soil, organisms, and the atmosphere. We also examine how microbes are used in commercial and industrial applications to produce foods, chemicals, and drugs (such as antibiotics); and to treat sewage, control pests, and clean up pollutants. We will discuss microbes as the cause of such diseases as avian (bird) flu, West Nile encephalitis, mad cow disease, diarrhea, hemorrhagic fever, and AIDS. We will also examine the growing public health problem of antibiotic-resistant bacteria. *Staphylococcus aureus* bacteria on human nasal epithelial cells are shown in the photograph. These bacteria live harmlessly on skin or inside the nose. Misuse of antibiotics allows the survival of bacteria with antibiotic-resistant genes such as methicillin-resistant *S. aureus* (MRSA). As illustrated in the Clinical Case, an infection caused by these bacteria is resistant to antibiotic treatment.

From Chapter 1 of *Microbiology: An Introduction*, Eleventh Edition. Gerard J. Tortora, Berdell R. Funke, Christine L. Case.

Microbes in Our Lives

1   List several ways in which microbes affect our lives.

For many people, the words *germ* and *microbe* bring to mind a group of tiny creatures that do not quite fit into any of the categories in that old question, "Is it animal, vegetable, or mineral?" **Microbes,** also called **microorganisms,** are minute living things that individually are usually too small to be seen with the unaided eye. The group includes bacteria, fungi (yeasts and molds), protozoa, and microscopic algae. It also includes viruses, those noncellular entities sometimes regarded as straddling the border between life and nonlife. You will be introduced to each of these groups of microbes shortly.

We tend to associate these small organisms only with major diseases such as AIDS, uncomfortable infections, or such common inconveniences as spoiled food. However, the majority of microorganisms actually help maintain the balance of living organisms and chemicals in our environment. Marine and freshwater microorganisms form the basis of the food chain in oceans, lakes, and rivers. Soil microbes help break down wastes and incorporate nitrogen gas from the air into organic compounds, thereby recycling chemical elements between the soil, water, life, and air. Certain microbes play important roles in *photosynthesis,* a food- and oxygen-generating process that is critical to life on Earth. Humans and many other animals depend on the microbes in their intestines for digestion and the synthesis of some vitamins that their bodies require, including some B vitamins for metabolism and vitamin K for blood clotting.

Microorganisms also have many commercial applications. They are used in the synthesis of such chemical products as vitamins, organic acids, enzymes, alcohols, and many drugs. For example, microbes are used to produce acetone and butanol, and the vitamins B_2 (riboflavin) and B_{12} (cobalamin) are made biochemically. The process by which microbes produce acetone and butanol was discovered in 1914 by Chaim Weizmann, a Russian-born chemist working in England. With the outbreak of World War I in August of that year, the production of acetone became very important for making cordite (a smokeless form of gunpowder used in munitions). Weizmann's discovery played a significant role in determining the outcome of the war.

The food industry also uses microbes in producing, for example, vinegar, sauerkraut, pickles, soy sauce, cheese, yogurt, bread, and alcoholic beverages. In addition, enzymes from microbes can now be manipulated to cause the microbes to produce substances they normally do not synthesize, including cellulose, digestive aids, and drain cleaner, plus important therapeutic substances such as insulin. Microbial enzymes may even have helped produce your favorite pair of jeans (see the box on the next page).

Though only a minority of microorganisms are **pathogenic** (disease-producing), practical knowledge of microbes is necessary for medicine and the related health sciences. For example, hospital workers must be able to protect patients from common microbes that are normally harmless but pose a threat to the sick and injured.

Today we understand that microorganisms are found almost everywhere. Yet not long ago, before the invention of the microscope, microbes were unknown to scientists. Thousands of people died in devastating epidemics, the causes of which were not understood. Entire families died because vaccinations and antibiotics were not available to fight infections.

We can get an idea of how our current concepts of microbiology developed by looking at a few historic milestones in microbiology that have changed our lives. First, however, we will look at the major groups of microbes and how they are named and classified.

CHECK YOUR UNDERSTANDING

✔ Describe some of the destructive and beneficial actions of microbes. 1*

Naming and Classifying Microorganisms

LEARNING OBJECTIVES

2   Recognize the system of scientific nomenclature that uses two names: a genus and a specific epithet.

3   Differentiate the major characteristics of each group of microorganisms.

4   List the three domains.

* The numbers following Check Your Understanding questions refer to the corresponding Learning Objectives.

Clinical Case: A Simple Spider Bite?

Andrea is a normally healthy 22-year-old college student who lives at home with her mother and younger sister, a high school gymnast. She is trying to work on a paper for her psychology class but is having a hard time because a red, swollen sore on her right wrist is making typing difficult. "Why won't this spider bite heal?" she wonders. "It's been there for days!" She makes an appointment with her doctor so she can show him the painful lesion. Although Andrea does not have a fever, she does have an elevated white blood cell count that indicates a bacterial infection. Andrea's doctor suspects that this isn't a spider bite at all, but a staph infection. He prescribes a β-lactam antibiotic, cephalosporin. Learn more about the development of Andrea's illness on the following pages.

What is staph? Read on to find out.

APPLICATIONS OF **MICROBIOLOGY**

Designer Jeans: Made by Microbes?

Denim blue jeans have become increasingly popular ever since Levi Strauss and Jacob Davis first made them for California gold miners in 1873. Now, companies that manufacture blue jeans are turning to microbiology to develop environmentally sound production methods that minimize toxic wastes and the associated costs.

Stone Washing?
A softer denim, called "stone-washed," was introduced in the 1980s. Enzymes, called cellulases, from *Trichoderma* fungus are used to digest some of the cellulose in the cotton, thereby softening it and giving the stone-washed appearance. Unlike many chemical reactions, enzymes usually operate at safe temperatures and pH. Moreover, enzymes are proteins, so they are readily degraded for removal from wastewater.

Fabric
Cotton production requires large tracts of land, pesticides, and fertilizer, and the crop yield depends on the weather. However, bacteria can produce both cotton and polyester with less environmental impact. *Gluconacetobacter xylinus* bacteria make cellulose by attaching glucose units to simple chains in the outer membrane of the bacterial cell wall. The cellulose microfibrils are extruded through pores in the outer membrane, and bundles of microfibrils then twist into ribbons.

Bleaching
Peroxide is a safer bleaching agent than chlorine and can be easily removed from fabric and wastewater by enzymes. Researchers at Novo Nordisk Biotech cloned a mushroom peroxidase gene in yeast and grew the yeasts in washing machine conditions. The yeast that survived the washing machine were selected as the peroxidase producers.

Indigo
Chemical synthesis of indigo requires a high pH and produces waste that explodes in contact with air. However, a California biotechnology company, Genencor, has developed a method to produce indigo by using bacteria. Researchers identified a gene from a soil bacterium, *Pseudomonas putida*, for conversion of the bacterial by-product indole to indigo. This gene was put into *Escherichia coli* bacteria, which then turned blue.

Bioplastic
Microbes can even make plastic zippers and packaging material for the jeans. Over 25 bacteria make polyhydroxyalkanoate (PHA) inclusion granules as a food reserve. PHAs are similar to common plastics, and because they are made by bacteria, they are also readily degraded by many bacteria. PHAs could provide a biodegradable alternative to conventional plastic, which is made from petroleum.

Precision Graphics

E. coli bacteria produce indigo from tryptophan.

Indigo-producing *E. coli* bacteria. 0.3 µm TEM Precision Graphics

Nomenclature

The system of nomenclature (naming) for organisms in use today was established in 1735 by Carolus Linnaeus. Scientific names are latinized because Latin was the language traditionally used by scholars. Scientific nomenclature assigns each organism two names—the **genus** (plural: *genera*) is the first name and is always capitalized; the **specific epithet** (**species** name) follows and is not capitalized. The organism is referred to by both the genus and the specific epithet, and both names are underlined or italicized. By custom, after a scientific name has been mentioned once, it can be abbreviated with the initial of the genus followed by the specific epithet.

Scientific names can, among other things, describe an organism, honor a researcher, or identify the habitat of a species. For example, consider *Staphylococcus aureus* (staf-i-lō-kok′kus ô′rē-us), a bacterium commonly found on human skin. *Staphylo-* describes the clustered arrangement of the cells; *coccus* indicates that they are shaped like spheres. The specific epithet, *aureus,* is Latin for golden, the color of many colonies of this bacterium. The genus of the bacterium *Escherichia coli* (esh-ë-rik′-ē-ä kō′lī or kō′lē) is named for a scientist, Theodor Escherich, whereas its specific epithet, *coli*, reminds us that *E. coli* live in the colon, or large intestine. **Table 1** contains more examples.

CHECK YOUR UNDERSTANDING

✔ Distinguish a genus from a specific epithet. **2**

Types of Microorganisms

Here is an overview of the major groups used to classify and identify microorganisms.

Bacteria

Bacteria (singular: **bacterium**) are relatively simple, single-celled (unicellular) organisms. Because their genetic material is not

TABLE **1** **Making Scientific Names Familiar**

Use a word roots guide to find out what the name means. The name will not seem so strange if you translate it. When you encounter a new name, practice saying it out loud. The exact pronunciation is not as important as the familiarity you will gain.

Following are some examples of microbial names you may encounter in the popular press as well as in the lab.

	Pronunciation	Source of Genus Name	Source of Specific Epithet
Salmonella enterica (bacterium)	sal-mōn-el′lă en-ter′i-kă	Honors public health microbiologist Daniel Salmon	Found in the intestines (*entero-*)
Streptococcus pyogenes (bacterium)	strep-tō-kok′kus pī-ăj′en-ēz	Appearance of cells in chains (*strepto-*)	Forms pus (*pyo-*)
Saccharomyces cerevisiae (yeast)	sak-ă-rō-mī′ses se-ri-vis′ē-ī	Fungus (*-myces*) that uses sugar (*saccharo-*)	Makes beer (*cerevisia*)
Penicillium chrysogenum (fungus)	pen-i-sil′lē-um krī-so′jen-um	Tuftlike or paintbrush (*penicill-*) appearance microscopically	Produces a yellow (*chryso-*) pigment
Trypanosoma cruzi (protozoan)	tri-pa-nō-sō′mă krūz′ē	Corkscrew- (*trypano-*, borer; *soma-*, body)	Honors epidemiologist Oswaldo Cruz

enclosed in a special nuclear membrane, bacterial cells are called **prokaryotes** (prō-kar′e-ōts), from Greek words meaning prenucleus. Prokaryotes include both bacteria and archaea.

Bacterial cells generally appear in one of several shapes. *Bacillus* (bä-sil′lus) (rodlike), illustrated in **Figure 1a**, *coccus* (kok′kus) (spherical or ovoid), and *spiral* (corkscrew or curved) are among the most common shapes, but some bacteria are star-shaped or square. Individual bacteria may form pairs, chains, clusters, or other groupings; such formations are usually characteristic of a particular genus or species of bacteria.

Bacteria are enclosed in cell walls that are largely composed of a carbohydrate and protein complex called *peptidoglycan*. (By contrast, cellulose is the main substance of plant and algal cell walls.) Bacteria generally reproduce by dividing into two equal cells; this process is called *binary fission*. For nutrition, most bacteria use organic chemicals, which in nature can be derived from either dead or living organisms. Some bacteria can manufacture their own food by photosynthesis, and some can derive nutrition from inorganic substances. Many bacteria can "swim" by using moving appendages called *flagella*.

Archaea

Like bacteria, **archaea** (är′kē-ä) consist of prokaryotic cells, but if they have cell walls, the walls lack peptidoglycan. Archaea, often found in extreme environments, are divided into three main groups. The *methanogens* produce methane as a waste product from respiration. The *extreme halophiles* (*halo* = salt; *philic* = loving) live in extremely salty environments such as the Great Salt Lake and the Dead Sea. The *extreme thermophiles* (*therm* = heat) live in hot sulfurous water, such as hot springs

at Yellowstone National Park. Archaea are not known to cause disease in humans.

Fungi

Fungi (singular: **fungus**) are **eukaryotes** (yū-kar′ē-ōts), organisms whose cells have a distinct nucleus containing the cell's genetic material (DNA), surrounded by a special envelope called the nuclear membrane. Organisms in the Kingdom Fungi may be unicellular or multicellular. Large multicellular fungi, such as mushrooms, may look somewhat like plants, but unlike most plants, fungi cannot carry out photosynthesis. True fungi have cell walls composed primarily of a substance called *chitin*. The unicellular forms of fungi, *yeasts*, are oval microorganisms that are larger than bacteria. The most typical fungi are *molds* (**Figure 1b**). Molds form visible masses called *mycelia*, which are composed of long filaments (*hyphae*) that branch and intertwine. The cottony growths sometimes found on bread and fruit are mold mycelia. Fungi can reproduce sexually or asexually. They obtain nourishment by absorbing solutions of organic material from their environment—whether soil, seawater, freshwater, or an animal or plant host. Organisms called *slime molds* have characteristics of both fungi and amoebas.

Protozoa

Protozoa (singular: **protozoan**) are unicellular eukaryotic microbes. Protozoa move by pseudopods, flagella, or cilia. Amebae (**Figure 1c**) move by using extensions of their cytoplasm called *pseudopods* (false feet). Other protozoa have long *flagella* or numerous shorter appendages for locomotion

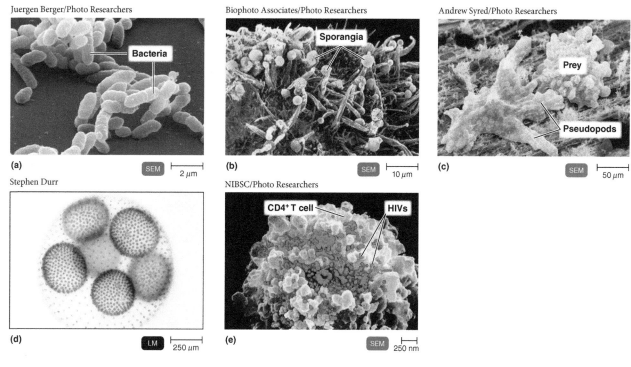

Juergen Berger/Photo Researchers

Biophoto Associates/Photo Researchers

Andrew Syred/Photo Researchers

Stephen Durr

NIBSC/Photo Researchers

Figure 1 Types of microorganisms.
NOTE: Throughout the text, a red icon under a micrograph indicates that the micrograph has been artificially colored. (**a**) The rod-shaped bacterium *Haemophilus influenzae,* one of the bacterial causes of pneumonia. (**b**) *Mucor,* a common bread mold, is a type of fungus. When released from sporangia, spores that land on a favorable surface germinate into a network of hyphae (filaments) that absorb nutrients. (**c**) An ameba, a protozoan, approaching a food particle. (**d**) The pond alga *Volvox.* (**e**) Several human immunodeficiency viruses (HIVs), the causative agent of AIDS, budding from a CD4⁺ T cell.

 How are bacteria, archaea, fungi, protozoa, algae, and viruses distinguished on the basis of cellular structure?

called *cilia.* Protozoa have a variety of shapes and live either as free entities or as *parasites* (organisms that derive nutrients from living hosts) that absorb or ingest organic compounds from their environment. Some protozoa, such as *Euglena,* are photosynthetic. They use light as a source of energy and carbon dioxide as their chief source of carbon to produce sugars. Protozoa can reproduce sexually or asexually.

Algae

Algae (singular: **alga**) are photosynthetic eukaryotes with a wide variety of shapes and both sexual and asexual reproductive forms (**Figure 1d**). The algae of interest to microbiologists are usually unicellular. The cell walls of many algae, are composed of a carbohydrate called *cellulose.* Algae are abundant in freshwater and salt water, in soil, and in association with plants. As photosynthesizers, algae need light, water, and carbon dioxide for food production and growth, but they do not generally require organic compounds from the environment. As a result of photosynthesis, algae produce oxygen and carbohydrates that are then utilized by other organisms, including animals. Thus, they play an important role in the balance of nature.

Viruses

Viruses (**Figure 1e**) are very different from the other microbial groups mentioned here. They are so small that most can be seen only with an electron microscope, and they are acellular (not cellular). Structurally very simple, a virus particle contains a core made of only one type of nucleic acid, either DNA or RNA. This core is surrounded by a protein coat, which is sometimes encased by a lipid membrane called an envelope. All living cells have RNA *and* DNA, can carry out chemical reactions, and can reproduce as self-sufficient units. Viruses can reproduce only by using the cellular machinery of other organisms. Thus, on the one hand, viruses are considered to be living only when they multiply within host cells they infect. In this sense, viruses are parasites of other forms of life. On the other hand, viruses are not considered to be living because they are inert outside living hosts.

Multicellular Animal Parasites

Although multicellular animal parasites are not strictly microorganisms, they are of medical importance and therefore will be discussed in this text. Animal parasites are eukaryotes. The two major groups of parasitic worms are the flatworms and the roundworms, collectively called **helminths**. During some stages of their life cycle, helminths are microscopic in size. Laboratory identification of these organisms includes many of the same techniques used for identifying microbes.

CHECK YOUR UNDERSTANDING

✔ Which groups of microbes are prokaryotes? Which are eukaryotes? 3

Classification of Microorganisms

Before the existence of microbes was known, all organisms were grouped into either the animal kingdom or the plant kingdom. When microscopic organisms with characteristics of animals and plants were discovered late in the seventeenth century, a new system of classification was needed. Still, biologists could not agree on the criteria for classifying these new organisms until the late 1970s.

In 1978, Carl Woese devised a system of classification based on the cellular organization of organisms. It groups all organisms in three domains as follows:

1. Bacteria (cell walls contain a protein–carbohydrate complex called peptidoglycan)
2. Archaea (cell walls, if present, lack peptidoglycan)
3. Eukarya, which includes the following:
   - Protists (slime molds, protozoa, and algae)
   - Fungi (unicellular yeasts, multicellular molds, and mushrooms)
   - Plants (mosses, ferns, conifers, and flowering plants)
   - Animals (sponges, worms, insects, and vertebrates)

CHECK YOUR UNDERSTANDING

✔ What are the three domains? 4

A Brief History of Microbiology

LEARNING OBJECTIVES

5 Explain the importance of observations made by Hooke and van Leeuwenhoek.

6 Compare spontaneous generation and biogenesis.

7 Identify the contributions to microbiology made by Needham, Spallanzani, Virchow, and Pasteur.

8 Explain how Pasteur's work influenced Lister and Koch.

9 Identify the importance of Koch's postulates.

10 Identify the importance of Jenner's work.

11 Identify the contributions to microbiology made by Ehrlich and Fleming.

12 Define *bacteriology, mycology, parasitology, immunology,* and *virology.*

13 Explain the importance of microbial genetics and molecular biology.

The science of microbiology dates back only 200 years, yet the recent discovery of *Mycobacterium tuberculosis* (mī-kō-bak-ti′rē-um tü-ber-ku-lō′sis) DNA in 3000-year-old Egyptian mummies reminds us that microorganisms have been around for much longer. In fact, bacterial ancestors were the first living cells to appear on Earth. Although we know relatively little about what earlier people thought about the causes, transmission, and treatment of disease, we know more about the history of the past few hundred years. Let's look now at some key developments in microbiology that have spurred the field to its current technological state.

The First Observations

One of the most important discoveries in biology occurred in 1665. After observing a thin slice of cork through a relatively crude microscope, an Englishman, Robert Hooke, reported to the world that life's smallest structural units were "little boxes," or "cells," as he called them. Using his improved version of a compound microscope (one that uses two sets of lenses), Hooke was able to see individual cells. Hooke's discovery marked the beginning of the **cell theory**—the theory that *all living things are composed of cells.* Subsequent investigations into the structure and function of cells were based on this theory.

Though Hooke's microscope was capable of showing large cells, it lacked the resolution that would have allowed him to see microbes clearly. The Dutch merchant and amateur scientist Anton van Leeuwenhoek was probably the first actually to observe live microorganisms through the magnifying lenses of more than 400 microscopes he constructed. Between 1673 and 1723, he wrote a series of letters to the Royal Society of London describing the "animalcules" he saw through his simple, single-lens microscope. Van Leeuwenhoek made detailed drawings of "animalcules" he found in rainwater, in his own feces, and in material scraped from his teeth. These drawings have since been identified as representations of bacteria and protozoa (**Figure 2**).

CHECK YOUR UNDERSTANDING

✔ What is the cell theory? 5

The Debate over Spontaneous Generation

After van Leeuwenhoek discovered the previously "invisible" world of microorganisms, the scientific community of the time became interested in the origins of these tiny living things. Until the second half of the nineteenth century, many scientists and philosophers believed that some forms of life could arise spontaneously from nonliving matter; they called this hypothetical process **spontaneous generation.** Not much more than 100 years ago, people commonly believed that toads, snakes, and mice could be born of moist soil; that flies could emerge from manure;

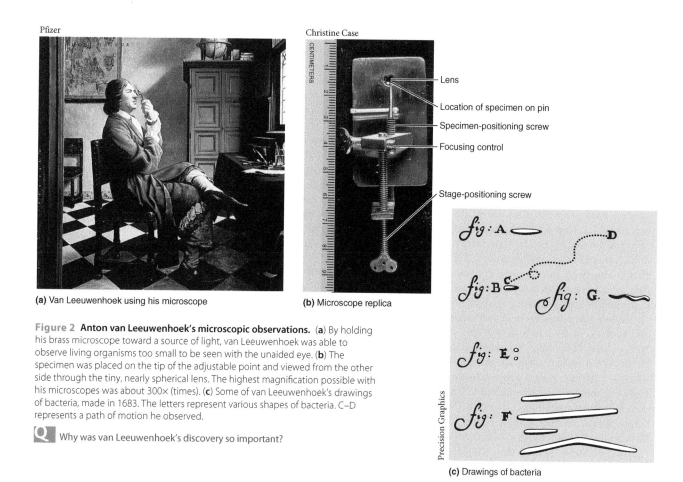

Pfizer

Christine Case

(a) Van Leeuwenhoek using his microscope

Lens
Location of specimen on pin
Specimen-positioning screw
Focusing control
Stage-positioning screw

(b) Microscope replica

Precision Graphics

fig: A
fig: B
fig: C
D
fig: G.
fig: E.
fig: F

(c) Drawings of bacteria

Figure 2 Anton van Leeuwenhoek's microscopic observations. (a) By holding his brass microscope toward a source of light, van Leeuwenhoek was able to observe living organisms too small to be seen with the unaided eye. (b) The specimen was placed on the tip of the adjustable point and viewed from the other side through the tiny, nearly spherical lens. The highest magnification possible with his microscopes was about 300× (times). (c) Some of van Leeuwenhoek's drawings of bacteria, made in 1683. The letters represent various shapes of bacteria. C–D represents a path of motion he observed.

Q Why was van Leeuwenhoek's discovery so important?

and that maggots (which we now know are the larvae of flies) could arise from decaying corpses.

Evidence Pro and Con

A strong opponent of spontaneous generation, the Italian physician Francesco Redi set out in 1668 to demonstrate that maggots did not arise spontaneously from decaying meat. Redi filled two jars with decaying meat. The first was left unsealed; the flies laid their eggs on the meat, and the eggs developed into larvae. The second jar was sealed, and because the flies could not lay their eggs on the meat, no maggots appeared. Still, Redi's antagonists were not convinced; they claimed that fresh air was needed for spontaneous generation. So Redi set up a second experiment, in which he covered a jar with a fine net instead of sealing it. No larvae appeared in the gauze-covered jar, even though air was present. Maggots appeared only when flies were allowed to leave their eggs on the meat.

Redi's results were a serious blow to the long-held belief that large forms of life could arise from nonlife. However, many scientists still believed that small organisms, such as

van Leeuwenhoek's "animalcules," were simple enough to be generated from nonliving materials.

The case for spontaneous generation of microorganisms seemed to be strengthened in 1745, when John Needham, an Englishman, found that even after he heated nutrient fluids (chicken broth and corn broth) before pouring them into covered flasks, the cooled solutions were soon teeming with microorganisms. Needham claimed that microbes developed spontaneously from the fluids. Twenty years later, Lazzaro Spallanzani, an Italian scientist, suggested that microorganisms from the air probably had entered Needham's solutions after they were boiled. Spallanzani showed that nutrient fluids heated *after* being sealed in a flask did not develop microbial growth. Needham responded by claiming the "vital force" necessary for spontaneous generation had been destroyed by the heat and was kept out of the flasks by the seals.

This intangible "vital force" was given all the more credence shortly after Spallanzani's experiment, when Anton Laurent Lavoisier showed the importance of oxygen to life. Spallanzani's observations were criticized on the grounds that there was not enough oxygen in the sealed flasks to support microbial life.

The Theory of Biogenesis

The issue was still unresolved in 1858, when the German scientist Rudolf Virchow challenged the case for spontaneous generation with the concept of **biogenesis,** the claim that living cells can arise only from preexisting living cells. Because he could offer no scientific proof, arguments about spontaneous generation continued until 1861, when the issue was finally resolved by the French scientist Louis Pasteur.

With a series of ingenious and persuasive experiments, Pasteur demonstrated that microorganisms are present in the air and can contaminate sterile solutions, but that air itself does not create microbes. He filled several short-necked flasks with beef broth and then boiled their contents. Some were then left open and allowed to cool. In a few days, these flasks were found to be contaminated with microbes. The other flasks, sealed after boiling, were free of microorganisms. From these results, Pasteur reasoned that microbes in the air were the agents responsible for contaminating nonliving matter.

Pasteur next placed broth in open-ended, long-necked flasks and bent the necks into S-shaped curves (**Figure 3**). The contents of these flasks were then boiled and cooled. The broth in the flasks did not decay and showed no signs of life, even after months. Pasteur's unique design allowed air to pass into the flask, but the curved neck trapped any airborne microorganisms that might contaminate the broth. (Some of these original vessels are still on display at the Pasteur Institute in Paris. They have been sealed but, like the flask shown in Figure 3, show no sign of contamination more than 100 years later.) **8**

Pasteur showed that microorganisms can be present in nonliving matter—on solids, in liquids, and in the air. Furthermore, he demonstrated conclusively that microbial life can be destroyed by heat and that methods can be devised to block the access of airborne microorganisms to nutrient environments. These discoveries form the basis of **aseptic techniques,** techniques that prevent contamination by unwanted microorganisms, which are now the standard practice in laboratory and many medical procedures. Modern aseptic techniques are among the first and most important concepts that a beginning microbiologist learns.

Pasteur's work provided evidence that microorganisms cannot originate from mystical forces present in nonliving materials. Rather, any appearance of "spontaneous" life in nonliving solutions can be attributed to microorganisms that were already present in the air or in the fluids themselves. Scientists now believe that a form of spontaneous generation probably did occur on the primitive Earth when life first began, but they agree that this does not happen under today's environmental conditions.

CHECK YOUR UNDERSTANDING

🖊 What evidence supported spontaneous generation? 6

🖊 How was spontaneous generation disproved? 7

The Golden Age of Microbiology

The work that began with Pasteur started an explosion of discoveries in microbiology. The period from 1857 to 1914 has been appropriately named the Golden Age of Microbiology. During this period, rapid advances, spearheaded mainly by Pasteur and Robert Koch, led to the establishment of microbiology as a science. Discoveries during these years included both the agents of many diseases and the role of immunity in preventing and curing disease. During this productive period, microbiologists studied the chemical activities of microorganisms, improved the techniques for performing microscopy and culturing microorganisms, and developed vaccines and surgical techniques. Some of the major events that occurred during the Golden Age of Microbiology are listed in **Figure 4**.

Fermentation and Pasteurization

One of the key steps that established the relationship between microorganisms and disease occurred when a group of French merchants asked Pasteur to find out why wine and beer soured. They hoped to develop a method that would prevent spoilage when those beverages were shipped long distances. At the time, many scientists believed that air converted the sugars in these fluids into alcohol. Pasteur found instead that microorganisms called yeasts convert the sugars to alcohol in the absence of air. This process, called **fermentation**, is used to make wine and beer. Souring and spoilage are caused by different microorganisms called bacteria. In the presence of air, bacteria change the alcohol into vinegar (acetic acid).

Pasteur's solution to the spoilage problem was to heat the beer and wine just enough to kill most of the bacteria that caused the spoilage. The process, called **pasteurization,** is now commonly used to reduce spoilage and kill potentially harmful bacteria in milk as well as in some alcoholic drinks. Showing the connection between food spoilage and microorganisms was a major step toward establishing the relationship between disease and microbes.

The Germ Theory of Disease

As we have seen, the fact that many kinds of diseases are related to microorganisms was unknown until relatively recently. Before the time of Pasteur, effective treatments for many diseases were discovered by trial and error, but the causes of the diseases were unknown.

The realization that yeasts play a crucial role in fermentation was the first link between the activity of a microorganism and physical and chemical changes in organic materials. This discovery alerted scientists to the possibility that microorganisms might have similar relationships with plants and animals—specifically, that microorganisms might cause disease. This idea was known as the **germ theory of disease.**

FOUNDATION FIGURE **3**

Disproving the Theory of Spontaneous Generation

According to the theory of spontaneous generation, life can arise spontaneously from nonliving matter, such as dead corpses and soil. Pasteur's experiment, described below, demonstrated that microbes are present in nonliving matter—air, liquids, and solids.

1 Pasteur first poured beef broth into a long-necked flask.

2 Next he heated the neck of the flask and bent it into an S-shape; then he boiled the broth for several minutes.

3 Microorganisms did not appear in the cooled solution, even after long periods.

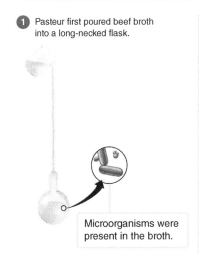

Microorganisms were present in the broth.

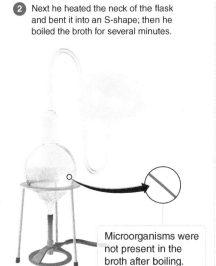

Microorganisms were not present in the broth after boiling.

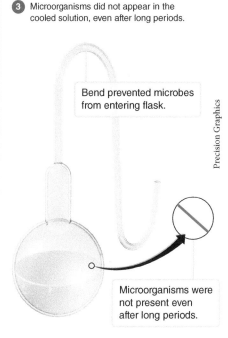

Bend prevented microbes from entering flask.

Microorganisms were not present even after long periods.

Precision Graphics

KEYCONCEPTS

- Pasteur demonstrated that microbes are responsible for food spoilage, leading researchers to the connection between microbes and disease.

- His experiments and observations provided the basis of aseptic techniques, which are used to prevent microbial contamination, as shown in the photo at right.

TEK Image/SPL/Alamy

The germ theory was a difficult concept for many people to accept at that time because for centuries disease was believed to be punishment for an individual's crimes or misdeeds. When the inhabitants of an entire village became ill, people often blamed the disease on demons appearing as foul odors from sewage or on poisonous vapors from swamps. Most people born in Pasteur's time found it inconceivable that "invisible" microbes could travel through the air to infect plants and animals or remain on clothing and bedding to be transmitted from one person to another. Despite these doubts scientists gradually accumulated the information needed to support the new germ theory.

In 1865, Pasteur was called upon to help fight silkworm disease, which was ruining the silk industry throughout Europe.

Years earlier, in 1835, Agostino Bassi, an amateur microscopist, had proved that another silkworm disease was caused by a fungus. Using data provided by Bassi, Pasteur found that the more recent infection was caused by a protozoan, and he developed a method for recognizing afflicted silkworm moths.

In the 1860s, Joseph Lister, an English surgeon, applied the germ theory to medical procedures. Lister was aware that in the 1840s, the Hungarian physician Ignaz Semmelweis had demonstrated that physicians, who at the time did not disinfect their hands, routinely transmitted infections (puerperal, or childbirth, fever) from one obstetrical patient to another. Lister had also heard of Pasteur's work connecting microbes to animal diseases. Disinfectants were not used at the time, but Lister knew

1665	Hooke—First observation of cells
1673	van Leeuwenhoek—First observation of live microorganisms
1735	Linnaeus—Nomenclature for organisms
1798	Jenner—First vaccine
1835	Bassi—Silkworm fungus
1840	Semmelweis—Childbirth fever
1853	DeBary—Fungal plant disease

1857	Pasteur—Fermentation
1861	Pasteur—Disproved spontaneous generation
1864	Pasteur—Pasteurization
1867	Lister—Aseptic surgery
1876	*Koch—Germ theory of disease
1879	Neisser—*Neisseria gonorrhoeae*
1881	*Koch—Pure cultures
	Finley—Yellow fever
1882	*Koch—*Mycobacterium tuberculosis*
	Hess—Agar (solid) media
1883	*Koch—*Vibrio cholerae*
1884	*Metchnikoff—Phagocytosis

GOLDEN AGE OF MICROBIOLOGY

	Gram—Gram-staining procedure
	Escherich—*Escherichia coli*
1887	Petri—Petri dish
1889	Kitasato—*Clostridium tetani*
1890	*von Bering—Diphtheria antitoxin
	*Ehrlich—Theory of immunity
1892	Winogradsky—Sulfur cycle
1898	Shiga—*Shigella dysenteriae*
1908	*Ehrlich—Syphilis
1910	Chagas—*Trypanosoma cruzi*
1911	* Rous—Tumor-causing virus (1966 Nobel Prize)

1928	*Fleming, Chain, Florey—Penicillin
	Griffith—Transformation in bacteria
1934	Lancefield—Streptococcal antigens
1935	*Stanley, Northrup, Sumner—Crystallized virus
1941	Beadle and Tatum—Relationship between genes and enzymes
1943	*Delbrück and Luria—Viral infection of bacteria
1944	Avery, MacLeod, McCarty—Genetic material is DNA
1946	Lederberg and Tatum—Bacterial conjugation
1953	*Watson and Crick—DNA structure
1957	*Jacob and Monod—Protein synthesis regulation
1959	Stewart—Viral cause of human cancer
1962	*Edelman and Porter—Antibodies
1964	Epstein, Achong, Barr—Epstein-Barr virus as cause of human cancer
1971	*Nathans, Smith, Arber—Restriction enzymes (used for recombinant DNA technology)
1973	Berg—Genetic engineering
1975	Dulbecco, Temin, Baltimore—Reverse transcriptase
1978	Woese—Archaea
	*Mitchell—Chemiosmotic mechanism
1981	Margulis—Origin of eukaryotic cells
1982	*Klug—Structure of tobacco mosaic virus
1983	*McClintock—Transposons

1988	*Deisenhofer, Huber, Michel—Bacterial photosynthesis pigments
1994	Cano—Reported to have cultured 40-million-year-old bacteria
1997	*Prusiner—Prions

Precision Graphics

Images from the History of Medicine (NLM)

Louis Pasteur (1822–1895)
Demonstrated that life did not arise spontaneously from nonliving matter.

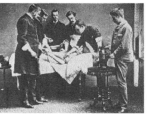

KRUIF, Paul de. Mikrobenjäger. Orell Füssli, Zürich, 1927

Robert Koch (1843–1910)
Established experimental steps for directly linking a specific microbe to a specific disease.

Performing an 1871 surgery in the Lister Surgery Theatre, Edinburgh, Scotland

Joseph Lister (1827–1912)
Performed surgery under antiseptic conditions using phenol. Proved that microbes caused surgical wound infections.

Rockefeller Archive Center

Rebecca C. Lancefield (1895–1981)
Classified streptococci according to serotypes (variants within a species)

Figure 4 Milestones in microbiology, highlighting those that occurred during the Golden Age of Microbiology. An asterisk (*) indicates a Nobel laureate.

[Q] Why do you think the Golden Age of Microbiology occurred when it did?

that phenol (carbolic acid) kills bacteria, so he began treating surgical wounds with a phenol solution. The practice so reduced the incidence of infections and deaths that other surgeons quickly adopted it. Lister's technique was one of the earliest medical attempts to control infections caused by microorganisms. In fact, his findings proved that microorganisms cause surgical wound infections.

The first proof that bacteria actually cause disease came from Robert Koch in 1876. Koch, a German physician, was Pasteur's young rival in the race to discover the cause of anthrax, a disease that was destroying cattle and sheep in Europe. Koch discovered rod-shaped bacteria now known as *Bacillus anthracis* (bä-sil′lus an-thrā′sis) in the blood of cattle that had died of anthrax. He cultured the bacteria on nutrients and then injected samples of the culture into healthy animals. When these animals became sick and died, Koch isolated the bacteria in their blood and compared them with the originally isolated bacteria. He found that the two sets of blood cultures contained the same bacteria.

Koch thus established **Koch's postulates,** a sequence of experimental steps for directly relating a specific microbe to a specific disease. During the past 100 years, these same criteria have been invaluable in investigations proving that specific microorganisms cause many diseases.

Vaccination

Often a treatment or preventive procedure is developed before scientists know why it works. The smallpox vaccine is an example. On May 4, 1796, almost 70 years before Koch established that a specific microorganism causes anthrax, Edward Jenner, a young British physician, embarked on an experiment to find a way to protect people from smallpox.

Smallpox epidemics were greatly feared. The disease periodically swept through Europe, killing thousands, and it wiped out 90% of the American Indians on the East Coast when European settlers first brought the infection to the New World.

When a young milkmaid informed Jenner that she couldn't get smallpox because she already had been sick from cowpox—a much milder disease—he decided to put the girl's story to the test. First Jenner collected scrapings from cowpox blisters. Then he inoculated a healthy 8-year-old volunteer with the cowpox material by scratching the person's arm with a pox-contaminated needle. The scratch turned into a raised bump. In a few days, the volunteer became mildly sick but recovered and never again contracted either cowpox or smallpox. The process was called *vaccination,* from the Latin word *vacca,* meaning cow. Pasteur gave it this name in honor of Jenner's work. The protection from disease provided by vaccination (or by recovery from the disease itself) is called **immunity.**

Years after Jenner's experiment, in about 1880, Pasteur discovered why vaccinations work. He found that the bacterium that causes fowl cholera lost its ability to cause disease (lost its *virulence,* or became *avirulent*) after it was grown in the laboratory for long periods. However, it—and other microorganisms with decreased virulence—was able to induce immunity against subsequent infections by its virulent counterparts. The discovery of this phenomenon provided a clue to Jenner's successful experiment with cowpox. Both cowpox and smallpox are caused by viruses. Even though cowpox virus is not a laboratory-produced derivative of smallpox virus, it is so closely related to the smallpox virus that it can induce immunity to both viruses. Pasteur used the term *vaccine* for cultures of avirulent microorganisms used for preventive inoculation.

Jenner's experiment marked the first time in a Western culture that a living viral agent—the cowpox virus—was used to produce immunity. Physicians in China had immunized patients from smallpox by removing scales from drying pustules of a person suffering from a mild case of smallpox, grinding the scales to a fine powder, and inserting the powder into the nose of the person to be protected.

Some vaccines are still produced from avirulent microbial strains that stimulate immunity to the related virulent strain. Other vaccines are made from killed virulent microbes, from isolated components of virulent microorganisms, or by genetic engineering techniques.

CHECK YOUR UNDERSTANDING

✔ Summarize in your own words the germ theory of disease. **8**

✔ What is the importance of Koch's postulates? **9**

✔ What is the significance of Jenner's discovery? **10**

The Birth of Modern Chemotherapy: Dreams of a "Magic Bullet"

After the relationship between microorganisms and disease was established, medical microbiologists next focused on the search for substances that could destroy pathogenic microorganisms without damaging the infected animal or human. Treatment of disease by using chemical substances is called **chemotherapy.** (The term also commonly refers to chemical treatment of noninfectious diseases, such as cancer.) Chemicals produced naturally by bacteria and fungi to act against other microorganisms are called **antibiotics.** Chemotherapeutic agents prepared from chemicals in the laboratory are called **synthetic drugs.** The success of chemotherapy is based on the fact that some chemicals are more poisonous to microorganisms than to the hosts infected by the microbes.

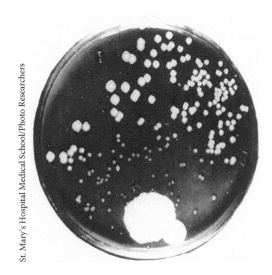

St. Mary's Hospital Medical School/Photo Researchers

Figure 5 The discovery of penicillin. Alexander Fleming took this photograph in 1928. The colony of *Penicillium* mold accidentally contaminated the plate and inhibited nearby bacterial growth.

Q Why do you think penicillin is no longer as effective as it once was?

The First Synthetic Drugs

Paul Ehrlich, a German physician, was the imaginative thinker who fired the first shot in the chemotherapy revolution. As a medical student, Ehrlich speculated about a "magic bullet" that could hunt down and destroy a pathogen without harming the infected host. He then launched a search for such a bullet. In 1910, after testing hundreds of substances, he found a chemotherapeutic agent called *salvarsan,* an arsenic derivative effective against syphilis. The agent was named salvarsan because it was considered to offer salvation from syphilis and it contained arsenic. Before this discovery, the only known chemical in Europe's medical arsenal was an extract from the bark of a South American tree, *quinine,* which had been used by Spanish conquistadors to treat malaria.

By the late 1930s, researchers had developed several other synthetic drugs that could destroy microorganisms. Most of these drugs were derivatives of dyes. This came about because the dyes synthesized and manufactured for fabrics were routinely tested for antimicrobial qualities by microbiologists looking for a "magic bullet." In addition, *sulfonamides* (sulfa drugs) were synthesized at about the same time.

A Fortunate Accident—Antibiotics

In contrast to the sulfa drugs, which were deliberately developed from a series of industrial chemicals, the first antibiotic was discovered by accident. Alexander Fleming, a Scottish physician and bacteriologist, almost tossed out some culture plates that had been contaminated by mold. Fortunately, he took a second look at the curious pattern of growth on the contaminated plates. Around the mold was a clear area where bacterial growth had been inhibited (**Figure 5**). Fleming was looking at a mold that

could inhibit the growth of a bacterium. The mold was later identified as *Penicillium notatum* (pen-i-sil′lē-um nō-tā′tum), later renamed *Penicillium chrysogenum* (krī-so′jen-um), and in 1928 Fleming named the mold's active inhibitor *penicillin.* Thus, penicillin is an antibiotic produced by a fungus. The enormous usefulness of penicillin was not apparent until the 1940s, when it was finally tested clinically and mass produced.

Since these early discoveries, thousands of other antibiotics have been discovered. Unfortunately, antibiotics and other chemotherapeutic drugs are not without problems. Many antimicrobial chemicals are too toxic to humans for practical use; they kill the pathogenic microbes, but they also damage the infected host. For reasons we will discuss later, toxicity to humans is a particular problem in the development of drugs for treating viral diseases. Viral growth depends on life processes of normal host cells. Thus, there are very few successful antiviral drugs, because a drug that would interfere with viral reproduction would also likely affect uninfected cells of the body.

Another major problem associated with antimicrobial drugs is the emergence and spread of new strains of microorganisms that are resistant to antibiotics. Over the years, more and more microbes have developed resistance to antibiotics that at one time were very effective against them. Drug resistance results from genetic changes in microbes that enables them to tolerate a certain amount of an antibiotic that would normally inhibit them. For example a microbe might produce chemicals (enzymes) that inactivate antibiotics, or a microbe might undergo changes to its surface that prevent an antibiotic from attaching to it or entering it.

The recent appearance of vancomycin-resistant *Staphylococcus aureus* and *Enterococcus faecalis* (en-te-rō-kok′kus fe-kā′lis) has alarmed health care professionals because it indicates that some previously treatable bacterial infections may soon be impossible to treat with antibiotics.

CHECK YOUR UNDERSTANDING

✔ What was Ehrlich's "magic bullet"? **11**

Modern Developments in Microbiology

The quest to solve drug resistance, identify viruses, and develop vaccines requires sophisticated research techniques and correlated studies that were never dreamed of in the days of Koch and Pasteur.

The groundwork laid during the Golden Age of Microbiology provided the basis for several monumental achievements during the twentieth century (**Table 2**). New branches of microbiology were developed, including immunology and virology. Most recently, the development of a set of new methods called recombinant DNA technology has revolutionized research and practical applications in all areas of microbiology.

Bacteriology, Mycology, and Parasitology

Bacteriology, the study of bacteria, began with van Leeuwenhoek's first examination of tooth scrapings. New pathogenic

TABLE **2** **Selected Nobel Prizes Awarded for Research in Microbiology**

Nobel Laureates	Year of Presentation	Country of Birth	Contribution
Ronald Ross	1902	England	Discovered how malaria is transmitted
Selman A. Waksman	1952	Ukraine	Discovered streptomycin
Hans A. Krebs	1953	Germany	Discovered chemical steps of the Krebs cycle in carbohydrate metabolism
John F. Enders, Thomas H. Weller, and Frederick C. Robbins	1954	United States	Cultured poliovirus in cell cultures
Joshua Lederberg, George Beadle, and Edward Tatum	1958	United States	Described genetic control of biochemical reactions
Frank Macfarlane Burnet and Peter Brian Medawar	1960	Australia Great Britain	Discovered acquired immune tolerance
César Milstein, Georges J. F. Köhler, and Niels Kai Jerne	1984	Argentina Germany Denmark	Developed a technique for producing monoclonal antibodies (single pure antibodies)
Susumu Tonegawa	1987	Japan	Described the genetics of antibody production
J. Michael Bishop and Harold E. Varmus	1989	United States	Discovered cancer-causing genes called oncogenes
Joseph E. Murray and E. Donnall Thomas	1990	United States	Performed the first successful organ transplants by using immunosuppressive agents
Edmond H. Fisher and Edwin G. Krebs	1992	United States	Discovered protein kinases, enzymes that regulate cell growth
Richard J. Roberts and Phillip A. Sharp	1993	Great Britain United States	Discovered that a gene can be separated onto different segments of DNA
Kary B. Mullis	1993	United States	Discovered the polymerase chain reaction to amplify (make multiple copies of) DNA
Peter C. Doherty and Rolf M. Zinkernagel	1996	Australia Switzerland	Discovered how cytotoxic T cells recognize virus-infected cells prior to destroying them
Peter Agre and Roderick MacKirron	2003	United States	Discovered water and ion channels in plasma membranes
Aaron Ciechanover, Avram Hershko, and Irwin Rose	2004	Israel Israel United States	Discovered how cells dispose of unwanted proteins in proteasomes
Barry Marshall and J. Robin Warren	2005	Australia	Discovered that *Helicobacter pylori* causes peptic ulcers
Andrew Fire and Craig Mello	2006	United States	Discovered RNA interference (RNAi), or gene silencing, by double-stranded RNA
Harald zur Hausen	2008	Germany	Discovered that human papilloma viruses cause cervical cancer
Françoise Barré-Sinoussi and Luc Montagnier	2008	France	Discovered human immunodeficiency virus (HIV)
Venkatraman Ramakrishnan, Thomas A. Steitz, and Ada E. Yonath	2010	India United States Israel	Detailed study of the structure and function of ribosomes

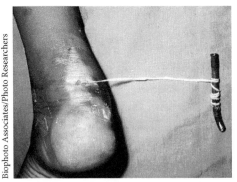

(a) Rod of Asclepius, symbol of the medical profession.

(b) A parasitic guinea worm (*Dracunculus medinensis*) is removed from the subcutaneous tissue of a patient by winding it onto a stick. This procedure may have been used for the design of the symbol in part (a).

Figure 6 Parasitology: the study of protozoa and parasitic worms.

 How do you think parasitic worms survive and live off a human host?

bacteria are still discovered regularly. Many bacteriologists, like Pasteur, look at the roles of bacteria in food and the environment. One intriguing discovery came in 1997, when Heide Schulz discovered a bacterium large enough to be seen with the unaided eye (0.2 mm wide). This bacterium, named *Thiomargarita namibiensis* (thī′o-mä-gär-e-tä na′mib-ē-ėn-sis), lives in the mud on the African coast. *Thiomargarita* is unusual because of its size and its ecological niche. The bacterium consumes hydrogen sulfide, which would be toxic to mud-dwelling animals.

Mycology, the study of fungi, includes medical, agricultural, and ecological branches. Recall that Bassi's work leading up to the germ theory of disease focused on a fungal pathogen. Fungal infection rates have been rising during the past decade, accounting for 10% of hospital-acquired infections. Climatic and environmental changes (severe drought) are thought to account for the tenfold increase in *Coccidioides immitis* (kok-sid-ē-oi′dēz im′mi-tis) infections in California. New techniques for diagnosing and treating fungal infections are currently being investigated.

Parasitology is the study of protozoa and parasitic worms. Because many parasitic worms are large enough to be seen with the unaided eye, they have been known for thousands of years. It has been speculated that the medical symbol, the rod of Asclepius, represents the removal of parasitic guinea worms (**Figure 6**). Asclepius was a Greek physician who practiced about 1200 B.C. and was deified as the god of medicine.

The clearing of rain forests has exposed laborers to previously undiscovered parasites. Previously unknown parasitic diseases are also being found in patients whose immune systems have been suppressed by organ transplants, cancer chemotherapy, or AIDS.

Bacteriology, mycology, and parasitology are currently going through a "golden age" of classification. Recent advances in **genomics,** the study of all of an organism's genes, have allowed scientists to classify bacteria and fungi according to their genetic relationships with other bacteria, fungi, and protozoa. These microorganisms were originally classified according to a limited number of visible characteristics.

Immunology

Immunology, the study of immunity, dates back in Western culture to Jenner's first vaccine in 1796. Since then, knowledge about the immune system has accumulated steadily and expanded rapidly. Vaccines are now available for numerous diseases, including measles, rubella (German measles), mumps, chickenpox, pneumococcal pneumonia, tetanus, tuberculosis, influenza, whooping cough, polio, and hepatitis B. The smallpox vaccine was so effective that the disease has been eliminated. Public health officials estimate that polio will be eradicated within a few years because of the polio vaccine.

A major advance in immunology occurred in 1933, when Rebecca Lancefield proposed that streptococci be classified according to serotypes (variants within a species) based on certain components in the cell walls of the bacteria. Streptococci are responsible for a variety of diseases, such as sore throat (strep throat), streptococcal toxic shock, and septicemia (blood poisoning). Her research permits the rapid identification of specific pathogenic streptococci based on immunological techniques.

In 1960, interferons, substances generated by the body's own immune system, were discovered. Interferons inhibit replication of viruses and have triggered considerable research related to the treatment of viral diseases and cancer. One of today's biggest challenges for immunologists is learning how the immune system might be stimulated to ward off the virus responsible for AIDS, a disease that destroys the immune system.

Virology

The study of viruses, **virology,** originated during the Golden Age of Microbiology. In 1892, Dmitri Iwanowski reported that the organism that caused mosaic disease of tobacco was so small that it passed through filters fine enough to stop all known bacteria. At the time, Iwanowski was not aware that the organism in question was a virus. In 1935, Wendell Stanley demonstrated that the organism, called tobacco mosaic virus (TMV), was fundamentally different from other microbes and so simple and homogeneous that it could be crystallized like a chemical compound. Stanley's work facilitated the study of viral structure and chemistry. Since the development of the electron microscope in the 1940s, microbiologists have been able to observe the structure of viruses in detail, and today much is known about their structure and activity.

Recombinant DNA Technology

Microorganisms can now be genetically modified to manufacture large amounts of human hormones and other urgently needed medical substances. In the late 1960s, Paul Berg showed that fragments of human or animal DNA (genes) that code for important proteins can be attached to bacterial DNA. The resulting hybrid was the first example of **recombinant DNA.** When recombinant DNA is inserted into bacteria (or other microbes), it can be used to make large quantities of the desired protein. The technology that developed from this technique is called **recombinant DNA technology.** Its origins can be found in two related fields. The first, **microbial genetics,** studies the mechanisms by which microorganisms inherit traits. The second, **molecular biology,** specifically studies how genetic information is carried in molecules of DNA and how DNA directs the synthesis of proteins.

Although molecular biology encompasses all organisms, much of our knowledge of how genes determine specific traits has been revealed through experiments with bacteria. Through the 1930s, all genetic research was based on the study of plant and animal cells. But in the 1940s, scientists turned to unicellular organisms, primarily bacteria, which have several advantages for genetic and biochemical research. For one thing, bacteria are less complex than plants and animals. For another, the life cycles of many bacteria last less than an hour, so scientists can cultivate very large numbers of bacteria for study in a relatively short time.

Once science turned to the study of unicellular life, rapid progress was made in genetics. In 1941, George W. Beadle and Edward L. Tatum demonstrated the relationship between genes and enzymes. DNA was established as the hereditary material in 1944 by Oswald Avery, Colin MacLeod, and Maclyn McCarty. In 1946, Joshua Lederberg and Edward L. Tatum discovered that genetic material could be transferred from one bacterium to another by a process called conjugation. Then, in 1953, James Watson and Francis Crick proposed a model for the structure and replication of DNA. The early 1960s witnessed a further explosion of discoveries relating to the way DNA controls protein synthesis. In 1961, François Jacob and Jacques Monod discovered messenger RNA (ribonucleic acid), a chemical involved in protein synthesis, and later they made the first major discoveries about the regulation of gene function in bacteria. During the same period, scientists were able to break the genetic code and thus understand how the information for protein synthesis in messenger RNA is translated into the amino acid sequence for making proteins.

CHECK YOUR UNDERSTANDING

✔ Define *bacteriology, mycology, parasitology, immunology,* and *virology.* 12

✔ Differentiate microbial genetics from molecular biology. 13

Microbes and Human Welfare

LEARNING OBJECTIVES

14 List at least four beneficial activities of microorganisms.

15 Name two examples of biotechnology that use recombinant DNA technology and two examples that do not.

As mentioned earlier, only a minority of all microorganisms are pathogenic. Microbes that cause food spoilage, such as soft spots on fruits and vegetables, decomposition of meats, and rancidity

of fats and oils, are also a minority. The vast majority of microbes benefit humans, other animals, and plants in many ways. For example, microbes produce methane and ethanol that can be used as alternative fuels to generate electricity and power vehicles. Biotechnology companies are using bacterial enzymes to break down plant cellulose so that yeast can metabolize the resulting simple sugars and produce ethanol. The following sections outline some of these beneficial activities.

Recycling Vital Elements

Discoveries made by two microbiologists in the 1880s have formed the basis for today's understanding of the biogeochemical cycles that support life on Earth. Martinus Beijerinck and Sergei Winogradsky were the first to show how bacteria help recycle vital elements between the soil and the atmosphere. **Microbial ecology,** the study of the relationship between microorganisms and their environment, originated with the work of these scientists. Today, microbial ecology has branched out and includes the study of how microbial populations interact with plants and animals in various environments. Among the concerns of microbial ecologists are water pollution and toxic chemicals in the environment.

The chemical elements carbon, nitrogen, oxygen, sulfur, and phosphorus are essential for life and abundant, but not necessarily in forms that organisms can use. Microorganisms are primarily responsible for converting these elements into forms that plants and animals can use. Microorganisms, primarily bacteria and fungi, return carbon dioxide to the atmosphere when they decompose organic wastes and dead plants and animals. Algae, cyanobacteria, and higher plants use the carbon dioxide during photosynthesis to produce carbohydrates for animals, fungi, and bacteria. Nitrogen is abundant in the atmosphere but in that form is not usable by plants and animals. Only bacteria can naturally convert atmospheric nitrogen to a form available to plants and animals.

Sewage Treatment: Using Microbes to Recycle Water

Our society's growing awareness of the need to preserve the environment has made people more conscious of the responsibility to recycle precious water and prevent the pollution of rivers and oceans. One major pollutant is sewage, which consists of human excrement, waste water, industrial wastes, and surface runoff. Sewage is about 99.9% water, with a few hundredths of 1% suspended solids. The remainder is a variety of dissolved materials.

Sewage treatment plants remove the undesirable materials and harmful microorganisms. Treatments combine various physical processes with the action of beneficial microbes. Large solids such as paper, wood, glass, gravel, and plastic are removed from sewage; left behind are liquid and organic materials that bacteria convert into such by-products as carbon dioxide, nitrates, phosphates, sulfates, ammonia, hydrogen sulfide, and methane.

Bioremediation: Using Microbes to Clean Up Pollutants

In 1988, scientists began using microbes to clean up pollutants and toxic wastes produced by various industrial processes. For example, some bacteria can actually use pollutants as energy sources; others produce enzymes that break down toxins into less harmful substances. By using bacteria in these ways—a process known as **bioremediation**—toxins can be removed from underground wells, chemical spills, toxic waste sites, and oil spills, such as the massive oil spill from an offshore drilling rig in the Gulf of Mexico on April 20, 2010. In addition, bacterial enzymes are used in drain cleaners to remove clogs without adding harmful chemicals to the environment. In some cases, microorganisms indigenous to the environment are used; in others, genetically modified microbes are used. Among the most commonly used microbes are certain species of bacteria of the genera *Pseudomonas* (sū-dō-mō′nas) and *Bacillus* (bä-sil′lus). *Bacillus* enzymes are also used in household detergents to remove spots from clothing.

Insect Pest Control by Microorganisms

Besides spreading diseases, insects can cause devastating crop damage. Insect pest control is therefore important for both agriculture and the prevention of human disease.

The bacterium *Bacillus thuringiensis* (thŭr-in-jē-en′sis) has been used extensively in the United States to control such pests as alfalfa caterpillars, bollworms, corn borers, cabbageworms, tobacco budworms, and fruit tree leaf rollers. It is incorporated into a dusting powder that is applied to the crops these insects eat. The bacteria produce protein crystals that are toxic to the digestive systems of the insects. The toxin gene also has been inserted into some plants to make them insect resistant.

By using microbial rather than chemical insect control, farmers can avoid harming the environment. Many chemical insecticides, such as DDT, remain in the soil as toxic pollutants and are eventually incorporated into the food chain.

Modern Biotechnology and Recombinant DNA Technology

Earlier, we touched on the commercial use of microorganisms to produce some common foods and chemicals. Such practical applications of microbiology are called **biotechnology.** Although biotechnology has been used in some form for centuries, techniques have become much more sophisticated in the past few decades. In the last several years, biotechnology has undergone a revolution through the advent of recombinant DNA technology to expand the potential of bacteria, viruses, and yeast cells and other fungi as miniature biochemical factories. Cultured plant and animal cells, as well as intact plants and animals, are also used as recombinant cells and organisms.

The applications of recombinant DNA technology are increasing with each passing year. Recombinant DNA techniques have been used thus far to produce a number of natural proteins, vaccines, and enzymes. Such substances have great potential for medical use.

A very exciting and important outcome of recombinant DNA techniques is **gene therapy**—inserting a missing gene or replacing a defective one in human cells. This technique uses a harmless virus to carry the missing or new gene into certain host cells, where the gene is picked up and inserted into the appropriate chromosome. Since 1990, gene therapy has been used to treat patients with adenosine deaminase (ADA) deficiency, a cause of severe combined immunodeficiency disease (SCID), in which cells of the immune system are inactive or missing; Duchenne's muscular dystrophy, a muscle-destroying disease; cystic fibrosis, a disease of the secreting portions of the respiratory passages, pancreas, salivary glands, and sweat glands; and LDL-receptor deficiency, a condition in which low-density lipoprotein (LDL) receptors are defective and LDL cannot enter cells. The LDL remains in the blood in high concentrations and increases the risk of atherosclerosis and coronary artery disease because it leads to fatty plaque formation in blood vessels. Results are still being evaluated. Other genetic diseases may also be treatable by gene therapy in the future, including hemophilia, an inability of the blood to clot normally; diabetes, elevated blood sugar levels; sickle cell disease, an abnormal kind of hemoglobin; and one type of hypercholesterolemia, high blood cholesterol.

Beyond medical applications, recombinant DNA techniques have also been applied to agriculture. For example, genetically altered strains of bacteria have been developed to protect fruit against frost damage, and bacteria are being modified to control insects that damage crops. Recombinant DNA has also been used to improve the appearance, flavor, and shelf life of fruits and vegetables. Potential agricultural uses of recombinant DNA include drought resistance, resistance to insects and microbial diseases, and increased temperature tolerance in crops.

CHECK YOUR UNDERSTANDING

☑ Name two beneficial uses of bacteria. 14

☑ Differentiate biotechnology from recombinant DNA technology. 15

Microbes and Human Disease

LEARNING OBJECTIVES

16   Define *normal microbiota* and *resistance*.

17   Define *biofilm*.

18   Define *emerging infectious disease*.

Normal Microbiota

We all live from birth until death in a world filled with microbes, and we all have a variety of microorganisms on and inside our bodies. These microorganisms make up our **normal microbiota,** or *flora** (**Figure 7**). The normal microbiota not only do us no harm, but also in some cases can actually benefit us. For example, some normal microbiota protect us against disease by preventing the overgrowth of harmful microbes, and others produce useful substances such as vitamin K and some B vitamins. Unfortunately, under some circumstances normal microbiota can make us sick or infect people we contact. For instance, when some normal microbiota leave their habitat, they can cause disease.

When is a microbe a welcome part of a healthy human, and when is it a harbinger of disease? The distinction between health and disease is in large part a balance between the natural defenses of the body and the disease-producing properties of microorganisms. Whether our bodies overcome the offensive tactics of a particular microbe depends on our **resistance**—the ability to ward off diseases. Important resistance is provided by the barrier of the skin, mucous membranes, cilia, stomach acid, and antimicrobial chemicals such as interferons. Microbes can be destroyed by white blood cells, by the inflammatory response, by fever, and by specific responses of our immune system. Sometimes, when our natural defenses are not strong enough to overcome an invader, they have to be supplemented by antibiotics or other drugs.

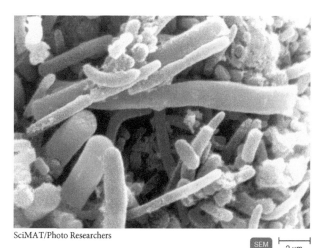

SciMAT/Photo Researchers

SEM 2 µm

Figure 7 Several types of bacteria found as part of the normal microbiota on the surface of the human tongue.

Q How do we benefit from the production of vitamin K by microbes?

Clinical Case

Staph is the common name for *Staphylococcus aureus* bacteria, which are carried on the skin of about 30% of the human population. Although Andrea is diligent about taking her antibiotic as prescribed, she doesn't seem to be improving. After 3 days, the lesion on her wrist is even larger than before and is now draining yellow pus. Andrea also develops a fever. Her mother insists that she call her doctor to tell him about the latest developments.

Why does Andrea's infection persist after treatment?

Biofilms

In nature, microorganisms may exist as single cells that float or swim independently in a liquid, or they may attach to each other and/or some usually solid surface. This latter mode of behavior is called a **biofilm,** a complex aggregation of microbes. The slime covering a rock in a lake is a biofilm. Use your tongue to feel the biofilm on your teeth. Biofilms can be beneficial. They protect your mucous membranes from harmful microbes, and biofilms in lakes are an important food for aquatic animals. Biofilms can also be harmful. They can clog water pipes, and on medical implants

* At one time, bacteria and fungi were thought to be plants, and thus the term *flora* was used.

such as joint prostheses and catheters (**Figure 8**), they can cause such infections as endocarditis (inflammation of the heart). Bacteria in biofilms are often resistant to antibiotics because the biofilm offers a protective barrier.

Infectious Diseases

An **infectious disease** is a disease in which pathogens invade a susceptible host, such as a human or an animal. In the process, the pathogen carries out at least part of its life cycle inside the host, and disease frequently results. By the end of World War II, many people believed that infectious diseases were under control. They thought malaria would be eradicated through the use of the insecticide DDT to kill mosquitoes, that a vaccine would prevent diphtheria, and that improved sanitation measures would help prevent cholera transmission. Malaria is far from eliminated. Since 1986, local outbreaks have been identified in New Jersey, California, Florida, New York, and Texas, and the disease infects 300 million people worldwide. In 1994, diphtheria appeared in the United States, brought by travelers from the newly independent states of the former Soviet Union, which were experiencing a massive diphtheria epidemic. The epidemic was brought under control in 1998. Cholera outbreaks still occur in less-developed parts of the world.

Emerging Infectious Diseases

These recent outbreaks point to the fact that infectious diseases are not disappearing, but rather seem to be reemerging and increasing. In addition, a number of new diseases—**emerging infectious diseases (EIDs)**—have cropped up in recent years. These are diseases that are new or changing and are increasing or

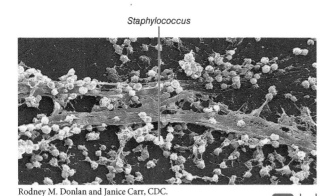

Staphylococcus

Rodney M. Donlan and Janice Carr, CDC.
1.AM: Sascha Drewlo

SEM 2 μm

Figure 8 Biofilm on a catheter. *Staphylococcus* bacteria stick to solid surfaces, forming a slimy layer. Bacteria that break away from this biofilm can cause infections.

 How does a biofilm's protective barrier make it resistant to antibiotics?

have the potential to increase in incidence in the near future. Some of the factors that have contributed to the development of EIDs are evolutionary changes in existing organisms (e.g., *Vibrio cholerae;* vib′rē-ō kol′-er-ĭ); the spread of known diseases to new geographic regions or populations by modern transportation (e.g., West Nile virus); and increased human exposure to new, unusual infectious agents in areas that are undergoing ecologic changes such as deforestation and construction (e.g., Venezuelan hemorrhagic virus). EIDs also develop as a result of antimicrobial resistance (e.g., vancomycin-resistant *S. aureus*). An increasing number of incidents in recent years highlights the extent of the problem.

H1N1 influenza (flu), also known as *swine flu,* is a type of influenza caused by a new virus called *influenza H1N1.* H1N1 was first detected in the United States in april 2009. In June 2009, the World Health Organization declared H1N1 flu to be a *global pandemic disease* (a disease that affects large numbers of individuals in a short period of time and occurs worldwide).

Avian influenza A (H5N1), or **bird flu,** caught the attention of the public in 2003, when it killed millions of poultry and 24 people in eight countries in southeast Asia. Avian influenza viruses occur in birds worldwide. Certain wild birds, particularly waterfowl, do not get sick but carry the virus in their intestines and shed it in saliva, nasal secretions, and feces. Most often, the wild birds spread influenza to domesticated birds, in which the virus causes death.

Influenza A viruses are found in many different animals, including ducks, chickens, pigs, whales, horses, and seals. Normally, each subtype of influenza A virus is specific to certain species. However, influenza A viruses normally seen in one species sometimes can cross over and cause illness in another species, and all subtypes of influenza A virus can infect pigs. Although

it is unusual for people to get influenza infections directly from animals, sporadic human infections and outbreaks caused by certain avian influenza A viruses and pig influenza viruses have been reported. As of 2008, avian influenza had sickened 242 people, and about half of them died. Fortunately, the virus has not yet evolved to be transmitted successfully among humans.

Human infections with avian influenza viruses detected since 1997 have not resulted in sustained human-to-human transmission. However, because influenza viruses have the potential to change and gain the ability to spread easily between people, monitoring for human infection and person-to-person transmission is important. The U.S. Food and Drug Administration (FDA) approved a human vaccine against the avian influenza virus in April 2007.

Antibiotics are critical in treating bacterial infections. However, years of overuse and misuse of these drugs have created environments in which antibiotic-resistant bacteria thrive. Random mutations in bacterial genes can make a bacterium resistant to an antibiotic. In the presence of that antibiotic, this bacterium has an advantage over other, susceptible bacteria and is able to proliferate. Antibiotic-resistant bacteria have become a global health crisis.

Staphylococcus aureus causes a wide range of human infections from pimples and boils to pneumonia, food poisoning, and surgical wound infections, and it is a significant cause of hospital-associated infections. After penicillin's initial success in treating *S. aureus* infection, penicillin-resistant *S. aureus* became a major threat in hospitals in the 1950s, requiring the use of methicillin. In the 1980s, **methicillin-resistant *S. aureus,*** called **MRSA,** emerged and became endemic in many hospitals, leading to increasing use of vancomycin. In the late 1990s, *S. aureus* infections that were less sensitive to vancomycin (**vancomycin-intermediate *S. aureus,* or VISA**) were reported. In 2002, an infection caused by **vancomycin-resistant *S. aureus* (VRSA)** in a patient in the United States was reported.

In March 2010, the World Health Organization (WHO) reported that in some parts of the world (such as northwestern Russia) about 28% of all individuals with tuberculosis (TB) had the multidrug-resistant form of the disease (MDR-TB). Multidrug-resistant TB is caused by bacteria that are resistant to at least the antibiotics isoniazid and rifampicin, the most effective drugs against tuberculosis.

The antibacterial substances added to various household cleaning products are similar to antibiotics in many ways. When used correctly, they inhibit bacterial growth. However, wiping every household surface with these antibacterial agents creates an environment in which the resistant bacteria survive. Unfortunately, when you really need to disinfect your homes and hands—for example, when a family member comes home from a hospital and is still vulnerable to infection—you may encounter mainly resistant bacteria.

Routine housecleaning and handwashing are necessary, but standard soaps and detergents (without added antibacterials) are fine for these tasks. In addition, quickly evaporating chemicals, such as chlorine bleach, alcohol, ammonia, and hydrogen peroxide, remove potentially pathogenic bacteria but do not leave residues that encourage the growth of resistant bacteria.

Clinical Case

The *S. aureus* bacterium responsible for Andrea's infection is resistant to the β-lactam antibiotic prescribed by Andrea's doctor. Concerned about what his patient is telling him, Andrea's doctor calls the local hospital to let them know he is sending a patient over. In the emergency department, a nurse swabs Andrea's wound and sends it to the hospital lab for culturing. The culture shows that Andrea's infection is caused by methicillin-resistant *Staphylococcus aureus* (MRSA). MRSA produces β-lactamase, an enzyme that destroys β-lactam antibiotics. The attending physician surgically drains the pus from the sore on Andrea's wrist.

How does antibiotic resistance develop?

West Nile encephalitis (WNE) is inflammation of the brain caused by West Nile virus. WNE was first diagnosed in the West Nile region of Uganda in 1937. In 1999 the virus made its first North American appearance in humans in New York City. In 2007, West Nile virus infected over 3600 people in 43 states. West Nile virus is now established in nonmigratory birds in 48 states. The virus, which is carried by birds, is transmitted between birds—and to horses and humans—by mosquitoes. West Nile virus may have arrived in the United States in an infected traveler or in migratory birds.

In 1996, countries worldwide were refusing to import beef from the United Kingdom, where hundreds of thousands of cattle born after 1988 had to be killed because of an epidemic of **bovine spongiform encephalopathy** (en-sef-a-lop′a-thē), also called **BSE** or **mad cow disease.** BSE first came to the attention of microbiologists in 1986 as one of a handful of diseases caused by an infectious protein called a *prion.* Studies suggest that the source of disease was cattle feed prepared from sheep infected with their own version of the disease. Cattle are herbivores (planteaters), but adding protein to their feed improves their growth and health. **Creutzfeldt-Jakob disease** (kroits′felt yä′kôb), or **CJD,** is a human disease also caused by a prion. The incidence of CJD in the United Kingdom is similar to the incidence in other countries. However, by 2005 the United Kingdom reported 154 human cases of CJD caused by a new variant related to the bovine disease.

Escherichia coli is a normal inhabitant of the large intestine of vertebrates, including humans, and its presence is beneficial because it helps produce certain vitamins and breaks down otherwise undigestible foodstuffs. However, a strain called *E. coli* **O157:H7** causes bloody diarrhea when it grows in the intestines. This strain was first recognized in 1982 and since then has emerged as a public health problem. It is now one of the leading causes of diarrhea worldwide. In 1996, some 9000 people in Japan became ill, and 7 died, as a result of infection by *E. coli* O157:H7. The recent outbreaks of *E. coli* O157:H7 in the United States, associated with contamination of undercooked meat and unpasteurized beverages, have led public health officials to call for the development of new methods of testing for bacteria in food.

In 1995, infections of so-called **flesh-eating bacteria** were reported on the front pages of major newspapers. The bacteria are more correctly named invasive group A *Streptococcus* (strep-tō-kok′kus), or IGAS. Rates of IGAS in the United States, Scandinavia, England, and Wales have been increasing.

In 1995, a hospital laboratory technician in Democratic Republic of Congo (DROC) who had fever and bloody diarrhea underwent surgery for a suspected perforated bowel. Afterward he started hemorrhaging, and his blood began clotting in his blood vessels. A few days later, health care workers in the hospital where he was staying developed similar symptoms. One of them was transferred to a hospital in a different city; personnel in the second hospital who cared for this patient also developed symptoms. By the time the epidemic was over, 315 people had contracted **Ebola hemorrhagic fever** (hem-ôr-raj′ik), or **EHF,** and over 75% of them died. The epidemic was controlled when microbiologists instituted training on the use of protective equipment and educational measures in the community. Close personal contact with infectious blood or other body fluids or tissue leads to human-to-human transmission.

Microbiologists first isolated Ebola viruses from humans during earlier outbreaks in DROC in 1976. (The virus is named after Congo's Ebola River.) In 2008, an Ebola virus outbreak occurred in Uganda with 149 cases. In 1989 and 1996, outbreaks among monkeys imported into the United States from the Philippines were caused by another Ebola virus but were not associated with human disease.

Recorded cases of **Marburg virus,** another hemorrhagic fever virus, are rare. The first cases were laboratory workers in Europe who handled African green monkeys from Uganda. Four outbreaks were identified in Africa between 1975 and 1998, involving 2 to 154 people with 56% mortality. In 2004, an outbreak killed 227 people. Microbiologists have been studying many animals but have not yet discovered the natural reservoir (source) of EHF and Marburg viruses.

In 1993, an outbreak of **cryptosporidiosis** (krip-tō-spô-rid-ē-ō′sis) transmitted through the public water supply in Milwaukee, Wisconsin, resulted in diarrheal illness in an estimated 403,000 persons. The microorganism responsible for this outbreak was the protozoan *Cryptosporidium* (krip-tō-spô-ri′dē-um). First reported as a cause of human disease in 1976, it is responsible for up to 30% of the diarrheal illness in developing countries. In the United States, transmission has occurred via drinking water, swimming pools, and contaminated hospital supplies.

AIDS (acquired immunodeficiency syndrome) first came to public attention in 1981 with reports from Los Angeles that a few young homosexual men had died of a previously rare type of pneumonia known as *Pneumocystis* (nü-mō-sis′tis) pneumonia. These men had experienced a severe weakening of the immune system, which normally fights infectious diseases. Soon these cases were correlated with an unusual number of occurrences of a rare form of cancer, Kaposi's sarcoma, among young homosexual men. Similar increases in such rare diseases were found among hemophiliacs and intravenous drug users.

Researchers quickly discovered that the cause of AIDS was a previously unknown virus (see Figure 1e). The virus, now called **human immunodeficiency virus (HIV),** destroys $CD4^+$ T cells, one type of white blood cell important to immune system defenses. Sickness and death result from microorganisms or cancerous cells that might otherwise have been defeated by the body's natural defenses. So far, the disease has been inevitably fatal once symptoms develop.

By studying disease patterns, medical researchers found that HIV could be spread through sexual intercourse, by contaminated needles, from infected mothers to their newborns via breast milk, and by blood transfusions—in short, by the transmission of body fluids from one person to another. Since 1985, blood used for transfusions has been carefully checked for the presence of HIV, and it is now quite unlikely that the virus can be spread by this means.

By the end of 2010, over 1 million people in the United States are living with AIDS. Over 50,000 Americans become infected and 18,000 die each year. As of 2010, health officials estimated that 1.3 million Americans have HIV infection. In 2009, the World Health Organization (WHO) estimated that over 33 million people worldwide are living with HIV/AIDS and that 7500 new infections occur every day.

Since 1994, new treatments have extended the life span of people with AIDS; however, approximately 40,000 new cases occur annually in the United States. The majority of individuals with AIDS are in the sexually active age group. Because heterosexual partners of AIDS sufferers are at high risk of infection, public health officials are concerned that even more women and minorities will contract AIDS. In 1997, HIV diagnoses began increasing among women and minorities. Among the AIDS cases reported in 2009, 26% were women, and 49% were African American.

In the months and years to come, scientists will continue to apply microbiological techniques to help them learn more about the structure of the deadly HIV, how it is transmitted, how it grows in cells and causes disease, how drugs can be directed against it, and whether an effective vaccine can be developed. Public health officials have also focused on prevention through education.

AIDS poses one of this century's most formidable health threats, but it is not the first serious epidemic of a sexually transmitted disease. Syphilis was also once a fatal epidemic disease. As recently as 1941, syphilis caused an estimated 14,000 deaths per year in the United States. With few drugs available for treatment and no vaccines to prevent it, efforts to control the disease focused mainly on altering sexual behavior and on the use of condoms. The eventual development of drugs to treat syphilis contributed significantly to preventing the spread of the disease. According to the Centers for Disease Control and Prevention (CDC), reported cases of syphilis dropped from a record high of 575,000 in 1943 to an all-time low of 5979 cases in 2004. Since then, however, the number of cases has been increasing.

Just as microbiological techniques helped researchers in the fight against syphilis and smallpox, they will help scientists discover the causes of new emerging infectious diseases in the twenty-first century. Undoubtedly there will be new diseases. Ebola virus and *Influenzavirus* are examples of viruses that may be changing their abilities to infect different host species.

Infectious diseases may reemerge because of antibiotic resistance and through the use of microorganisms as weapons. The breakdown of public health measures for previously controlled infections has resulted in unexpected cases of tuberculosis, whooping cough, and diphtheria.

Clinical Case

Mutations develop randomly in bacteria: some mutations are lethal, some have no effect, and some may be beneficial. Once these mutations develop, the offspring of the mutated parent cells also carry the same mutation. Because they have an advantage in the presence of the antibiotic, bacteria that are resistant to antibiotics soon outnumber those that are susceptible to antibiotic therapy. The widespread use of antibiotics selectively allows the resistant bacteria to grow, whereas the susceptible bacteria are killed. Eventually, almost the entire population of bacteria is resistant to the antibiotic.

The emergency department physician prescribes a different antibiotic, vancomycin, which will kill the MRSA in Andrea's wrist. She also explains to Andrea what MRSA is and why it's important they find out where Andrea acquired the potentially lethal bacteria.

What can the emergency department physician tell Andrea about MRSA?

☑ Differentiate normal microbiota and infectious disease. **16**

☑ Why are biofilms important? **17**

☑ What factors contribute to the emergence of an infectious disease? **18**

* * *

The diseases we have mentioned are caused by viruses, bacteria, protozoa, and prions—types of microorganisms. This text introduces you to the enormous variety of microscopic organisms. It shows you how microbiologists use specific techniques and procedures to study the microbes that cause such diseases as AIDS and diarrhea—and diseases that have yet to be discovered. You will also learn how the body responds to microbial infection and how certain drugs combat microbial diseases. Finally, you will learn about the many beneficial roles that microbes play in the world around us.

Clinical Case Resolved

The first MRSA was health care–associated MRSA (HA-MRSA), transmitted between staff and patients in health care settings. In the 1990s, infections by a genetically different strain, community-associated MRSA (CA-MRSA), emerged as a major cause of skin disease in the United States. CA-MRSA enters skin abrasions from environmental surfaces or other people. Andrea has never been hospitalized before now, so they are able to rule out the hospital as the source of infection. Her college courses are all online, so she didn't contract MRSA at the university, either. The local health department sends someone to her family home to swab for the bacteria there.

MRSA is isolated from Andrea's living room sofa, but how did it get there? After speaking with the family, the representative from the health department, knowing that clusters of CA-MRSA infections have been seen among athletes suggests swabbing the mats used by the gymnasts at the school Andrea's sister attends. The cultures come back positive for MRSA. Andrea's sister, although not infected, transferred the bacteria from her skin to the sofa, where Andrea laid her arm. (A person can carry MRSA on the skin without becoming infected.) The bacteria entered through a scratch on Andrea's wrist.

Study Outline

Test your understanding with quizzes, microbe review, and a chapter post-test at www.masteringmicrobiology.com.

Microbes in Our Lives

1. Living things too small to be seen with the unaided eye are called microorganisms.
2. Microorganisms are important in maintaining Earth's ecological balance.
3. Some microorganisms live in humans and other animals and are needed to maintain good health.
4. Some microorganisms are used to produce foods and chemicals.
5. Some microorganisms cause disease.

Naming and Classifying Microorganisms

Nomenclature

1. In a nomenclature system designed by Carolus Linnaeus (1735), each living organism is assigned two names.
2. The two names consist of a genus and a specific epithet, both of which are underlined or italicized.

Types of Microorganisms

3. Bacteria are unicellular organisms. Because they have no nucleus, the cells are described as prokaryotic.
4. The three major basic shapes of bacteria are bacillus, coccus, and spiral.
5. Most bacteria have a peptidoglycan cell wall; they divide by binary fission, and they may possess flagella.
6. Bacteria can use a wide range of chemical substances for their nutrition.
7. Archaea consist of prokaryotic cells; they lack peptidoglycan in their cell walls.
8. Archaea include methanogens, extreme halophiles, and extreme thermophiles.
9. Fungi (mushrooms, molds, and yeasts) have eukaryotic cells (cells with a true nucleus). Most fungi are multicellular.
10. Fungi obtain nutrients by absorbing organic material from their environment.
11. Protozoa are unicellular eukaryotes.
12. Protozoa obtain nourishment by absorption or ingestion through specialized structures.
13. Algae are unicellular or multicellular eukaryotes that obtain nourishment by photosynthesis.
14. Algae produce oxygen and carbohydrates that are used by other organisms.
15. Viruses are noncellular entities that are parasites of cells.
16. Viruses consist of a nucleic acid core (DNA or RNA) surrounded by a protein coat. An envelope may surround the coat.
17. The principal groups of multicellular animal parasites are flatworms and roundworms, collectively called helminths.
18. The microscopic stages in the life cycle of helminths are identified by traditional microbiological procedures.

Classification of Microorganisms

19. All organisms are classified into Bacteria, Archaea, and Eukarya. Eukarya include protists, fungi, plants, and animals.

A Brief History of Microbiology

The First Observations

1. Robert Hooke observed that cork was composed of "little boxes"; he introduced the term *cell* (1665).

2. Hooke's observations laid the groundwork for development of the cell theory, the concept that all living things are composed of cells.

3. Anton van Leeuwenhoek, using a simple microscope, was the first to observe microorganisms (1673).

The Debate over Spontaneous Generation

4. Until the mid-1880s, many people believed in spontaneous generation, the idea that living organisms could arise from nonliving matter.

5. Francesco Redi demonstrated that maggots appear on decaying meat only when flies are able to lay eggs on the meat (1668).

6. John Needham claimed that microorganisms could arise spontaneously from heated nutrient broth (1745).

7. Lazzaro Spallanzani repeated Needham's experiments and suggested that Needham's results were due to microorganisms in the air entering his broth (1765).

8. Rudolf Virchow introduced the concept of biogenesis: living cells can arise only from preexisting cells (1858).

9. Louis Pasteur demonstrated that microorganisms are in the air everywhere and offered proof of biogenesis (1861).

10. Pasteur's discoveries led to the development of aseptic techniques used in laboratory and medical procedures to prevent contamination by microorganisms.

The Golden Age of Microbiology

11. The science of microbiology advanced rapidly between 1857 and 1914.

12. Pasteur found that yeasts ferment sugars to alcohol and that bacteria can oxidize the alcohol to acetic acid.

13. A heating process called pasteurization is used to kill bacteria in some alcoholic beverages and milk.

14. Agostino Bassi (1835) and Pasteur (1865) showed a causal relationship between microorganisms and disease.

15. Joseph Lister introduced the use of a disinfectant to clean surgical wounds in order to control infections in humans (1860s).

16. Robert Koch proved that microorganisms cause disease. He used a sequence of procedures, now called Koch's postulates (1876), that are used today to prove that a particular microorganism causes a particular disease.

17. In a vaccination, immunity (resistance to a particular disease) is conferred by inoculation with a vaccine.

18. In 1798, Edward Jenner demonstrated that inoculation with cowpox material provides humans with immunity to smallpox.

19. About 1880, Pasteur discovered that avirulent bacteria could be used as a vaccine for fowl cholera; he coined the word *vaccine*.

20. Modern vaccines are prepared from living avirulent microorganisms or killed pathogens, from isolated components of pathogens, and by recombinant DNA techniques.

The Birth of Modern Chemotherapy: Dreams of a "Magic Bullet"

21. Chemotherapy is the chemical treatment of a disease.

22. Two types of chemotherapeutic agents are synthetic drugs (chemically prepared in the laboratory) and antibiotics (substances produced naturally by bacteria and fungi to inhibit the growth of other microorganisms).

23. Paul Ehrlich introduced an arsenic-containing chemical called salvarsan to treat syphilis (1910).

24. Alexander Fleming observed that the *Penicillium* fungus inhibited the growth of a bacterial culture. He named the active ingredient penicillin (1928).

25. Penicillin has been used clinically as an antibiotic since the 1940s.

26. Researchers are tackling the problem of drug-resistant microbes.

Modern Developments in Microbiology

27. Bacteriology is the study of bacteria, mycology is the study of fungi, and parasitology is the study of parasitic protozoa and worms.

28. Microbiologists are using genomics, the study of all of an organism's genes, to classify bacteria, fungi, and protozoa.

29. The study of AIDS, analysis of the action of interferons, and the development of new vaccines are among the current research interests in immunology.

30. New techniques in molecular biology and electron microscopy have provided tools for advancing our knowledge of virology.

31. The development of recombinant DNA technology has helped advance all areas of microbiology.

Microbes and Human Welfare

1. Microorganisms degrade dead plants and animals and recycle chemical elements to be used by living plants and animals.

2. Bacteria are used to decompose organic matter in sewage.

3. Bioremediation processes use bacteria to clean up toxic wastes.

4. Bacteria that cause diseases in insects are being used as biological controls of insect pests. Biological controls are specific for the pest and do not harm the environment.

5. Using microbes to make products such as foods and chemicals is called biotechnology.

6. Using recombinant DNA, bacteria can produce important substances such as proteins, vaccines, and enzymes.

7. In gene therapy, viruses are used to carry replacements for defective or missing genes into human cells.

8. Genetically modified bacteria are used in agriculture to protect plants from frost and insects and to improve the shelf life of produce.

Microbes and Human Disease

1. Everyone has microorganisms in and on the body; these make up the normal microbiota, or flora.

2. The disease-producing properties of a species of microbe and the host's resistance are important factors in determining whether a person will contract a disease.

3. Bacterial communities that form slimy layers on surfaces are called biofilms.

4. An infectious disease is one in which pathogens invade a susceptible host.

5. An emerging infectious disease (EID) is a new or changing disease showing an increase in incidence in the recent past or a potential to increase in the near future.

Study Questions

Answers to the Review and Multiple Choice questions can be found at the end of this chapter.

Review

1. How did the idea of spontaneous generation come about?

2. Briefly state the role microorganisms play in each of the following:
   a. biological control of pests
   b. recycling of elements
   c. normal microbiota
   d. sewage treatment
   e. human insulin production
   f. vaccine production
   g. biofilms

3. Into which field of microbiology would the following scientists best fit?

Researcher Who	Field
_____ a. Studies biodegradation of toxic wastes	1. Biotechnology
_____ b. Studies the causative agent of Ebola hemorrhagic fever	2. Immunology
_____ c. Studies the production of human proteins by bacteria	3. Microbial ecology
_____ d. Studies the symptoms of AIDS	4. Microbial genetics
_____ e. Studies the production of toxin by *E. coli*	5. Microbial physiology
_____ f. Studies the life cycle of *Cryptosporidium*	6. Molecular biology
_____ g. Develops gene therapy for a disease	7. Mycology
_____ h. Studies the fungus *Candida albicans*	8. Virology

4. Match the microorganisms in column A to their descriptions in column B.

Column A	Column B
_____ a. Archaea	1. Not composed of cells
_____ b. Algae	2. Cell wall made of chitin
_____ c. Bacteria	3. Cell wall made of peptidoglycan
_____ d. Fungi	4. Cell wall made of cellulose; photosynthetic
_____ e. Helminths	5. Unicellular, complex cell structure lacking a cell wall
_____ f. Protozoa	6. Multicellular animals
_____ g. Viruses	7. Prokaryote without peptidoglycan cell wall

5. Match the people in column A to their contribution toward the advancement of microbiology, in column B.

Column A	Column B
_____ a. Avery, MacLeod, and McCarty	1. Developed vaccine against smallpox
_____ b. Beadle and Tatum	2. Discovered how DNA controls protein synthesis in a cell
_____ c. Berg	3. Discovered penicillin

_____ d. Ehrlich	4. Discovered that DNA can be transferred from one bacterium to another
_____ e. Fleming	5. Disproved spontaneous generation
_____ f. Hooke	6. First to characterize a virus
_____ g. Iwanowski	7. First to use disinfectants in surgical procedures
_____ h. Jacob and Monod	8. First to observe bacteria
_____ i. Jenner	9. First to observe cells in plant material and name them
_____ j. Koch	10. Observed that viruses are filterable
_____ k. Lancefield	11. Proved that DNA is the hereditary material
_____ l. Lederberg and Tatum	12. Proved that microorganisms can cause disease
_____ m. Lister	13. Said living cells arise from preexisting living cells
_____ n. Pasteur	14. Showed that genes code for enzymes
_____ o. Stanley	15. Spliced animal DNA to bacterial DNA
_____ p. van Leeuwenhoek	16. Used bacteria to produce acetone
_____ q. Virchow	17. Used the first synthetic chemotherapeutic agent
_____ r. Weizmann	18. Proposed a classification system for streptococci based on antigens in their cell walls

6. The genus name of a bacterium is "erwinia," and the specific epithet is "amylovora." Write the scientific name of this organism correctly. Using this name as an example, explain how scientific names are chosen.

7. It is possible to purchase the following microorganisms in a retail store. Provide a reason for buying each.
   a. *Bacillus thuringiensis*
   b. *Saccharomyces*

8. **DRAW IT** Show where airborne microbes ended up in Pasteur's experiment.

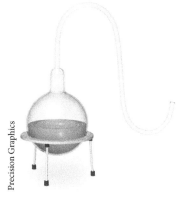

Precision Graphics

9. **NAME IT** What type of microorganism has a peptidoglycan cell wall, has DNA that is not contained in a nucleus, and has flagella?

Multiple Choice

1. Which of the following is a scientific name?
   a. *Mycobacterium tuberculosis*
   b. Tubercle bacillus
2. Which of the following is *not* a characteristic of bacteria?
   a. are prokaryotic
   b. have peptidoglycan cell walls
   c. have the same shape
   d. grow by binary fission
   e. have the ability to move
3. Which of the following is the most important element of Koch's germ theory of disease? The animal shows disease symptoms when
   a. the animal has been in contact with a sick animal.
   b. the animal has a lowered resistance.
   c. a microorganism is observed in the animal.
   d. a microorganism is inoculated into the animal.
   e. microorganisms can be cultured from the animal.
4. Recombinant DNA is
   a. DNA in bacteria.
   b. the study of how genes work.
   c. the DNA resulting when genes of two different organisms are mixed.
   d. the use of bacteria in the production of foods.
   e. the production of proteins by genes.
5. Which of the following statements is the best definition of *biogenesis*?
   a. Nonliving matter gives rise to living organisms.
   b. Living cells can only arise from preexisting cells.
   c. A vital force is necessary for life.
   d. Air is necessary for living organisms.
   e. Microorganisms can be generated from nonliving matter.
6. Which of the following is a beneficial activity of microorganisms?
   a. Some microorganisms are used as food for humans.
   b. Some microorganisms use carbon dioxide.
   c. Some microorganisms provide nitrogen for plant growth.
   d. Some microorganisms are used in sewage treatment processes.
   e. all of the above
7. It has been said that bacteria are essential for the existence of life on Earth. Which of the following is the essential function performed by bacteria?
   a. control insect populations
   b. directly provide food for humans
   c. decompose organic material and recycle elements
   d. cause disease
   e. produce human hormones such as insulin
8. Which of the following is an example of bioremediation?
   a. application of oil-degrading bacteria to an oil spill
   b. application of bacteria to a crop to prevent frost damage
   c. fixation of gaseous nitrogen into usable nitrogen
   d. production by bacteria of a human protein such as interferon
   e. all of the above
9. Spallanzani's conclusion about spontaneous generation was challenged because Lavoisier had just shown that oxygen was the vital component of air. Which of the following statements is true?
   a. All life requires air.
   b. Only disease-causing organisms require air.
   c. Some microbes do not require air.
   d. Pasteur kept air out of his biogenesis experiments.
   e. Lavoisier was mistaken.
10. Which of the following statements about *E. coli* is *false*?
    a. *E. coli* was the first disease-causing bacterium identified by Koch.
    b. *E. coli* is part of the normal microbiota of humans.
    c. *E. coli* is beneficial in human intestines.
    d. A disease-causing strain of *E. coli* causes bloody diarrhea.
    e. none of the above

Critical Thinking

1. How did the theory of biogenesis lead the way for the germ theory of disease?
2. Even though the germ theory of disease was not demonstrated until 1876, why did Semmelweis (1840) and Lister (1867) argue for the use of aseptic techniques?
3. Find at least three supermarket products made by microorganisms. (*Hint:* The label will state the scientific name of the organism or include the word *culture, fermented,* or *brewed.*)
4. People once believed all microbial diseases would be controlled by the twenty-first century. Name one emerging infectious disease. List three reasons why we are identifying new diseases now.

Clinical Applications

1. The prevalence of arthritis in the United States is 1 in 100,000 children. However, 1 in 10 children in Lyme, Connecticut, developed arthritis between June and September 1973. Allen Steere, a rheumatologist at Yale University, investigated the cases in Lyme and found that 25% of the patients remembered having a skin rash during their arthritic episode and that the disease was treatable with penicillin. Steere concluded that this was a new infectious disease and did not have an environmental, genetic, or immunologic cause.
   a. What was the factor that caused Steere to reach his conclusion?
   b. What is the disease?
   c. Why was the disease more prevalent between June and September?
2. In 1864, Lister observed that patients recovered completely from simple fractures, but that compound fractures had "disastrous consequences." He knew that the application of phenol (carbolic acid) to fields in the town of Carlisle prevented cattle disease. Lister treated compound fractures with phenol, and his patients recovered without complications. How was Lister influenced by Pasteur's work? Why was Koch's work still needed?

Answers to Review and Multiple Choice Study Questions

Review

1. People came to believe that living organisms arise from nonliving matter because they would see flies coming out of manure, maggots coming out of dead animals, and microorganisms appearing in liquids after a day or two.

2. **a.** Certain microorganisms cause diseases in insects. Microorganisms that kill insects can be effective biological control agents because they are specific for the pest and do not persist in the environment.
   b. Carbon, oxygen, nitrogen, sulfur, and phosphorus are required for all living organisms. Microorganisms convert these elements into forms that are useful for other organisms. Many bacteria decompose material and release carbon dioxide into the atmosphere, which plants use. Some bacteria can take nitrogen from the atmosphere and convert it into a form that plants and other microorganisms can use.
   c. Normal microbiota are microorganisms that are found in and on the human body. They do not usually cause disease and can be beneficial.
   d. Organic matter in sewage is decomposed by bacteria into carbon dioxide, nitrates, phosphates, sulfate, and other inorganic compounds in a wastewater treatment plant.
   e. Recombinant DNA techniques have resulted in insertion of the gene for insulin production into bacteria. These bacteria can produce human insulin inexpensively.
   f. Microorganisms can be used as vaccines. Some microbes can be genetically modified to produce components of vaccines.
   g. Biofilms are aggregated bacteria adhering to each other and to a solid surface.

3. **a.** 1, 3   **c.** 1, 4, 5   **e.** 5   **g.** 4
   b. 8   **d.** 2   **f.** 3   **h.** 7

4. **a.** 7   **c.** 3   **e.** 6   **g.** 1
   b. 4   **d.** 2   **f.** 5

5. **a.** 11   **e.** 3   **i.** 1   **m.** 7   **q.** 13
   b. 14   **f.** 9   **j.** 12   **n.** 5   **r.** 16
   c. 15   **g.** 10   **k.** 18   **o.** 6
   d. 17   **h.** 2   **l.** 4   **p.** 8

6. *Erwinia amylovora* is the correct way to write this scientific name. Scientific names can be derived from the names of scientists. In this case, *Erwinia* is derived from Erwin F. Smith, an American plant pathologist. Scientific names also can describe the organism, its habitat, or its niche. *E. amylovora* is a pathogen of plants (*amylo-* = starch; *vora* = eat).

7. **a.** *B. thuringiensis* is sold as a biological insecticide.
   b. *Saccharomyces* is the yeast sold for making bread, wine, and beer.

8.

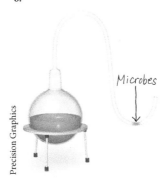

Microbes

Precision Graphics

9. Bacteria

Multiple Choice

1. a   6. e
2. c   7. c
3. d   8. a
4. c   9. c
5. b   10. a

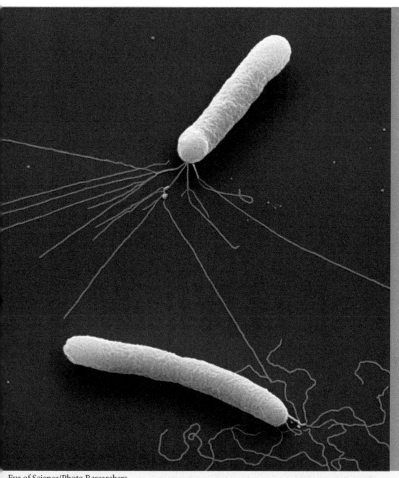

Eye of Science/Photo Researchers

Microbial Mechanisms of Pathogenicity

Visualize microbiology and check your
understanding with a pre-test at
www.masteringmicrobiology.com.

N ow that you have a basic understanding of how microorganisms
cause disease, we will take a look at some of the specific properties of
microorganisms that contribute to **pathogenicity,** the ability to cause
disease by overcoming the defenses of a host, and **virulence,** the degree or extent
of pathogenicity. (As discussed throughout the chapter, the term *host* usually refers
to humans.) Microbes don't try to cause disease; the microbial cells are getting
food and defending themselves. Sometimes the presence of microbial cells or
cell parts can induce symptoms in a host. An example due to *Burkholderia* (in the
photograph) is described in the Clinical Case.**1**

To humans, it doesn't make sense for a parasite to kill its host. However,
nature does not have a plan for evolution; the genetic variations that give rise
to evolution are due to random mutations, not to logic. According to natural
selection, organisms best adapted to their environments will reproduce.
Coevolution between a parasite and its host seems to occur: the behavior of one
influences that of the other. For example, the cholera pathogen, *Vibrio cholerae,*
quickly induces diarrhea, threatening the host's life from a loss of fluids and salts
but providing a way to transmit the pathogen to another person by contaminating
the water supply.

Keep in mind that many of the properties contributing to microbial
pathogenicity and virulence are unclear or unknown. We do know, however, that if
the microbe overpowers the host defenses, disease results.

From Chapter 15 of *Microbiology: An Introduction*, Eleventh Edition. Gerard J. Tortora, Berdell R. Funke, Christine L. Case.

How Microorganisms Enter a Host

1   Identify the principal portals of entry.

2   Define ID_{50} and LD_{50}.

3   Using examples, explain how microbes adhere to host cells.

To cause disease, most pathogens must gain access to the host, adhere to host tissues, penetrate or evade host defenses, and damage the host tissues. However, some microbes do not cause disease by directly damaging host tissue. Instead, disease is due to the accumulation of microbial waste products. Some microbes, such as those that cause dental caries and acne, can cause disease without penetrating the body. Pathogens can gain entrance to the human body and other hosts through several avenues, which are called **portals of entry.**

Portals of Entry

The portals of entry for pathogens are mucous membranes, skin, and direct deposition beneath the skin or membranes (the parenteral route).

Mucous Membranes

Many bacteria and viruses gain access to the body by penetrating mucous membranes lining the respiratory tract, gastrointestinal tract, genitourinary tract, and conjunctiva, a delicate membrane that covers the eyeballs and lines the eyelids. Most pathogens enter through the mucous membranes of the gastrointestinal and respiratory tracts.

Clinical Case: The Eyes Have It

Kerry Santos, a board-certified ophthalmologist for 20 years, has had a long day. She performed outpatient cataract surgery on ten patients (see the figure) today. As she checks over her patients in the recovery area, she notes that eight of the ten patients have an unusual degree of inflammation and that their pupils are fixed and do not respond to light. Of these eight patients, Dr. Santos replaced the lens on the left eye of five patients and on the right eye of three patients.

What could have caused this complication? Read on to find out.

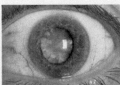

National Eye Institute, National Institutes of Health

The respiratory tract is the easiest and most frequently traveled portal of entry for infectious microorganisms. Microbes are inhaled into the nose or mouth in drops of moisture and dust particles. Diseases that are commonly contracted via the respiratory tract include the common cold, pneumonia, tuberculosis, influenza, and measles.

Microorganisms can gain access to the gastrointestinal tract in food and water and via contaminated fingers. Most microbes that enter the body in these ways are destroyed by hydrochloric acid (HCl) and enzymes in the stomach or by bile and enzymes in the small intestine. Those that survive can cause disease. Microbes in the gastrointestinal tract can cause poliomyelitis, hepatitis A, typhoid fever, amebic dysentery, giardiasis, shigellosis (bacillary dysentery), and cholera. These pathogens are then eliminated with feces and can be transmitted to other hosts via contaminated water, food, or fingers.

The genitourinary tract is a portal of entry for pathogens that are contracted sexually. Some microbes that cause sexually transmitted infections (STIs) may penetrate an unbroken mucous membrane. Others require a cut or abrasion of some type. Examples of STIs are HIV infection, genital warts, chlamydia, herpes, syphilis, and gonorrhea.

Skin

The skin is the largest organ of the body in terms of surface area and weight and is an important defense against disease. Unbroken skin is impenetrable by most microorganisms. Some microbes gain access to the body through openings in the skin, such as hair follicles and sweat gland ducts. Larvae of the hookworm actually bore through intact skin, and some fungi grow on the keratin in skin or infect the skin itself.

The conjunctiva is a delicate mucous membrane that lines the eyelids and covers the white of the eyeballs. Although it is a relatively effective barrier against infection, certain diseases such as conjunctivitis, trachoma, and ophthalmia neonatorium are acquired through the conjunctiva.

The Parenteral Route

Other microorganisms gain access to the body when they are deposited directly into the tissues beneath the skin or into mucous membranes when these barriers are penetrated or injured. This route is called the **parenteral route.** Punctures, injections, bites, cuts, wounds, surgery, and splitting of the skin or mucous membrane due to swelling or drying can all establish parenteral routes. HIV, the hepatitis viruses, and bacteria that cause tetanus and gangrene can be transmitted parenterally.

The Preferred Portal of Entry

Even after microorganisms have entered the body, they do not necessarily cause disease. The occurrence of disease depends on several factors, only one of which is the portal of entry. Many

TABLE 1 Portals of Entry for the Pathogens of Some Common Diseases

Portal of Entry	Pathogen[*]	Disease	Incubation Period
Mucous Membranes			
Respiratory tract	*Streptococcus pneumoniae*	Pneumococcal pneumonia	Variable
	Mycobacterium tuberculosis[†]	Tuberculosis	Variable
	Bordetella pertussis	Whooping cough (pertussis)	12–20 days
	Influenza virus (*Influenzavirus*)	Influenza	18–36 hours
	Measles virus (*Morbillivirus*)	Measles (rubeola)	11–14 days
	Rubella virus (*Rubivirus*)	German measles (rubella)	2–3 weeks
	Epstein-Barr virus (*Lymphocryptovirus*)	Infectious mononucleosis	2–6 weeks
	Varicella-zoster virus (*Varicellovirus*)	Chickenpox (varicella) (primary infection)	14–16 days
	Histoplasma capsulatum (fungus)	Histoplasmosis	5–18 days
Gastrointestinal tract	*Shigella* spp.	Shigellosis (bacillary dysentery)	1–2 days
	Brucella spp.	Brucellosis (undulant fever)	6–14 days
	Vibrio cholerae	Cholera	1–3 days
	Salmonella enterica	Salmonellosis	7–22 hours
	Salmonella typhi	Typhoid fever	14 days
	Hepatitis A virus (*Hepatovirus*)	Hepatitis A	15–50 days
	Mumps virus (*Rubulavirus*)	Mumps	2–3 weeks
	Trichinella spiralis (helminth)	Trichinellosis	2–28 days
Genitourinary tract	*Neisseria gonorrhoeae*	Gonorrhea	3–8 days
	Treponema pallidum	Syphilis	9–90 days
	Chlamydia trachomatis	Nongonococcal urethritis	1–3 weeks
	Herpes simplex virus type 2	Herpes virus infections	4–10 days
	Human immunodeficiency virus (HIV)[‡]	AIDS	10 years
	Candida albicans (fungus)	Candidiasis	2–5 days
Skin or Parenteral Route			
	Clostridium perfringens	Gas gangrene	1–5 days
	Clostridium tetani	Tetanus	3–21 days
	Rickettsia rickettsii	Rocky Mountain spotted fever	3–12 days
	Hepatitis B virus (*Hepadnavirus*)[‡]	Hepatitis B	6 weeks–6 months
	Rabiesvirus (*Lyssavirus*)	Rabies	10 days–1 year
	Plasmodium spp. (protozoan)	Malaria	2 weeks

[*]All pathogens are bacteria, unless indicated otherwise. For viruses, the viral species and/or genus name is given.
[†]These pathogens can also cause disease after entering the body via the gastrointestinal tract.
[‡]These pathogens can also cause disease after entering the body via the parenteral route. Hepatitis B virus and HIV can also cause disease after entering the body via the genitourinary tract.

pathogens have a preferred portal of entry that is a prerequisite to their being able to cause disease. If they gain access to the body by another portal, disease might not occur. For example, the bacteria of typhoid fever, *Salmonella typhi,* produce all the signs and symptoms of the disease when swallowed (preferred route), but if the same bacteria are rubbed on the skin, no reaction (or only a slight inflammation) occurs. Streptococci that are inhaled (preferred route) can cause pneumonia; those that are swallowed generally do not produce signs or symptoms. Some pathogens, such as *Yersinia pestis,* the microorganism that causes plague, and *Bacillus anthracis,* the causative agent of anthrax, can initiate disease from more than one portal of entry. The preferred portals of entry for some common pathogens are listed in **Table 1**.

Precision Graphics

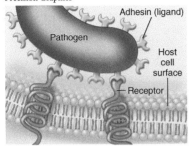

(a) Surface molecules on a pathogen, called adhesins or ligands, bind specifically to complementary surface receptors on cells of certain host tissues.

SPL/Photo Researchers

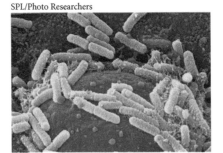

(b) *E. coli* bacteria (yellow-green) on human urinary bladder cells

SEM |—| 1 μm

Gillette Corporation/Photo Researchers

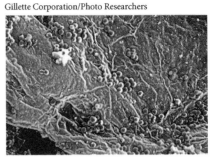

(c) Bacteria (purple) adhering to human skin

SEM |—| 9 μm

Figure 1 Adherence.

Q Of what chemicals are adhesins composed?

Numbers of Invading Microbes

If only a few microbes enter the body, they will probably be overcome by the host's defenses. However, if large numbers of microbes gain entry, the stage is probably set for disease. Thus, the likelihood of disease increases as the number of pathogens increases.

The virulence of a microbe is often expressed as the ID_{50} (infectious dose for 50% of a sample population). The 50 is not an absolute value; rather, it is used to compare relative virulence under experimental conditions. *Bacillus anthracis* can cause infection via three different portals of entry. The ID_{50} through the skin (cutaneous anthrax) is 10 to 50 endospores; the ID_{50} for inhalation anthrax is inhalation of 10,000 to 20,000 endospores; and the ID_{50} for gastrointestinal anthrax is ingestion of 250,000 to 1,000,000 endospores. These data show that cutaneous anthrax is significantly easier to acquire than either the inhalation or the gastrointestinal forms. A study of *Vibrio cholerae* showed that the ID_{50} is 10^8 cells; but if stomach acid is neutralized with bicarbonate, the number of cells required to cause an infection decreases significantly.

The potency of a toxin is often expressed as the LD_{50} (lethal dose for 50% of a sample population). For example, the LD_{50} for botulinum toxin in mice is 0.03 ng/kg; for Shiga toxin, 250 ng/kg; and staphylococcal enterotoxin, 1350 ng/kg. In other words, compared to the other two toxins, a much smaller dose of botulinum toxin is needed to cause symptoms.

Adherence

Almost all pathogens have some means of attaching themselves to host tissues at their portal of entry. For most pathogens, this attachment, called **adherence** (or **adhesion**), is a necessary step in pathogenicity. (Of course, nonpathogens also have structures for attachment.) The attachment between pathogen and host is accomplished by means of surface molecules on the pathogen called **adhesins** or **ligands** that bind specifically to complementary surface **receptors** on the cells of certain host tissues (**Figure 1**). Adhesins may be located on a microbe's glycocalyx or on other microbial surface structures, such as pili, fimbriae, and flagella.

The majority of adhesins on the microorganisms studied so far are glycoproteins or lipoproteins. The receptors on host cells are typically sugars, such as mannose. Adhesins on different strains of the same species of pathogen can vary in structure. Different cells of the same host can also have different receptors that vary in structure. If adhesins, receptors, or both can be altered to interfere with adherence, infection can often be prevented (or at least controlled).

The following examples illustrate the diversity of adhesins. *Streptococcus mutans*, a bacterium that plays a key role in tooth decay, attaches to the surface of teeth by its glycocalyx. An enzyme produced by *S. mutans*, called glucosyltransferase, converts glucose (derived from sucrose or table sugar) into a sticky polysaccharide called dextran, which forms the glycocalyx. *Actinomyces* bacterial cells have fimbriae that adhere to the glycocalyx of *S. mutans*. The combination of *S. mutans*, *Actinomyces*, and dextran make up dental plaque and contribute to dental caries (tooth decay).

Microbes have the ability to come together in masses, cling to surfaces, and take in and share available nutrients. These communities, which constitute masses of microbes and their extracellular products that can attach to living and nonliving surfaces, are called **biofilms**. Examples of biofilms include the dental plaque on teeth, the algae on the walls of swimming pools, and the scum that accumulates on shower doors. A biofilm forms when microbes adhere to a particular surface that is typically moist and contains organic matter. The first microbes to attach are usually bacteria. Once they adhere to the surface, they multiply and secrete a glycocalyx that further attaches the bacteria to each other and to the surface. In some cases, biofilms can be several layers thick and may contain several types of microbes. Biofilms represent another method of adherence and are important because they resist disinfectants and antibiotics. This characteristic is significant, especially when biofilms colonize structures such as teeth, medical catheters, stents, heart valves, hip replacement components, and contact lenses. Dental plaque is actually a biofilm that mineralizes over time. It is estimated that biofilms are involved in 65% of all human bacterial infections.

Enteropathogenic strains of *E. coli* (those responsible for gastrointestinal disease) have adhesins on fimbriae that adhere only to specific kinds of cells in certain regions of the small intestine. After adhering, *Shigella* and *E. coli* induce receptor-mediated endocytosis as a vehicle to enter host cells and then multiply within them. *Treponema pallidum,* the causative agent of syphilis, uses its tapered end as a hook to attach to host cells. *Listeria monocytogenes,* which causes meningitis, spontaneous abortions, and stillbirths, produces an adhesin for a specific receptor on host cells. *Neisseria gonorrhoeae,* the causative agent of gonorrhea, also has fimbriae containing adhesins, which in this case permit attachment to cells with appropriate receptors in the genitourinary tract, eyes, and pharynx. *Staphylococcus aureus,* which can cause skin infections, binds to skin by a mechanism of adherence that resembles viral attachment.

CHECK YOUR UNDERSTANDING

- List three portals of entry, and describe how microorganisms gain access through each. **1**
- The LD_{50} of botulinum toxin is 0.03 ng/kg; the LD_{50} of *Salmonella* toxin is 12 mg/kg. Which is the more potent toxin? **2**
- How would a drug that binds mannose on human cells affect a pathogenic bacterium? **3**

How Bacterial Pathogens Penetrate Host Defenses

LEARNING OBJECTIVES

4   Explain how capsules and cell wall components contribute to pathogenicity.

5   Compare the effects of coagulases, kinases, hyaluronidase, and collagenase.

6   Define and give an example of *antigenic variation.*

7   Describe how bacteria use the host cell's cytoskeleton to enter the cell.

Although some pathogens can cause damage on the surface of tissues, most must penetrate tissues to cause disease. Here we will consider several factors that contribute to the ability of bacteria to invade a host.

Capsules

Some bacteria make glycocalyx material that forms capsules around their cell walls; this property increases the virulence of the species. The capsule resists the host's defenses by impairing phagocytosis, the process by which certain cells of the body engulf and destroy microbes. The chemical nature of the capsule appears to prevent the phagocytic cell from adhering to the bacterium. However, the human body can produce antibodies against the capsule, and when these antibodies are present on the capsule surface, the encapsulated bacteria are easily destroyed by phagocytosis.

One bacterium that owes its virulence to the presence of a polysaccharide capsule is *Streptococcus pneumoniae,* the causative agent of pneumococcal pneumonia. Some strains of this organism have capsules, and others do not. Strains with capsules are virulent, but strains without capsules are avirulent because they are susceptible to phagocytosis. Other bacteria that produce capsules related to virulence are *Klebsiella pneumoniae,* a causative agent of bacterial pneumonia; *Haemophilus influenzae,* a cause of pneumonia and meningitis in children; *Bacillus anthracis,* the cause of anthrax; and *Yersinia pestis,* the causative agent of plague. Keep in mind that capsules are not the only cause of virulence. Many nonpathogenic bacteria produce capsules, and the virulence of some pathogens is not related to the presence of a capsule.

Cell Wall Components

The cell walls of certain bacteria contain chemical substances that contribute to virulence. For example, *Streptococcus pyogenes* produces a heat-resistant and acid-resistant protein called **M protein.** This protein is found on both the cell surface and fimbriae. The M protein mediates attachment of the bacterium to epithelial cells of the host and helps the bacterium resist phagocytosis by white blood cells. The protein thereby increases the virulence of the microorganism. Immunity to *S. pyogenes* depends on the body's production of an antibody specific to M protein. *Neisseria gonorrhoeae* grows inside human epithelial cells and leukocytes. These bacteria use **fimbriae** and an outer membrane protein called **Opa** to attach to host cells. Following attachment by both Opa and fimbriae, the host cells take in the bacteria. (Bacteria that produce Opa form *opaque* colonies on culture media.) The **waxy lipid** (mycolic acid) that makes up the cell wall of *Mycobacterium tuberculosis* also increases virulence by resisting digestion by phagocytes, and can even multiply inside phagocytes.

Enzymes

The virulence of some bacteria is thought to be aided by the production of extracellular enzymes *(exoenzymes)* and related substances. These chemicals can digest materials between cells and form or digest blood clots, among other functions.

APPLICATIONS OF **MICROBIOLOGY**

Streptococcus: Harmful or Helpful?

Louie, a 56-year-old man, wakes in the middle of the night with a burning pain in his chest. He is having a heart attack. Louie is rushed to the hospital, where his family is told that he has a blockage in one of his coronary arteries. As reported in an anonymous 1899 *Journal of the American Medical Association* article, the main cause of heart attack is blood clots that block the flow of blood in the coronary arteries (**Figure A**). Louie's physician treats Louie with an injection of the enzyme streptokinase to dissolve the blockage.

Ashley, a 4-month-old girl, has been having flulike symptoms, including tiredness and an intermittent, low-grade fever, for 4 days. Now her left leg has become red and swollen, and no puncture or scrape is visible. Her parents take her to the pediatrician, who orders that Ashley be

hospitalized and given intravenous antibiotics. Despite the antibiotics treatment, after 2 days the area becomes dark and fluid–filled vesicles appear (**Figure B**). Damaged tissue is blocking blood flow to her left leg. Ashley undergoes a fasciotomy (removal of the connective tissue over the muscles) of her left leg. Ashley has necrotizing fasciitis caused by *Streptococcus pyogenes*. Tissue destruction from *S. pyogenes* can occur as fast as 2 cm of tissue per hour— much faster than the bacteria are growing. What is causing this rapid spread?

In 1933, a researcher named Tillet reported that one of the enzymes responsible for the rapid spread is streptokinase. Streptokinase digests the fibrin clot that the body uses to isolate an infection. He found three strains of *S. pyogenes* that produce this enzyme.

What Do Louie and Ashley Have in Common?

Normally the body produces plasmin to break down unneeded blood clots. Streptokinase

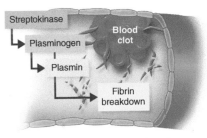

Figure C Mechanism of streptokinase

breaks down the body's precursor, plasminogen, to produce plasmin (**Figure C**). Both Louie and Ashley have been affected by streptokinase. Louie has a positive experience: the enzyme is used to dissolve the blood clot that is blocking the artery to his heart. Ashley, however, is affected negatively: the streptokinase produced by *S. pyogenes* has destroyed tissue in her left leg.

In the 1950s, four physicians reported using streptokinase to successfully treat coronary artery blockage. Streptokinase became the mainstay for digesting blood clots when the U.S. Food and Drug Administration (FDA) approved its use in 1982.

Streptokinase is produced commercially from *Streptococcus equisimilis* H46A. The enzyme must be purified to ensure that toxins are not present. Isolation of the streptokinase gene has also allowed the enzyme to be produced by recombinant *E. coli*.

Blocked coronary artery

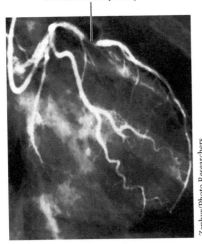

Figure A X ray of coronary arteries.

From: Necrotizing fasciitis in a newborn infant: a case report. V.L Krebs, et al. *Rev Hosp Clin Fac Med Sao Paulo.* 2001 Mar-Apr;56(2):59–62

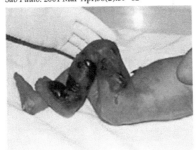

Figure B Necrotizing fasciitis

Coagulases are bacterial enzymes that coagulate (clot) the fibrinogen in blood. Fibrinogen, a plasma protein produced by the liver, is converted by coagulases into fibrin, the threads that form a blood clot. The fibrin clot may protect the bacterium from phagocytosis and isolate it from other defenses of the host. Coagulases are produced by some members of the genus *Staphylococcus*; they may be involved in the walling-off process in boils produced by staphylococci. However, some staphylococci

that do not produce coagulases are still virulent. (Capsules may be more important to their virulence.)

Bacterial **kinases** are bacterial enzymes that break down fibrin and thus digest clots formed by the body to isolate the infection. One of the better-known kinases is *fibrinolysin (streptokinase)*, which is produced by such streptococci as *Streptococcus pyogenes*. See the box above. Another kinase, *staphylokinase*, is produced by *Staphylococcus aureus*.

Hyaluronidase is another enzyme secreted by certain bacteria, such as streptococci. It hydrolyzes hyaluronic acid, a type of polysaccharide that holds together certain cells of the body, particularly cells in connective tissue. This digesting action is thought to be involved in the tissue blackening of infected wounds and to help the microorganism spread from its initial site of infection. Hyaluronidase is also produced by some clostridia that cause gas gangrene. For therapeutic use, hyaluronidase may be mixed with a drug to promote the spread of the drug through a body tissue.

Another enzyme, **collagenase,** produced by several species of *Clostridium,* facilitates the spread of gas gangrene. Collagenase breaks down the protein collagen, which forms the connective tissue of muscles and other body organs and tissues.

As a defense against adherence of pathogens to mucosal surfaces, the body produces a class of antibodies called IgA antibodies. There are some pathogens with the ability to produce enzymes, called **IgA proteases,** that can destroy these antibodies. *N. gonorrhoeae* has this ability, as do *N. meningitidis,* the causative agent of meningococcal meningitis, and other microbes that infect the central nervous system.

Antigenic Variation

Adaptive (acquired) immunity refers to a specific defensive response of the body to an infection or to antigens. In the presence of antigens, the body produces proteins called antibodies, which bind to the antigens and inactivate or destroy them. However, some pathogens can alter their surface antigens, by a process called **antigenic variation.** Thus, by the time the body mounts an immune response against a pathogen, the pathogen has already altered its antigens and is unaffected by the antibodies. Some microbes can activate alternative genes, resulting in antigenic changes. For example, *N. gonorrhoeae* has several copies of the Opa-encoding gene, resulting in cells with different antigens and in cells that express different antigens over time.

A wide range of microbes is capable of antigenic variation. Examples include *Influenzavirus,* the causative agent of influenza (flu); *Neisseria gonorrhoeae,* the causative agent of gonorrhea; and *Trypanosoma brucei gambiense* (tri-pa'nō-sō-mä brüs'ē gam-bē-ens'), the causative agent of African trypanosomiasis (sleeping sickness).

Penetration into the Host Cell Cytoskeleton

As previously noted, microbes attach to host cells by adhesins. The interaction triggers signals in the host cell that activate factors that can result in the entrance of some bacteria. The actual mechanism is provided by the host cell cytoskeleton. Eukaryotic cytoplasm has a complex internal structure (the cytoskeleton), consisting of protein filaments called microfilaments, intermediate filaments, and microtubules. A major component of the cytoskeleton is a protein called actin, which is used by some microbes to penetrate host cells and by others to move through and between host cells.

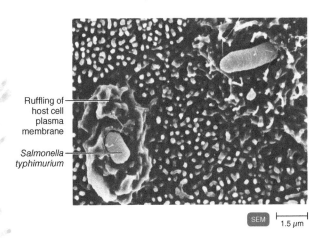

Ruffling of host cell plasma membrane

Salmonella typhimurium

SEM 1.5 µm

Figure 2 *Salmonella* **entering intestinal epithelial cells as a result of ruffling.**

Q What are invasins?

Reproduced by permission from C. Ginocchio, S. Olmstead, C. Wells, and J. E. Galan, "Contact with Epithelial Cells Induces the Formation of Surface Appendages on Salmonella Typhimurium," *CELL*, 1994 Feb 25; 76(4):717–24. Copyright © 1994 by Elsevier Science Ltd.

Salmonella strains and *E. coli* make contact with the host cell plasma membrane. This leads to dramatic changes in the membrane at the point of contact. The microbes produce surface proteins called **invasins** that rearrange nearby actin filaments of the cytoskeleton. For example, when *S. typhimurium* makes contact with a host cell, invasins of the microbe cause the appearance of the host cell plasma membrane to resemble the splash of a drop of a liquid hitting a solid surface. This effect, called *membrane ruffling,* is the result of disruption in the cytoskeleton of the host cell (**Figure 2**). The microbe sinks into the ruffle and is engulfed by the host cell.

Once inside the host cell, certain bacteria such as *Shigella* species and *Listeria* species can actually use actin to propel themselves through the host cell cytoplasm and from one host cell to another. The condensation of actin on one end of the bacteria propels them through the cytoplasm. The bacteria also make contact with membrane junctions that form part of a transport network between host cells. The bacteria use a glycoprotein called *cadherin,* which bridges the junctions, to move from cell to cell.

The study of the numerous interactions between microbes and host cell cytoskeleton is a very intense area of investigation on virulence mechanisms.

CHECK YOUR UNDERSTANDING

✔ What function do capsules and M proteins have in common? **4**

✔ Would you expect a bacterium to make coagulase and kinase simultaneously? **5**

✔ Many vaccines provide years of protection against a disease. Why doesn't the influenza vaccine offer more than a few months of protection? **6**

✔ How does *E. coli* cause membrane ruffling? **7**

How Bacterial Pathogens Damage Host Cells

LEARNING OBJECTIVES

8   Describe the function of siderophores.

9   Provide an example of direct damage, and compare this to toxin production.

10 Contrast the nature and effects of exotoxins and endotoxins.

11 Outline the mechanisms of action of A-B toxins, membrane-disrupting toxins, and superantigens. Classify diphtheria toxin, erythrogenic toxin, botulinum toxin, tetanus toxin, *Vibrio* enterotoxin, and staphylococcal enterotoxin.

12 Identify the importance of the LAL assay.

13 Using examples, describe the roles of plasmids and lysogeny in pathogenicity.

When a microorganism invades a body tissue, it initially encounters phagocytes of the host. If the phagocytes are successful in destroying the invader, no further damage is done to the host. But if the pathogen overcomes the host's defense, then the microorganism can damage host cells in four basic ways: (1) by using the host's nutrients; (2) by causing direct damage in the immediate vicinity of the invasion; (3) by producing toxins, transported by blood and lymph, that damage sites far removed from the original site of invasion; and (4) by inducing hypersensitivity reactions. For now, we will discuss only the first three mechanisms.

Using the Host's Nutrients: Siderophores

Iron is required for the growth of most pathogenic bacteria. However, the concentration of free iron in the human body is fairly low because most of the iron is tightly bound to iron-transport proteins, such as lactoferrin, transferrin, and ferritin, as well as hemoglobin. To obtain free iron, some pathogens secrete proteins called **siderophores** (Figure 3). When a pathogen needs iron, siderophores are released into the medium, where they take the iron away from iron-transport proteins by binding the iron even more tightly. Once the iron-siderophore complex is formed, it is taken up by siderophore receptors on the bacterial surface. Then the iron is brought into the bacterium. In some cases, the iron is released from the complex to enter the bacterium; in other cases, the iron enters as part of the complex.

As an alternative to iron acquisition by siderophores, some pathogens have receptors that bind directly to iron-transport proteins and hemoglobin. Then these are taken into the bacterium directly along with the iron. Also, it is possible that some bacteria produce toxins (described shortly) when iron levels are low. The toxins kill host cells, releasing their iron and thereby making it available to the bacteria.

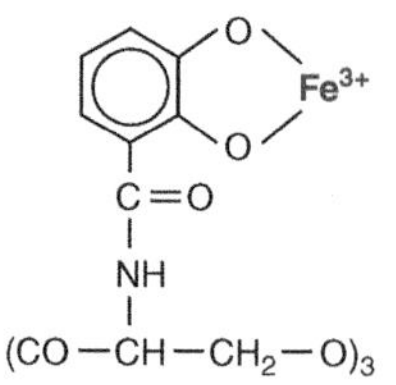

Figure 3 **Structure of enterobactin, one type of bacterial siderophore.** Note where the iron (Fe^{3+}) is attached to the siderophore.

Q Of what value are siderophores?

Direct Damage

Once pathogens attach to host cells, they can cause direct damage as the pathogens use the host cell for nutrients and produce waste products. As pathogens metabolize and multiply in cells, the cells usually rupture. Many viruses and some intracellular bacteria and protozoa that grow in host cells are released when the host cell ruptures. Following their release, pathogens that rupture cells can spread to other tissues in even greater numbers. Some bacteria, such as *E. coli, Shigella, Salmonella,* and *Neisseria gonorrhoeae,* can induce host epithelial cells to engulf them by a process that resembles phagocytosis. These pathogens can disrupt host cells as they pass through and can then be extruded from the host cells by a reverse phagocytosis process, enabling them to enter other host cells. Some bacteria can also penetrate host cells by excreting enzymes and by their own motility; such penetration can itself damage the host cell. Most damage by bacteria, however, is done by toxins. (MM) **Animations** Virulence Factors: Penetrating Host Tissues, Hiding from Host Defenses, Enteric Pathogens

The Production of Toxins

Toxins are poisonous substances that are produced by certain microorganisms. They are often the primary factor contributing to the pathogenic properties of those microbes. The capacity of microorganisms to produce toxins is called **toxigenicity**. Toxins transported by the blood or lymph can cause serious, and sometimes fatal, effects. Some toxins produce fever, cardiovascular

Clinical Case

Dr. Santos suspects toxic anterior segment syndrome (TASS), which is a reaction to a toxin or other chemical. TASS is caused by (1) chemicals on surgical instruments, resulting from improper or insufficient cleaning; (2) products introduced into the eye during surgery, such as washing solutions or medications; or (3) other substances that enter the eye during or after surgery, such as topical ointments or talc from surgical gloves.

Why does Dr. Santos suspect an intoxication and not an infection?

FOUNDATION FIGURE **4**

Mechanisms of Exotoxins and Endotoxins

exotoxins

Exotoxins are proteins produced inside pathogenic bacteria, most commonly gram-positive bacteria, as part of their growth and metabolism. The exotoxins are then secreted into the surrounding medium during log phase.

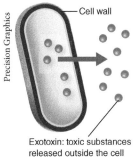

Cell wall

Exotoxin: toxic substances
released outside the cell

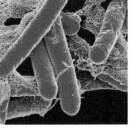

Clostridium botulinum, an example of a gram-positive bacterium that produces exotoxins

KEYCONCEPTS

- Toxins are of two general types: exotoxins and endotoxins.
- Bacterial toxins can cause damage to host cells.
- Toxins can elicit an inflammatory response in the host, as well as activate the complement system.
- Some gram-negative bacteria may release minute amounts of endotoxins, which may stimulate natural immunity.

endotoxins

Endotoxins are the lipid portions of lipopolysaccharides (LPS) that are part of the outer membrane of the cell wall of gram-negative bacteria (lipid A). The endotoxins are liberated when the bacteria die and the cell wall breaks apart.

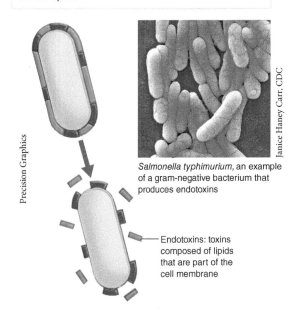

Salmonella typhimurium, an example of a gram-negative bacterium that produces endotoxins

Endotoxins: toxins composed of lipids that are part of the cell membrane

Precision Graphics

Gary Gaugler/Photo Researchers

Janice Haney Carr, CDC

---

disturbances, diarrhea, and shock. Toxins can also inhibit protein synthesis, destroy blood cells and blood vessels, and disrupt the nervous system by causing spasms. Of the 220 or so known bacterial toxins, nearly 40% cause disease by damaging eukaryotic cell membranes. The term **toxemia** refers to the presence of toxins in the blood. Toxins are of two general types, based on their position relative to the microbial cell: exotoxins and endotoxins.

Exotoxins

Exotoxins are produced inside some bacteria as part of their growth and metabolism and are secreted by the bacterium into the surrounding medium or released following lysis (**Figure 4**). Exotoxins are proteins, and many are enzymes that catalyze only certain biochemical reactions. Because of the enzymatic nature of most exotoxins, even small amounts are quite harmful because they can act over and over again. Bacteria that produce exotoxins may be gram-positive or gram-negative. The genes for

most (perhaps all) exotoxins are carried on bacterial plasmids or phages. Because exotoxins are soluble in body fluids, they can easily diffuse into the blood and are rapidly transported throughout the body.

Exotoxins work by destroying particular parts of the host's cells or by inhibiting certain metabolic functions. They are highly specific in their effects on body tissues. Exotoxins are among the most lethal substances known. Only 1 mg of the botulinum exotoxin is enough to kill 1 million guinea pigs. Fortunately, only a few bacterial species produce such potent exotoxins.

Diseases caused by bacteria that produce exotoxins are often caused by minute amounts of exotoxins, not by the bacteria themselves. It is the exotoxins that produce the specific signs and symptoms of the disease. Thus, exotoxins are disease-specific. For example, botulism is usually due to ingestion of the exotoxin, not to a bacterial infection. Likewise, staphylococcal food poisoning is an *intoxication,* not an infection.

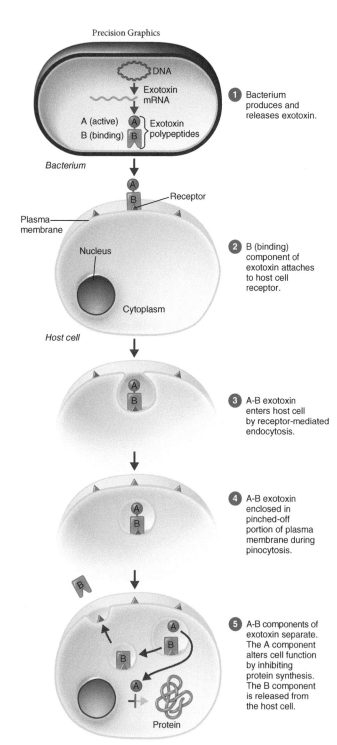

Figure 5 The action of an A-B exotoxin. A proposed model for the mechanism of action of diphtheria toxin.

Q Why is this called an A-B toxin?

The body produces antibodies called **antitoxins** that provide immunity to exotoxins. When exotoxins are inactivated by heat or by formaldehyde, iodine, or other chemicals, they no longer cause the disease but can still stimulate the body to produce antitoxins. Such altered exotoxins are called **toxoids.** When toxoids are injected into the body as a vaccine, they stimulate antitoxin production so that immunity is produced. Diphtheria and tetanus can be prevented by toxoid vaccination.

Naming Exotoxins Exotoxins are named on the basis of several characteristics. One is the type of host cell that is attacked. For example, *neurotoxins* attack nerve cells, *cardiotoxins* attack heart cells, *hepatotoxins* attack liver cells, *leukotoxins* attack leukocytes, *enterotoxins* attack the lining of the gastrointestinal tract, and *cytotoxins* attack a wide variety of cells. Some exotoxins are named for the diseases with which they are associated. Examples include *diphtheria toxin* (cause of diphtheria) and *tetanus toxin* (cause of tetanus). Other exotoxins are named for the specific bacterium that produces them, for example, *botulinum toxin (Clostridium botulinum)* and *Vibrio enterotoxin (Vibrio cholerae).*

Types of Exotoxins Exotoxins are divided into three principal types on the basis of their structure and function: (1) A-B toxins, (2) membrane-disrupting toxins, and (3) superantigens.

A-B Toxins **A-B toxins** were the first toxins to be studied intensively and are so named because they consist of two parts designated A and B, both of which are polypeptides. Most exotoxins are A-B toxins. The A part is the active (enzyme) component, and the B part is the binding component. An example of an A-B toxin is the diphtheria toxin, which is illustrated in **Figure 5**.

❶ In the first step, the A-B toxin is released from the bacterium.

❷ The B component attaches to a host cell receptor.

❸ The plasma membrane of the host cell invaginates (folds inward) at the point where the A-B exotoxin and plasma receptor make contact, and the exotoxin enters the cell by receptor-mediated endocytosis.

❹ The A-B exotoxin and receptor are enclosed by a pinched-off portion of the membrane.

❺ The A-B components of the exotoxin separate. The A component alters the function of the host cell, often by inhibiting protein synthesis. The B component is released from the host cell, and the receptor is inserted into the plasma membrane for reuse.

Membrane-Disrupting Toxins Membrane-disrupting toxins cause lysis of host cells by disrupting their plasma membranes. Some do this by forming protein channels in the plasma membrane; others disrupt the phospholipid portion of the membrane. The cell-lysing exotoxin of *Staphylococcus aureus* is an example of an exotoxin that forms protein channels, whereas that of *Clostridium perfringens* is an example of an exotoxin that disrupts the phospholipids. Membrane-disrupting toxins contribute to virulence by killing host cells, especially phagocytes, and by aiding the escape of bacteria from sacs within phagocytes (phagosomes) into the host cell's cytoplasm.

Membrane-disrupting toxins that kill phagocytic leukocytes (white blood cells) are called **leukocidins.** They act by forming protein channels. Leukocidins are also active against macrophages, phagocytes present in tissues. Most leukocidins are produced by staphylococci and streptococci. The damage to phagocytes decreases host resistance. Membrane-disrupting toxins that destroy erythrocytes (red blood cells), also by forming protein channels, are called **hemolysins.** Important producers of hemolysins include staphylococci and streptococci. Hemolysins produced by streptococci are called **streptolysins.** One kind, called *streptolysin O (SLO),* is so named because it is inactivated by atmospheric oxygen. Another kind of streptolysin is called *streptolysin S (SLS)* because it is stable in an oxygen environment. Both streptolysins can cause lysis not only of red blood cells, but also of white blood cells (whose function is to kill the streptococci) and other body cells.

Superantigens Superantigens are antigens that provoke a very intense immune response. They are bacterial proteins. Through a series of interactions with various cells of the immune system, superantigens nonspecifically stimulate the proliferation of immune cells called T cells. These cells are types of white blood cells (lymphocytes) that act against foreign organisms and tissues (transplants) and regulate the activation and proliferation of other cells of the immune system. In response to superantigens, T cells are stimulated to release enormous amounts of chemicals called cytokines. *Cytokines* are small protein molecules produced by various body cells, especially T cells, that regulate immune responses and mediate cell-to-cell communication. The excessively high levels of cytokines released by T cells enter the bloodstream and give rise to a number of symptoms, including fever, nausea, vomiting, diarrhea, and sometimes shock and even death. Bacterial superantigens include the staphylococcal toxins that cause food poisoning and toxic shock syndrome.

Representative Exotoxins Next we briefly describe a few of the more notable exotoxins.

Diphtheria Toxin *Corynebacterium diphtheriae* produces the *diphtheria toxin* only when it is infected by a lysogenic phage carrying the *tox* gene. This cytotoxin inhibits protein synthesis in eukaryotic cells. It does this using an A-B toxin mechanism (see Figure 5).

Erythrogenic Toxins *Streptococcus pyogenes* has the genetic material to synthesize three types of cytotoxins, designated A, B, and C. These *erythrogenic* (*erythro* = red; *gen* = producing) *toxins* are superantigens that damage the plasma membranes of blood capillaries under the skin and produce a red skin rash. Scarlet fever, caused by *S. pyogenes* exotoxins, is named for this characteristic rash.

Botulinum Toxin *Botulinum toxin* is produced by *Clostridium botulinum.* Although toxin production is associated with the germination of endospores and the growth of vegetative cells, little of the toxin appears in the medium until it is released by lysis late in growth. Botulinum toxin is an A-B neurotoxin; it acts at the neuromuscular junction (the junction between nerve cells and muscle cells) and prevents the transmission of impulses from the nerve cell to the muscle. The toxin accomplishes this by binding to nerve cells and inhibiting the release of a neurotransmitter called acetylcholine. As a result, botulinum toxin causes paralysis in which muscle tone is lacking (flaccid paralysis). *C. botulinum* produces several different types of botulinum toxin, and each possesses a different potency.

Tetanus Toxin *Clostridium tetani* produces tetanus neurotoxin, also known as *tetanospasmin.* This A-B toxin reaches the central nervous system and binds to nerve cells that control the contraction of various skeletal muscles. These nerve cells normally send inhibiting impulses that prevent random contractions and terminate completed contractions. The binding of tetanospasmin blocks this relaxation pathway. The result is uncontrollable muscle contractions, producing the convulsive symptoms (spasmodic contractions) of tetanus, or "lockjaw."

Vibrio Enterotoxin *Vibrio cholerae* produces an A-B enterotoxin called *cholera toxin.* Subunit B binds to epithelial cells, and subunit A causes cells to secrete large amounts of fluids and electrolytes (ions). Normal muscular contractions are disturbed, leading to severe diarrhea that may be accompanied by vomiting. *Heat-labile enterotoxin* (so named because it is more sensitive to heat than are most toxins), produced by some strains of *E. coli,* has an action identical to that of *Vibrio* enterotoxin.

Staphylococcal Enterotoxin *Staphylococcus aureus* produces a superantigen that affects the intestines in the same way as *Vibrio* enterotoxin. A strain of *S. aureus* also produces a superantigen that results in the symptoms associated with toxic shock syndrome. A summary of diseases produced by exotoxins is shown in **Table 2.**

Endotoxins

Endotoxins differ from exotoxins in several ways. Endotoxins are part of the outer portion of the cell wall of gram-negative bacteria (**Figure 4**). Gram-negative bacteria have an outer membrane surrounding the peptidoglycan layer of the cell wall. This outer membrane consists of lipoproteins, phospholipids, and lipopolysaccharides (LPSs). The lipid portion

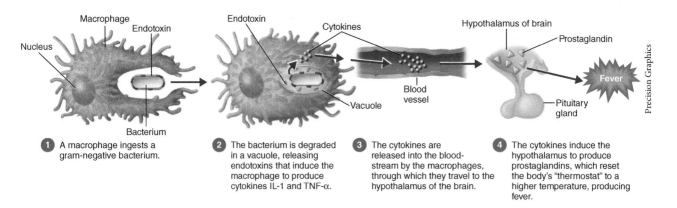

① A macrophage ingests a gram-negative bacterium.

② The bacterium is degraded in a vacuole, releasing endotoxins that induce the macrophage to produce cytokines IL-1 and TNF-α.

③ The cytokines are released into the bloodstream by the macrophages, through which they travel to the hypothalamus of the brain.

④ The cytokines induce the hypothalamus to produce prostaglandins, which reset the body's "thermostat" to a higher temperature, producing fever.

Figure 6 Endotoxins and the pyrogenic response. The proposed mechanism by which endotoxins cause fever.

 What is an endotoxin?

of LPS, called **lipid A,** is the endotoxin. Thus, endotoxins are lipopolysaccharides, whereas exotoxins are proteins.

Endotoxins are released when gram-negative bacteria die and their cell walls undergo lysis, thus liberating the endotoxin. (Endotoxins are also released during bacterial multiplication.) Antibiotics used to treat diseases caused by gram-negative bacteria can lyse the bacterial cells; this reaction releases endotoxin and may lead to an immediate worsening of the symptoms, but the condition usually improves as the endotoxin breaks down. Endotoxins exert their effects by stimulating macrophages to release cytokines in very high concentrations. At these levels, cytokines are toxic. All endotoxins produce the same signs and symptoms, regardless of the species of microorganism, although not to the same degree. These include chills, fever, weakness, generalized aches, and, in some cases, shock and even death. Endotoxins can also induce miscarriage.

Another consequence of endotoxins is the activation of blood-clotting proteins, causing the formation of small blood clots. These blood clots obstruct capillaries, and the resulting decreased blood supply induces the death of tissues. This condition is referred to as *disseminated intravascular coagulation (DIC).*

The fever (pyrogenic response) caused by endotoxins is believed to occur as depicted in **Figure 6.**

① Gram-negative bacteria are ingested by phagocytes.

② As the bacteria are degraded in vacuoles, the LPSs of the bacterial cell wall are released. These endotoxins cause macrophages to produce cytokines called **interleukin-1 (IL-1),** formerly called *endogenous pyrogen,* and **tumor necrosis factor alpha (TNF-α).**

③ The cytokines are carried via the blood to the hypothalamus, a temperature control center in the brain.

④ The cytokines induce the hypothalamus to release lipids called prostaglandins, which reset the thermostat in the hypothalamus at a higher temperature. The result is a fever.

Bacterial cell death caused by lysis or antibiotics can also produce fever by this mechanism. Both aspirin and acetaminophen reduce fever by inhibiting the synthesis of prostaglandins.

Shock refers to any life-threatening decrease in blood pressure. Shock caused by bacteria is called **septic shock.** Gram-negative bacteria cause *endotoxic shock.* Like fever, the shock produced by endotoxins is related to the secretion of a cytokine by macrophages. Phagocytosis of gram-negative bacteria causes the phagocytes to secrete tumor necrosis factor (TNF), sometimes called *cachectin.* TNF binds to many tissues in the body and alters their metabolism in a number of ways. One effect of TNF is damage to blood capillaries; their permeability is increased, and they lose large amounts of fluid. The result is a drop in blood pressure that results in shock. Low blood pressure has serious effects on the kidneys, lungs, and gastrointestinal tract. In addition, the presence of gram-negative bacteria such as *Haemophilus influenzae* type b in cerebrospinal fluid causes the release of IL-1 and TNF. These, in turn, cause a weakening of the blood–brain barrier that normally protects the central nervous system from infection. The weakened barrier lets phagocytes in, but this also lets more bacteria enter from the bloodstream. In the United States, 750,000 cases of septic shock occur each year. One-third of the patients die within a month, and nearly half die within 6 months.

Endotoxins do not promote the formation of effective antitoxins against the carbohydrate component of an endotoxin.

TABLE 2 Diseases Caused by Exotoxins

Disease	Bacterium	Type of Exotoxin	Mechanism
Botulism	*Clostridium botulinum*	A-B	Neurotoxin prevents the transmission of nerve impulses; flaccid paralysis results.
Tetanus	*Clostridium tetani*	A-B	Neurotoxin blocks nerve impulses to muscle relaxation pathway; results in uncontrollable muscle contractions.
Diphtheria	*Corynebacterium diphtheriae*	A-B	Cytotoxin inhibits protein synthesis, especially in nerve, heart, and kidney cells.
Scalded skin syndrome	*Staphylococcus aureus*	A-B	One exotoxin causes skin layers to separate and slough off (scalded skin).
Cholera	*Vibrio cholerae*	A-B	Enterotoxin causes secretion of large amounts of fluids and electrolytes that result in diarrhea.
Traveler's diarrhea	Enterotoxigenic *Escherichia coli* and *Shigella* spp.	A-B	Enterotoxin causes secretion of large amounts of fluids and electrolytes that result in diarrhea.
Anthrax	*Bacillus anthracis*	A-B	Two A components enter the cell via the same B. The A proteins cause shock and reduce the immune response.
Gas gangrene and food poisoning	*Clostridium perfringens* and other species of *Clostridium*	Membrane-disrupting	One exotoxin (cytotoxin) causes massive red blood cell destruction (hemolysis); another exotoxin (enterotoxin) is related to food poisoning and causes diarrhea.
Antibiotic-associated diarrhea	*Clostridium difficile*	Membrane-disrupting	Enterotoxin causes secretion of fluids and electrolytes that results in diarrhea; cytotoxin disrupts host cytoskeleton.
Food poisoning	*Staphylococcus aureus*	Superantigen	Enterotoxin causes secretion of fluids and electrolytes that results in diarrhea.
Toxic shock syndrome (TSS)	*Staphylococcus aureus*	Superantigen	Toxin causes secretion of fluids and electrolytes from capillaries that decreases blood volume and lowers blood pressure.

Antibodies are produced, but they tend not to counter the effect of the toxin; sometimes, in fact, they actually enhance its effect.

Representative microorganisms that produce endotoxins are *Salmonella typhi* (the causative agent of typhoid fever), *Proteus* spp. (frequently the causative agents of urinary tract infections), and *Neisseria meningitidis* (the causative agent of meningococcal meningitis).

It is important to have a sensitive test to identify the presence of endotoxins in drugs, medical devices, and body fluids. Materials that have been sterilized may contain endotoxins, even though no bacteria can be cultured from them. One such laboratory test is called the **Limulus amebocyte lysate (LAL) assay,** which can detect even minute amounts of endotoxin. The hemolymph (blood) of the Atlantic coast horseshoe crab, *Limulus polyphemus,* contains white blood cells called amebocytes, which have large amounts of a protein (lysate) that causes clotting. In the presence of endotoxin, amebocytes in the crab hemolymph lyse and liberate their clotting protein. The resulting gel-clot (precipitate) is a positive test for the presence of endotoxin. The degree of the reaction is measured using a spectrophotometer.

Table 3 compares exotoxins and endotoxins. (MM) **Animations** Virulence Factors: Exotoxins, Endotoxins

Plasmids, Lysogeny, and Pathogenicity

Plasmids are small, circular DNA molecules that are not connected to the main bacterial chromosome and are capable of independent replication. One group of plasmids, called R (resistance) factors, is responsible for the resistance of some microorganisms to antibiotics. In addition, a plasmid may carry the information that determines a microbe's pathogenicity. Examples of virulence factors that are encoded by plasmid genes are tetanus neurotoxin, heat-labile enterotoxin, and staphylococcal enterotoxin. Other examples are dextransucrase, an enzyme produced by *Streptococcus mutans* that is involved in tooth decay; adhesins and coagulase

TABLE 3 Exotoxins and Endotoxins

Property	Exotoxin	Endotoxin
Bacterial Source	Mostly from gram-positive bacteria	Gram-negative bacteria
Relation to Microorganism	Metabolic product of growing cell	Present in LPS of outer membrane of cell wall and released with destruction of cell or during cell division
Chemistry	Proteins, usually with two parts (A-B)	Lipid portion (lipid A) of LPS of outer membrane (lipopolysaccharide).
Pharmacology (Effect on Body)	Specific for a particular cell structure or function in the host (mainly affects cell functions, nerves, and gastrointestinal tract)	General, such as fever, weaknesses, aches, and shock; all produce the same effects
Heat Stability	Unstable; can usually be destroyed at 60–80°C (except staphylococcal enterotoxin)	Stable; can withstand autoclaving (121°C for 1 hour)
Toxicity (Ability to Cause Disease)	High	Low
Fever-Producing	No	Yes
Immunology (Relation to Antibodies)	Can be converted to toxoids to immunize against toxin; neutralized by antitoxin	Not easily neutralized by antitoxin; therefore, effective toxoids cannot be made to immunize against toxin
Lethal Dose	Small	Considerably larger
Representative Diseases	Gas gangrene, tetanus, botulism, diphtheria, scarlet fever	Typhoid fever, urinary tract infections, and meningococcal meningitis

Clinical Case

An infection could not have happened this quickly; infections usually take 3 to 4 days to show symptoms. Dr. Santos checks to make sure that the autoclave used to sterilize the ophthalmic equipment is functioning normally, single-use topical iodine antiseptic was used, and a new sterile tip for the corneal extraction was used for each patient. Both the epinephrine used during surgery and the enzymatic solution for the ultrasonic bath used to clean surgical instruments are sterile, and medications with different lot numbers were used in each surgery. Dr. Santos knows that the toxin had to have come from somewhere or something connected to the surgeries. Even though the enzymatic solution is sterile, Dr. Santos sends it to a laboratory for a LAL assay.

Why does Dr. Santos send the enzymatic solution for a LAL assay?

produced by *Staphylococcus aureus;* and a type of fimbria specific to enteropathogenic strains of *E. coli.*

Some bacteriophages (viruses that infect bacteria) can incorporate their DNA into the bacterial chromosome, becoming a prophage, and thus remain latent (do not cause lysis of the bacterium). Such a state is called *lysogeny,* and cells containing a prophage are said to be lysogenic. One outcome of lysogeny is that the host bacterial cell and its progeny may exhibit new properties encoded by the bacteriophage DNA. Such a change in the characteristics of a microbe due to a prophage is called **lysogenic conversion.** As a result of lysogenic conversion, the bacterial cell is immune to infection by the same type of phage. In addition, lysogenic cells are of medical importance because some bacterial pathogenesis is caused by the prophages they contain.

Among the bacteriophage genes that contribute to pathogenicity are the genes for diphtheria toxin, erythrogenic toxins, staphylococcal enterotoxin and pyrogenic toxin, botulinum neurotoxin, and the capsule produced by *Streptococcus pneumoniae.* The gene for Shiga toxin in *E. coli* O157 is encoded by phage genes. Pathogenic strains of *Vibrio cholerae* carry lysogenic phages. These phages can transmit the cholera toxin gene to nonpathogenic *V. cholerae* strains, increasing the number of pathogenic bacteria.

✔ Of what value are siderophores? 8

✔ How does toxigenicity differ from direct damage? 9

✔ Differentiate an exotoxin from an endotoxin. 10

✔ Food poisoning can be divided into two categories: food infection and food intoxication. On the basis of toxin production by bacteria, explain the difference between these two categories. 11

✔ Washwater containing *Pseudomonas* was sterilized and used to wash cardiac catheters. Three patients developed fever, chills, and hypotension following cardiac catheterization. The water and catheters were sterile. Why did the patients show these reactions? How should the water have been tested? 12

✔ How can lysogeny turn the normally harmless *E. coli* into a pathogen? 13

Pathogenic Properties of Viruses

LEARNING OBJECTIVE

14   List nine cytopathic effects of viral infections

The pathogenic properties of viruses depend on their gaining access to a host, evading the host's defenses, and then causing damage to or death of the host cell while reproducing themselves.

Viral Mechanisms for Evading Host Defenses

Viruses have a variety of mechanisms that enable them to evade destruction by the host's immune response. For example, viruses can penetrate and grow inside host cells, where components of the immune system cannot reach them. Viruses gain access to cells because they have attachment sites for receptors on their target cells. When such an attachment site is brought together with an appropriate receptor, the virus can bind to and penetrate the cell. Some viruses gain access to host cells because their attachment sites mimic substances useful to those cells. For example, the attachment sites of rabies virus can mimic the neurotransmitter acetylcholine. As a result, the virus can enter the host cell along with the neurotransmitter.

The AIDS virus (HIV) goes further by hiding its attachment sites from the immune response and by attacking components of the immune system directly. Like most viruses, HIV is cell-specific; that is, it attacks only particular body cells. HIV attacks only those cells that have a surface marker called the CD4 protein, most of which are cells of the immune system called T cells (T lymphocytes). Binding sites on HIV are complementary to the CD4 protein. The surface of the virus is folded to form ridges and valleys, and the HIV binding sites are located on the floors of the valleys. CD4 proteins are long enough and slender enough to reach these binding sites, whereas antibody molecules made against HIV are too large to make contact with the sites. As a result, it is difficult for these antibodies to destroy HIV.

Cytopathic Effects of Viruses

Infection of a host cell by an animal virus usually kills the host cell. Death can be caused by the accumulation of large numbers of multiplying viruses, by the effects of viral proteins on the permeability of the host cell's plasma membrane, or by inhibition of host DNA, RNA, or protein synthesis. The visible effects of viral infection are known as **cytopathic effects (CPE).** Those cytopathic effects that result in cell death are called *cytocidal effects;* those that result in cell damage but not cell death are called *noncytocidal effects.* CPEs are used to diagnose many viral infections.

Cytopathic effects vary with the virus. One difference is the point in the viral infection cycle at which the effects occur. Some viral infections result in early changes in the host cell; in other infections, changes are not seen until a much later stage. A virus can produce one or more of the following cytopathic effects:

1. At some stage in their multiplication, cytocidal viruses cause the macromolecular synthesis within the host cell to stop. Some viruses, such as herpes simplex virus, irreversibly stop mitosis.

2. When a cytocidal virus infects a cell, it causes the cell's lysosomes to release their enzymes, resulting in destruction of intracellular contents and host cell death.

3. **Inclusion bodies** are granules found in the cytoplasm or nucleus of some infected cells (**Figure 7a**). These granules are sometimes viral parts—nucleic acids or proteins in the process of being assembled into virions. The granules vary in size, shape, and staining properties, according to the virus. Inclusion bodies are characterized by their ability to stain with an acidic stain (acidophilic) or with a basic stain (basophilic). Other inclusion bodies arise at sites of earlier viral synthesis but do not contain assembled viruses or their components. Inclusion bodies are important because their presence can help identify the virus causing an infection. For example, in most cases, rabies virus produces inclusion bodies (Negri bodies) in the cytoplasm of nerve cells, and their presence in the brain tissue of animals suspected of being rabid has been used as one diagnostic tool for rabies. Diagnostic inclusion bodies are also associated with measles virus, vaccinia virus, smallpox virus, herpesvirus, and adenoviruses.

4. At times, several adjacent infected cells fuse to form a very large multinucleate cell called a **syncytium** (**Figure 7b**). Such giant cells are produced from infections by viruses that cause diseases, such as measles, mumps, and the common cold.

5. Some viral infections result in changes in the host cell's functions with no visible changes in the infected cells. For example, when measles virus attaches to its receptor called CD46, the CD46 prompts the cell to reduce production of an immune substance called IL-12, reducing the host's ability to fight the infection.

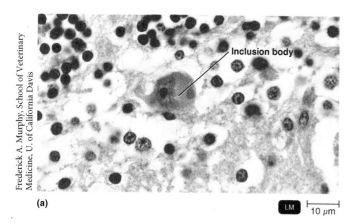

Frederick A. Murphy, School of Veterinary Medicine, U. of California Davis

(a) LM ⊢ 10 μm

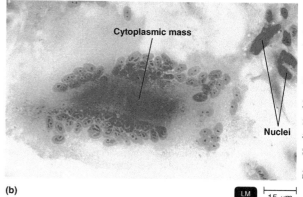

Cytoplasmic mass

Nuclei

Diana Hardie, U. of Cape Town Medical School, South Africa

(b) LM ⊢ 15 μm

Figure 7 Some cytopathic effects of viruses. (**a**) Cytoplasmic inclusion body in brain tissue from a person who died of rabies. (**b**) Portion of a syncytium (giant cell) formed in a cell infected with measles virus. The cytoplasmic mass is probably the Golgi complexes of fused cells.

Q   What are cytopathic effects?

6. Some virus-infected cells produce substances called **interferons.** Viral infection induces cells to produce interferons, but the host cell's DNA actually codes for the interferon. This protects neighboring uninfected cells from viral infection.

7. Many viral infections induce antigenic changes on the surface of the infected cells. These antigenic changes elicit a host antibody response against the infected cell, and thus they target the cell for destruction by the host's immune system.

8. Some viruses induce chromosomal changes in the host cell. For example, some viral infections result in chromosomal damage to the host cell, most often chromosomal breakage. Frequently, oncogenes (cancer-causing genes) may be contributed or activated by a virus.

9. Most normal cells cease growing in vitro when they come close to another cell, a phenomenon known as **contact inhibition.** Viruses capable of causing cancer *transform* host cells. Transformation results in an abnormal, spindle-shaped cell that does not recognize contact inhibition (**Figure 8**). The loss of contact inhibition results in unregulated cell growth.

Some representative viruses that cause cytopathic effects are presented in **Table 4.** In Part Four of the book we will discuss the pathological properties of viruses in more detail.

CHECK YOUR UNDERSTANDING

✔ Define *cytopathic effects*, and give five examples. 14

Clinical Case

Even sterile materials can contain endotoxins. The results come back from the lab: the solution from the ultrasonic bath is positive for endotoxins. Gram-negative bacteria such as *Burkholderia* found in liquid reservoirs and moist environments can colonize water pipes (see the figure) and, in turn, the laboratory containers used to hold water. In this case, the bacteria from the biofilms were washed into the enzymatic solution.

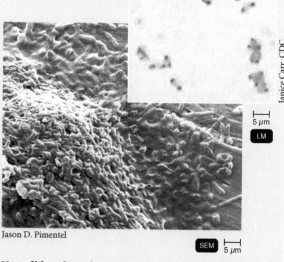

Janice Carr, CDC

5 μm LM

Jason D. Pimentel

SEM ⊢ 5 μm

How did endotoxins get in the sterile solutions?

John P. Bader/Biological Photo Service

LM | 100 μm

Figure 8 Transformed cells in culture. In the center of this photomicrograph is a cluster of chick embryo cells transformed by Rous sarcoma virus. Such a cluster results from the multiplication of a single cell infected with a transforming virus. Notice how the transformed cells appear dark, in contrast to the monolayer of light, flat, normal cells around them. This appearance is caused by their spindle shapes and their uninhibited growth due to the absence of contact inhibition.

 What is contact inhibition?

Pathogenic Properties of Fungi, Protozoa, Helminths, and Algae

LEARNING OBJECTIVE

15   Discuss the causes of symptoms in fungal, protozoan, helminthic, and algal diseases.

This section describes some general pathological effects of fungi, protozoa, helminths, and algae that cause human disease.

Fungi

Although fungi cause disease, they do not have a well-defined set of virulence factors. Some fungi have metabolic products that are toxic to human hosts. In such cases, however, the toxin is only an indirect cause of disease, because the fungus is already growing in or on the host. Chronic fungal infections, such as from molds growing in homes, can also provoke an allergic response in the host.

Trichothecenes are fungal toxins that inhibit protein synthesis in eukaryotic cells. Ingestion of these toxins causes headaches, chills, severe nausea, vomiting, and visual disturbances. These toxins are produced by *Fusarium* (fu'sār-ē-um) and *Stachybotrys* (stak'ē-bo-tris) growing on grains and wallboard in homes.

There is evidence that some fungi do have virulence factors. Two fungi that can cause skin infections, *Candida albicans* and *Trichophyton* (trik-ō-fō'ton), secrete proteases. These enzymes

TABLE 4 Cytopathic Effects of Selected Viruses

Virus (Genus)	Cytopathic Effect
Poliovirus (*Enterovirus*)	Cytocidal (cell death)
Genital warts virus (*Papillomavirus*)	Acidophilic inclusion bodies in nucleus
Adenovirus (*Mastadenovirus*)	Basophilic inclusion bodies in nucleus
Lyssavirus	Acidophilic inclusion bodies in cytoplasm
CMV (*Cytomegalovirus*)	Acidophilic inclusion bodies in nucleus and cytoplasm
Measles virus (*Morbillivirus*)	Cell fusion
Polyomavirus	Transformation
HIV (*Lentivirus*)	Destruction of T cells

may modify host cell membranes to allow attachment of the fungi. *Cryptococcus neoformans* (krip-tō-kok'kus nē-ō-fôr'manz) is a fungus that causes a type of meningitis; it produces a capsule that helps it resist phagocytosis. Some fungi have become resistant to antifungal drugs by decreasing their synthesis of receptors for these drugs.

The disease called ergotism, which was common in Europe during the Middle Ages, is caused by a toxin produced by an ascomycete plant pathogen, *Claviceps purpurea* (kla'vi-seps pủr-pủ-rē'ä), that grows on grains. The toxin is contained in **sclerotia,** highly resistant portions of the mycelia of the fungus that can detach. The toxin itself, **ergot,** is an alkaloid that can cause hallucinations resembling those produced by LSD (lysergic acid diethylamide); in fact, ergot is a natural source of LSD. Ergot also constricts capillaries and can cause gangrene of the limbs by preventing proper blood circulation in the body. Although *C. purpurea* still occasionally occurs on grains, modern milling usually removes the sclerotia.

Several other toxins are produced by fungi that grow on grains or other plants. For example, peanut butter is occasionally recalled because of excessive amounts of **aflatoxin,** a toxin that has carcinogenic properties. Aflatoxin is produced by the growth of the mold *Aspergillus flavus.* When ingested, the toxin might be altered in a human body to a mutagenic compound.

A few mushrooms produce toxins called **mycotoxins** (toxins produced by fungi). Examples are **phalloidin** and **amanitin,** produced by *Amanita phalloides* (am-an-ī'ta fal-loi'dēz), commonly known as the deathcap. These neurotoxins are so potent that ingestion of the *Amanita* mushroom may result in death.

Protozoa

The presence of protozoa and their waste products often produces disease symptoms in the host. Some protozoa, such as *Plasmo-*

dium, the causative agent of malaria, invade host cells and reproduce within them, causing their rupture. *Toxoplasma* attaches to macrophages and gains entry by phagocytosis. The parasite prevents normal acidification and digestion; thus, it can grow in the phagocytic vacuole. Other protozoa, such as *Giardia lamblia,* the causative agent of giardiasis, attach to host cells by a sucking disc and digest the cells and tissue fluids.

Some protozoa can evade host defenses and cause disease for very long periods of time. For example, *Giardia,* which causes diarrhea, and *Trypanosoma,* which causes African trypanosomiasis (sleeping sickness), both use antigenic variation to stay one step ahead of the host's immune system. The immune system is alerted to recognize foreign substances called antigens; the presence of antigens causes the immune system to produce antibodies designed to destroy them. When *Trypanosoma* is introduced into the bloodstream by a tsetse fly, it produces and displays a specific antigen. In response, the body produces antibodies against that antigen. However, within 2 weeks, the microbe stops displaying the original antigen and instead produces and displays a different one. Thus, the original antibodies are no longer effective. Because the microbe can make up to 1000 different antigens, such an infection can last for decades.

Helminths

The presence of helminths also often produces disease symptoms in a host. Some of these organisms actually use host tissues for their own growth or produce large parasitic masses; the resulting cellular damage evokes the symptoms. An example is the roundworm *Wuchereria bancrofti* (vū-kėr-ār′ē-ä ban-krof′tē), the causative agent of elephantiasis. This parasite blocks lymphatic circulation, leading to an accumulation of lymph and eventually causing grotesque swelling of the legs and other body parts. Waste products of the metabolism of these parasites can also contribute to the symptoms of a disease.

Algae

A few species of algae produce neurotoxins. For example, some genera of dinoflagellates, such as *Alexandrium,* are important medically because they produce a neurotoxin called **saxitoxin.** Although mollusks that feed on the dinoflagellates that produce saxitoxin show no symptoms of disease, people who eat the mollusks develop paralytic shellfish poisoning, with symptoms similar to botulism. Public health agencies frequently prohibit human consumption of mollusks during red tides.

CHECK YOUR UNDERSTANDING

✔ Identify one virulence factor that contributes to the pathogenicity of each of the following: fungi, protozoa, helminths, and algae. **15**

Portals of Exit

LEARNING OBJECTIVE

16 Differentiate portal of entry and portal of exit.

In the beginning of the chapter, you learned how microbes enter the body through a preferred route, or portal of entry. Microbes also leave the body via specific routes called **portals of exit** in secretions, excretions, discharges, or tissue that has been shed. In general, portals of exit are related to the part of the body that has been infected. Thus, in general, a microbe uses the same portal for entry and exit. By using various portals of exit, pathogens can spread through a population by moving from one susceptible host to another. This type of information about the dissemination of a disease is very important to epidemiologists.

The most common portals of exit are the respiratory and gastrointestinal tracts. For example, many pathogens living in the respiratory tract exit in discharges from the mouth and nose; such discharges are expelled during coughing or sneezing. These microorganisms are found in droplets formed from mucus. Pathogens that cause tuberculosis, whooping cough, pneumonia, scarlet fever, meningococcal meningitis, chickenpox, measles, mumps, smallpox, and influenza are discharged through the respiratory route. Other pathogens exit via the gastrointestinal tract in feces or saliva. Feces may be contaminated with pathogens associated with salmonellosis, cholera, typhoid fever, shigellosis, amebic dysentery, and poliomyelitis. Saliva can also contain pathogens, such as those that cause rabies, mumps, and infectious mononucleosis.

Another important route of exit is the genitourinary tract. Microbes responsible for sexually transmitted infections are

Clinical Case Resolved

Although the bacteria are killed by autoclaving, endotoxins can be released from the dead cells into solutions during autoclaving.

Dr. Santos treats her patients with prednisone, a topical anti-inflammatory drug, and they all fully recover from the reaction. (She did not prescribe antibiotics, because TASS is not an infection.) She holds a staff meeting to make sure the correct sterilizing procedures are being followed. Dr. Santos also stresses to her employees that preventing TASS depends primarily on using appropriate protocols for cleaning and sterilizing surgical equipment and paying careful attention to all solutions, medications, and ophthalmic devices used during surgery.

FOUNDATION FIGURE **9**

Microbial Mechanisms of Pathogenicity

When the balance between host and microbe is tipped in favor of the microbe, an infection or disease results. Learning these mechanisms of microbial pathogenicity is fundamental to understanding how pathogens are able to overcome the host's defenses.

H1N1 flu virus

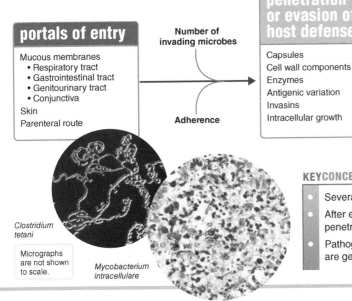

portals of entry		penetration or evasion of host defenses	damage to host cells	portals of exit
Mucous membranes • Respiratory tract • Gastrointestinal tract • Genitourinary tract • Conjunctiva Skin Parenteral route	**Number of invading microbes** **Adherence**	Capsules Cell wall components Enzymes Antigenic variation Invasins Intracellular growth	Siderophores Direct damage Toxins • Exotoxins • Endotoxins Lysogenic conversion Cytopathic effects	Generally the same as the portals of entry for a given microbe: • Mucous membranes • Skin • Parenteral route

Clostridium tetani

Micrographs are not shown to scale.

Mycobacterium intracellulare

KEYCONCEPTS

- Several factors are required for a microbe to cause disease.
- After entering the host, most pathogens adhere to host tissue, penetrate or evade host defenses, and damage host tissues.
- Pathogens usually leave the body via specific portals of exit, which are generally the same sites where they entered initially.

C. S. Goldsmith and A. Balish, CDC; Biophoto Associates/ Photo Researchers; Cecil H. Fox/Photo Researchers

found in secretions from the penis and vagina. Urine can also contain the pathogens responsible for typhoid fever and brucellosis, which can exit via the urinary tract. Skin or wound infections are other portals of exit. Infections transmitted from the skin include yaws, impetigo, ringworm, herpes simplex, and warts. Drainage from wounds can spread infections to another person directly or by contact with a contaminated fomite. Infected blood can be removed and reinjected by biting insects and contaminated needles and syringes to spread infection within a population. Examples of diseases transmitted by biting insects are yellow fever, plague, tularemia, and malaria. AIDS and hepatitis B may be transmitted by contaminated needles and syringes.

CHECK YOUR UNDERSTANDING

✔ Which are the most often used portals of exit? 16

* * *

Examine **Figure 9** carefully. It summarizes some key concepts of the microbial mechanisms of pathogenicity we have discussed in this chapter.

DO STUDY Qs ON QUIZLET ONCE COMPLETED.

Study Outline

Introduction

1. Pathogenicity is the ability of a pathogen to produce a disease by overcoming the defenses of the host.
2. Virulence is the degree of pathogenicity.

How Microorganisms Enter a Host

1. The specific route by which a particular pathogen gains access to the body is called its portal of entry.

Portals of Entry

2. Many microorganisms can penetrate mucous membranes of the conjunctiva and the respiratory, gastrointestinal, and genitourinary tracts.
3. Most microorganisms cannot penetrate intact skin; they enter hair follicles and sweat ducts.
4. Some microorganisms can gain access to tissues by inoculation through the skin and mucous membranes in bites, injections, and other wounds. This route of penetration is called the parenteral route.

The Preferred Portal of Entry

5. Many microorganisms can cause infections only when they gain access through their specific portal of entry.

Numbers of Invading Microbes

6. Virulence can be expressed as LD_{50} (lethal dose for 50% of the inoculated hosts) or ID_{50} (infectious dose for 50% of the inoculated hosts).

Adherence

7. Surface projections on a pathogen called adhesins (ligands) adhere to complementary receptors on the host cells.
8. Adhesins can be glycoproteins or lipoproteins and are frequently associated with fimbriae.
9. Mannose is the most common receptor.
10. Biofilms provide attachment and resistance to antimicrobial agents.

How Bacterial Pathogens Penetrate Host Defenses

Capsules

1. Some pathogens have capsules that prevent them from being phagocytized.

Cell Wall Components

2. Proteins in the cell wall can facilitate adherence or prevent a pathogen from being phagocytized.

Enzymes

3. Local infections can be protected in a fibrin clot caused by the bacterial enzyme coagulase.
4. Bacteria can spread from a focal infection by means of kinases (which destroy blood clots), hyaluronidase (which destroys a mucopolysaccharide that holds cells together), and collagenase (which hydrolyzes connective tissue collagen).
5. IgA proteases destroy IgA antibodies.

Antigenic Variation

6. Some microbes vary expression of antigens, thus avoiding the host's antibodies.

Penetration into the Host Cell Cytoskeleton

7. Bacteria may produce proteins that alter the actin of the host cell's cytoskeleton allowing bacteria into the cell.

How Bacterial Pathogens Damage Host Cells

Using the Host's Nutrients: Siderophores

1. Bacteria get iron from the host using siderophores.

Direct Damage

2. Host cells can be destroyed when pathogens metabolize and multiply inside the host cells.

The Production of Toxins

3. Poisonous substances produced by microorganisms are called toxins; toxemia refers to the presence of toxins in the blood. The ability to produce toxins is called toxigenicity.
4. Exotoxins are produced by bacteria and released into the surrounding medium. Exotoxins, not the bacteria, produce the disease symptoms.
5. Antibodies produced against exotoxins are called antitoxins.
6. A-B toxins consist of an active component that inhibits a cellular process and a binding component that attaches the two portions to the target cell, e.g., diphtheria toxin.
7. Membrane-disrupting toxins cause cell lysis, e.g., hemolysins.
8. Superantigens cause release of cytokines, which cause fever, nausea, and other symptoms; e.g., toxic shock syndrome toxin.
9. Endotoxins are lipopolysaccharides (LPS), the lipid A component of the cell wall of gram-negative bacteria.
10. Bacterial cell death, antibiotics, and antibodies may cause the release of endotoxins.
11. Endotoxins cause fever (by inducing the release of interleukin-1) and shock (because of a TNF-induced decrease in blood pressure).
12. Endotoxins allow bacteria to cross the blood–brain barrier.
13. The Limulus amebocyte lysate (LAL) assay is used to detect endotoxins in drugs and on medical devices.

Plasmids, Lysogeny, and Pathogenicity

14. Plasmids may carry genes for antibiotic resistance, toxins, capsules, and fimbriae.
15. Lysogenic conversion can result in bacteria with virulence factors, such as toxins or capsules.

Pathogenic Properties of Viruses

1. Viruses avoid the host's immune response by growing inside cells.
2. Viruses gain access to host cells because they have attachment sites for receptors on the host cell.
3. Visible signs of viral infections are called cytopathic effects (CPE).
4. Some viruses cause cytocidal effects (cell death), and others cause noncytocidal effects (damage but not death).
5. Cytopathic effects include stopping mitosis, lysis, formation of inclusion bodies, cell fusion, antigenic changes, chromosomal changes, and transformation.

Pathogenic Properties of Fungi, Protozoa, Helminths, and Algae

1. Symptoms of fungal infections can be caused by capsules, toxins, and allergic responses.
2. Symptoms of protozoan and helminthic diseases can be caused by damage to host tissue or by the metabolic waste products of the parasite.
3. Some protozoa change their surface antigens while growing in a host, thus avoiding destruction by the host's antibodies.
4. Some algae produce neurotoxins that cause paralysis when ingested by humans.

Portals of Exit

1. Pathogens have definite portals of exit.
2. Three common portals of exit are the respiratory tract via coughing or sneezing, the gastrointestinal tract via saliva or feces, and the genitourinary tract via secretions from the vagina or penis.
3. Arthropods and syringes provide a portal of exit for microbes in blood.

Study Questions

Answers to the Review and Multiple Choice questions can be found at the end of this chapter.

Review

1. Compare pathogenicity with virulence.
2. How are capsules and cell wall components related to pathogenicity? Give specific examples.
3. Describe how hemolysins, leukocidins, coagulase, kinases, hyaluronidase, siderophores, and IgA proteases might contribute to pathogenicity.
4. Explain how drugs that bind each of the following would affect pathogenicity:
   a. iron in the host's blood
   b. *Neisseria gonorrhoeae* fimbriae
   c. *Streptococcus pyogenes* M protein
5. Compare and contrast the following aspects of endotoxins and exotoxins: bacterial source, chemistry, toxicity, and pharmacology. Give an example of each toxin.
6. DRAW IT   Label this diagram to show how the Shiga toxin enters and inhibits protein synthesis in a human cell.

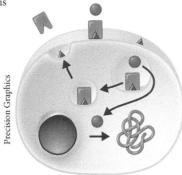

Precision Graphics

7. Describe the factors contributing to the pathogenicity of fungi, protozoa, and helminths.

8. Which of the following genera is the most infectious?

Genus	ID$_{50}$	Genus	ID$_{50}$
Legionella	1 cell	*Shigella*	200 cells
Salmonella	10^5 cells	*Treponema*	52 cells

9. How can viruses and protozoa avoid being killed by the host's immune response?
10. NAME IT   The *Opa* gene is used to identify this endotoxin-producing bacterium that grows well in the high-CO_2 conditions inside phagocytes.

Multiple Choice

1. The removal of plasmids reduces virulence in which of the following organisms?
   a. *Clostridium tetani*
   b. *Escherichia coli*
   c. *Salmonella enterica*
   d. *Streptococcus mutans*
   e. *Clostridium botulinum*
2. What is the LD$_{50}$ for the bacterial toxin tested in the example below?

Dilution (µg/kg)	No. of Animals Died	No. of Animals Survived
a. 6	0	6
b. 12.5	0	6
c. 25	3	3
d. 50	4	2
e. 100	6	0

3. Which of the following is *not* a portal of entry for pathogens?
   a. mucous membranes of the respiratory tract
   b. mucous membranes of the gastrointestinal tract
   c. skin
   d. blood
   e. parenteral route

4. All of the following can occur during bacterial infection. Which would prevent all of the others?
   a. vaccination against fimbriae
   b. phagocytosis
   c. inhibition of phagocytic digestion
   d. destruction of adhesins
   e. alteration of cytoskeleton

5. The ID_{50} for *Campylobacter* sp. is 500 cells; the ID_{50} for *Cryptosporidium* sp. is 100 cells. Which of the following statements is *false*?
   a. Both microbes are pathogens.
   b. Both microbes produce infections in 50% of the inoculated hosts.
   c. *Cryptosporidium* is more virulent than *Campylobacter*.
   d. *Campylobacter* and *Cryptosporidium* are equally virulent; they cause infections in the same number of test animals.
   e. *Cryptosporidium* infections are more severe than *Campylobacter* infections.

6. An encapsulated bacterium can be virulent because the capsule
   a. resists phagocytosis.
   b. is an endotoxin.
   c. destroys host tissues.
   d. interferes with physiological processes.
   e. has no effect; because many pathogens do not have capsules, capsules do not contribute to virulence.

7. A drug that binds to mannose on human cells would prevent
   a. the entrance of *Vibrio* enterotoxin.
   b. the attachment of pathogenic *E. coli*.
   c. the action of botulinum toxin.
   d. streptococcal pneumonia.
   e. the action of diphtheria toxin.

8. The earliest smallpox vaccines were infected tissue rubbed into the skin of a healthy person. The recipient of such a vaccine usually developed a mild case of smallpox, recovered, and was immune thereafter. What is the most likely reason this vaccine did not kill more people?
   a. Skin is the wrong portal of entry for smallpox.
   b. The vaccine consisted of a mild form of the virus.
   c. Smallpox is normally transmitted by skin-to-skin contact.
   d. Smallpox is a virus.
   e. The virus mutated.

9. Which of the following does *not* represent the same mechanism for avoiding host defenses as the others?
   a. Rabies virus attaches to the receptor for the neurotransmitter acetylcholine.
   b. *Salmonella* attaches to the receptor for epidermal growth factor.
   c. Epstein-Barr (EB) virus binds to the host receptor for complement.
   d. Surface protein genes in *Neisseria gonorrhoeae* mutate frequently.
   e. none of the above

10. Which of the following statements is true?
    a. The primary goal of a pathogen is to kill its host.
    b. Evolution selects for the most virulent pathogens.
    c. A successful pathogen doesn't kill its host before it is transmitted.
    d. A successful pathogen never kills its host.

Critical Thinking

1. The graph below shows confirmed cases of enteropathogenic *E. coli*. Why is the incidence seasonal?

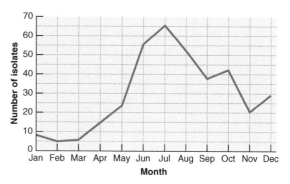

2. The cyanobacterium *Microcystis aeruginosa* produces a peptide that is toxic to humans. According to the graph below, when is this bacterium most toxic?

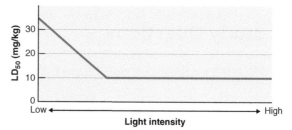

3. When injected into rats, the ID_{50} for *Salmonella typhimurium* is 10^6 cells. If sulfonamides are injected with the salmonellae, the ID_{50} is 35 cells. Explain the change in ID_{50} value.

4. How do each of the following strategies contribute to the virulence of the pathogen? What disease does each organism cause?

Strategy	Pathogen
Changes its cell wall after entry into host	*Yersinia pestis*
Uses urea to produce ammonia	*Helicobacter pylori*
Causes host to make more receptors	*Rhinovirus*

Clinical Applications

1. On July 8, a woman was given an antibiotic for presumptive sinusitis. However, her condition worsened, and she was unable to eat for 4 days because of severe pain and tightness of the jaw. On July 12, she was admitted to a hospital with severe facial spasms. She reported that on July 5 she had incurred a puncture wound at the base of her big toe; she cleaned the wound but did not seek medical attention. What caused her symptoms? Was her condition due to an infection or an intoxication? Can she transmit this condition to another person?

2. Explain whether each of the following examples is a food infection or intoxication. What is the probable etiological agent in each case?
   a. Eighty-two people who ate shrimp in Louisiana developed diarrhea, nausea, headache, and fever from 4 hours to 2 days after eating.
   b. Two people in Vermont who ate barracuda caught in Florida developed malaise, nausea, blurred vision, breathing difficulty, and numbness 3 to 6 hours after eating.

3. Cancer patients undergoing chemotherapy are normally *more* susceptible to infections. However, a patient receiving an antitumor drug that inhibited cell division was resistant to *Salmonella*. Provide a possible mechanism for the resistance.

Answers to Review and Multiple Choice Study Questions

Review

1. The ability of a microorganism to produce a disease is called *pathogenicity*. The degree of pathogenicity is *virulence*.

2. Encapsulated bacteria can resist phagocytosis and continue growing. *Streptococcus pneumoniae* and *Klebsiella pneumoniae* produce capsules that are related to their virulence. M protein found in the cell walls of *Streptococcus pyogenes* and A protein in the cell walls of *Staphylococcus aureus* help these bacteria resist phagocytosis.

3. Hemolysins lyse red blood cells; hemolysis might supply nutrients for bacterial growth. Leukocidins destroy neutrophils and macrophages that are active in phagocytosis; this decreases host resistance to infection. Coagulase causes fibrinogen in blood to clot; the clot may protect the bacterium from phagocytosis and other host defenses. Bacterial kinases break down fibrin; kinases can destroy a clot that was made to isolate the bacteria, thus allowing the bacteria to spread. Hyaluronidase hydrolyzes the hyaluronic acid that binds cells together; this could allow the bacteria to spread through tissues. Siderophores take iron from host iron-transport proteins, thus allowing bacteria to get iron for growth. IgA proteases destroy IgA antibodies; IgA antibodies protect mucosal surfaces.

4. **a.** Would inhibit bacteria.
   b. Would prevent adherence of *N. gonorrhoeae*.
   c. *S. pyogenes* would not be able to attach to host cells and would be more susceptible to phagocytosis.

5.

	Exotoxin	Endotoxin
Bacterial source	Gram +	Gram −
Chemistry	Proteins	Lipid A
Toxigenicity	High	Low
Pharmacology	Destroy certain cell parts or physiological functions	Systemic, fever, weakness, aches and shock
Example	Botulinum toxin	Salmonellosis

6.

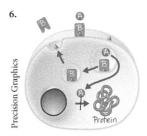

7. Pathogenic fungi do not have specific virulence factors; capsules, metabolic products, toxins, and allergic responses contribute to the virulence of pathogenic fungi. Some fungi produce toxins that, when ingested, produce disease. Protozoa and helminths elicit symptoms by destroying host tissues and producing toxic metabolic wastes.

8. *Legionella*.

9. Viruses avoid the host's immune response by growing inside host cells; some can remain latent in a host cell for prolonged periods. Some protozoa avoid the immune response by mutations that change their antigens.

10. *Neisseria gonorrhoeae*

Multiple Choice

1. d	**3.** d	**5.** c	**7.** b	**9.** d
2. c	**4.** a	**6.** a	**8.** a	**10.** c

6

DISEASES OF THE CARDIOVASCULAR SYSTEM

This photomicrograph reveals histopathological changes indicative of endocarditis caused by the fungus *Candida albicans*.

(Courtesy of the CDC/Sherry Brinkman, 1963)

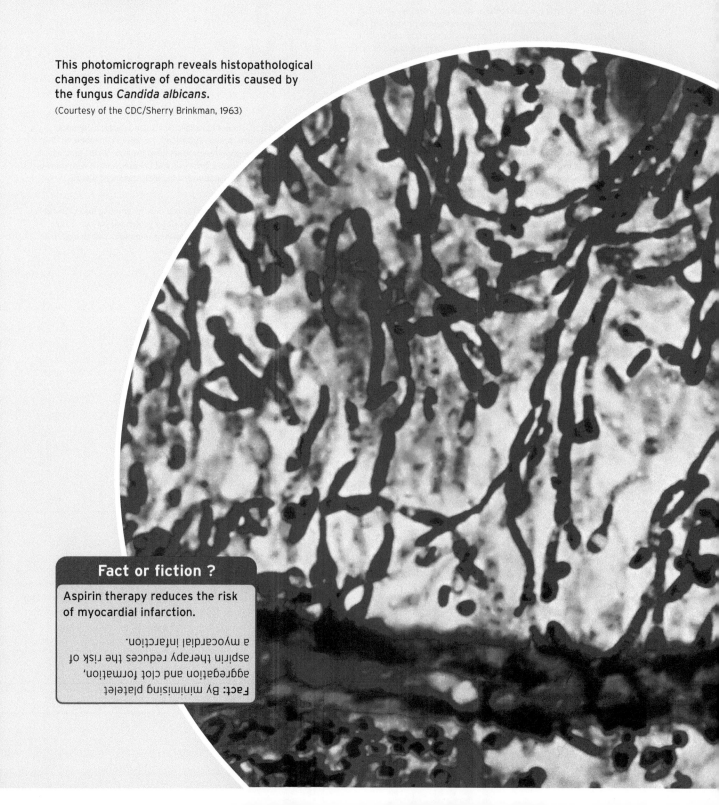

Fact or fiction ?

Aspirin therapy reduces the risk of myocardial infarction.

Fact: By minimising platelet aggregation and clot formation, aspirin therapy reduces the risk of a myocardial infarction.

Learning objectives

After studying this chapter, you should be able to:

+ Describe the normal structure and function of the heart and blood vessels
+ Describe the key characteristics of the diseases of the arterial circulation and heart
+ Explain the association between arteriosclerosis and atherosclerosis
+ Identify the role of hyperlipidaemia in atherosclerosis
+ Describe the aetiology, signs and risks associated with arterial hypertension
+ Compare and contrast pulmonary hypertension and arterial hypertension
+ Describe the role of varicose veins in peripheral vascular disease
+ Understand the risks associated with venous thrombosis
+ Differentiate between endocardial and myocardial diseases of the heart
+ Understand the distinguishing features of heart valve stenosis and heart valve regurgitation
+ Explain the different types of atrial and ventricular arrhythmias
  + Name the aetiologies of shock
    + Describe normal fetal circulation
      + Describe the epidemiology, symptoms, aetiology, diagnosis and treatment of congenital heart abnormalities
        + Review and understand the differences between cyanotic and non-cyanotic congenital heart disease
          + Review the risks and pathological changes associated with heart disease in older adults

Disease chronicle

Dr Christiaan Barnard

Dr Christiaan Barnard performed the first human heart transplant in 1967. In the Union of South Africa, Dr Barnard performed this famous surgery on a 53-year-old dentist named Louis Washkansky. The dentist received the donated heart of a 25-year-old car accident victim named Denise Davall. Although the surgery was a technical triumph and a beacon of hope for many with terminal heart disease, Washkansky died 18 days later from infection. Still risky today, heart transplants owe their successes to the generosity of Denise Davall, the courage of Louis Washkansky, and the brilliance of Dr Barnard, who died of a heart attack in 2001.

THE CIRCULATORY SYSTEM

The main function of the circulatory system, which includes the heart and blood vessels, is transport. The circulatory system delivers oxygen and nutrients needed for metabolism to the tissues; carries waste products from cellular metabolism to the kidneys and other excretory organs for elimination; and circulates electrolytes and hormones needed to regulate various bodily functions. The circulatory system is divided into two parts: the systemic and the pulmonary circulation. The heart pumps blood, and the blood vessels serve as tubes through which blood flows. The arterial system carries blood from the heart to the tissues, and the veins carry it back to the heart.

Structure and function of the heart

The heart is a hollow muscular organ located in the centre of the chest. The heart consists of four chambers: a right and left atrium and a right and left ventricle. The chamber walls consist of cardiac muscle, known as **myocardium**, and their internal lining, which consists of a smooth, delicate membrane called the **endocardium**. The **pericardium**, a double-layered membrane, encloses the heart (Figure 6.1).

The right and left sides of the heart have an upper atrium that collects blood from the body and the lungs, respectively, and a lower ventricle that ejects blood throughout the body and the lungs, respectively.

Valves between the atria and the ventricles, the atrioventricular (AV) valves, permit one-way blood flow from atria to ventricles. The **mitral valve**, between the left atrium and left ventricle, has two flaps called cusps that meet when the valve is closed. The **tricuspid valve**, between the right atrium and right ventricle, is named for its three cusps. Figure 6.2 shows these valves in the closed position.

The pulmonary semilunar valve permits one-way blood flow from the right ventricle to the pulmonary artery, while the aortic semilunar valve controls blood flow from the left ventricle to the aorta.

During every heartbeat cycle (the cardiac cycle), each heart chamber relaxes as it fills, and then contracts as it pumps blood. This filling period is

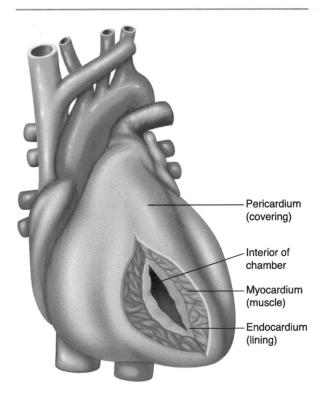

Figure 6.1 Heart covering and layer of the heart.

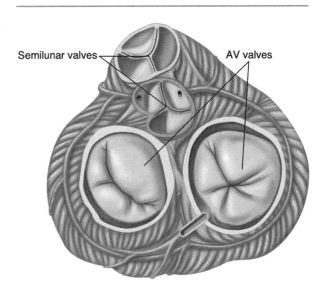

Figure 6.2 Heart valves in closed position viewed from the top.

diastole, or the diastolic phase, while the contracting phase of each chamber is **systole**, or systolic phase. The alternate contraction and relaxation of atria and ventricles comprises the **cardiac cycle**, which takes

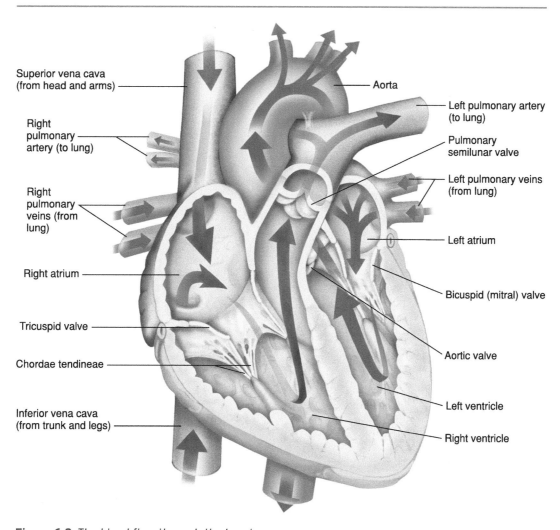

Superior vena cava
(from head and arms)

Aorta

Left pulmonary artery
(to lung)

Right
pulmonary
artery (to lung)

Pulmonary
semilunar valve

Left pulmonary veins
(from lung)

Right
pulmonary
veins (from
lung)

Left atrium

Right atrium

Bicuspid (mitral) valve

Tricuspid valve

Aortic valve

Chordae tendineae

Left ventricle

Inferior vena cava
(from trunk and legs)

Right ventricle

Figure 6.3 The blood flow through the heart.

about 0.8 of a second. The flow of blood through the heart chambers, vessels and lungs is reviewed in Figure 6.3.

Coronary arteries provide the heart muscle (myocardium) with a reliable blood supply. The left coronary artery begins at the aorta on the front of the heart and divides within an inch into the anterior interventricular coronary artery and the circumflex artery, which continues left around the back of the heart. The right coronary artery also branches from the front of the aorta and sends divisions to the right side and back of the heart (Figure 6.4).

Unlike skeletal muscle, cardiac muscle contracts continuously and rhythmically without conscious effort. A small patch of tissue, the **sinoatrial node**

(SA node), acts as the pacemaker of the heart. The impulse for contraction initiates at the SA node and spreads over the atria, then passes to the ventricles via conductive tissue called the atrioventricular (AV) node. The impulse continues along left and right bundle branches and terminates in the **Purkinje fibres**, which further branch throughout the ventricle walls. This conduction system is illustrated in Figure 6.5.

Heart muscle does not depend on nerve stimulation for contraction, but is influenced by the autonomic nervous system and hormones such as adrenaline (epinephrine). Two sets of nerves work antagonistically, one slowing the heart and the other accelerating it. The vagus nerve slows the heart

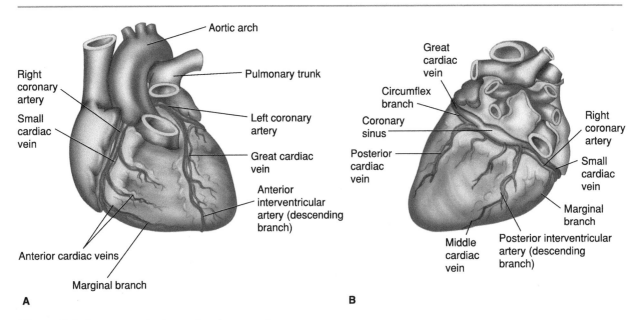

Figure 6.4 Coronary arteries and major vessels.

rate during rest and sleep by means of a chemical it secretes, acetylcholine. The excitatory portion of the autonomic nervous system increases heart rate during periods of stress, strenuous physical activity and excitement. This excitation is brought about by the release of adrenaline and noradrenaline (nor-epinephrine), which stimulate the heart's pacemaker.

Blood flows through two circulatory routes: the systemic circulation and the pulmonary circulation. The systemic circulation distributes oxygen-rich

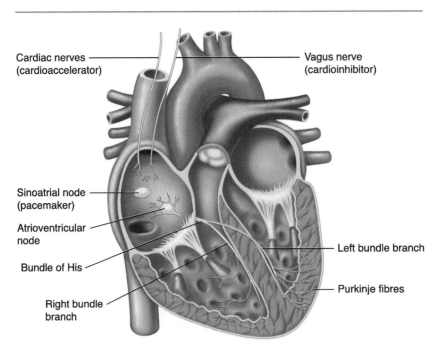

Figure 6.5 Conducting system of the heart.

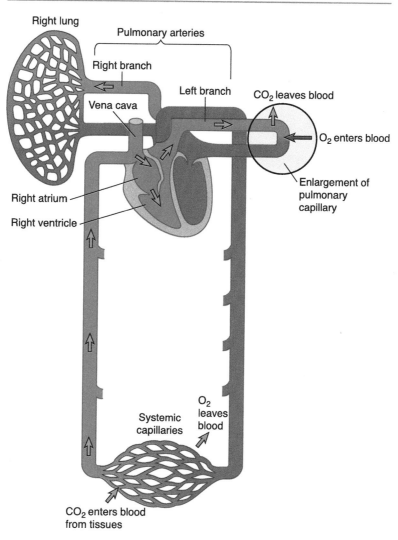

Figure 6.6 Venous return to the heart and blood flow to the lungs (red = oxygenated blood, blue = deoxygenated blood).

blood from the left ventricle, beginning at the **aorta** (large artery of the systemic arterial system) and continuing through arteries to all parts of the body, and returns oxygen-poor blood by veins to the right atrium. The pulmonary circulation carries oxygen-poor blood from the right ventricle, beginning at the pulmonary trunk and continuing through smaller arteries to the lungs to be oxygenated, and returns the blood through pulmonary veins to the left atrium. Partitions called the interatrial septum and interventricular septum separate oxygen-rich from oxygen-poor blood in the atria and ventricles, respectively (Figures 6.6 and 6.7).

Branches of the aorta carry blood to the head, upper extremities, chest, abdomen, pelvis and lower extremities. These arteries continue to divide into smaller and smaller arteries, and eventually into vessels called **arterioles**, the smallest arteries. Arterioles lead into **capillaries**, the connecting links between arteries and veins. Capillaries deliver oxygen and nutrients to tissues. Blood continues into **venules**, the smallest veins, and then into larger veins. Veins from the upper body empty blood into the superior vena cava, and veins of the lower body carry blood to the inferior vena cava. The superior and inferior **venae cavae** deliver systemic blood to the right atrium.

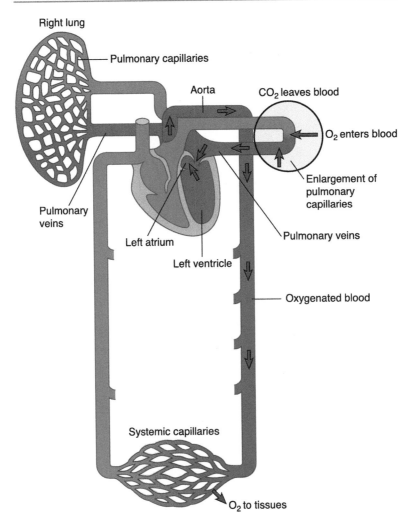

Figure 6.7 Return of oxygenated blood to heart and entry into aorta (red = oxygenated blood, blue = deoxygenated blood).

Structure and function of the blood vessels

The walls of arteries are muscular, thick and strong, with considerable elastic tissue, and are lined with endothelium. Arterioles have a smaller diameter than arteries, with thinner walls consisting mostly of smooth muscle fibres arranged circularly and a lining consisting of endothelium. Arterioles can change their diameter by constricting or dilating, which alters blood flow to the tissues. Capillaries are minute vessels about 0.5–1.0 mm long with a lumen as wide as a red blood cell. Their wall consists only of a layer of endothelium. Vein walls are much thinner than companion arteries, but their lumens are considerably larger. With less muscle and elasticity in their walls, veins tend to collapse when empty. Veins, particularly those of the legs, contain valves that help return blood upward to the heart against gravity.

DIAGNOSTIC TESTS AND PROCEDURES FOR CARDIAC DISORDERS

Many techniques for diagnosing and treating heart problems exist. **Auscultation**, listening through a stethoscope for abnormal sounds, and the electrocardiogram (ECG) provide valuable information regarding heart condition. The **electrocardiogram** is an electrical recording of heart action and aids in the diagnosis of coronary artery disease, myocardial infarction, valve disorders and some congenital heart diseases. It is also useful in diagnosing arrhythmias and heart block. **Echocardiography** (ultrasound cardiography) is also a non-invasive procedure that utilises high frequency sound waves to examine the size, shape and motion of heart structures. It gives a time–motion study of the heart, which permits direct recordings of heart valve movement, measurements of the heart chambers and changes that occur in the heart chambers during the cardiac cycle. Colour **Doppler echocardiography** explores blood flow patterns and changes in velocity of blood flow within the heart and great vessels. It enables the cardiologist to evaluate valve stenosis or insufficiency.

An exercise tolerance test is used to diagnose coronary artery disease and other heart disorders. This test monitors the ECG and blood pressure during exercise. Problems that normally do not occur at rest are revealed.

Cardiac catheterisation is a procedure in which a catheter is passed into the heart through blood vessels to sample the blood in each chamber for oxygen content and pressure. The findings can indicate valve disorders or abnormal shunting of blood and aid in determining cardiac output.

X-rays of the heart and great vessels, the aorta and the pulmonary artery, in conjunction with **angiocardiography**, in which a contrast indicator (dye) is injected into the cardiovascular system, can detect blockage in vessels. **Coronary arteriography** employs a selective injection of contrast material into coronary arteries for a film recording of blood vessel action.

CARDIOVASCULAR DISEASE

Cardiovascular disease includes a range of diseases that affect the heart and the blood vessels. Globally, mortality from cardiovascular disease is expected to reach 23.6 million by 2030 (WHO, 2009). Heart disease is the leading cause of death and a major cause of disability in the UK, with 16% of all female deaths and 20.2% of all male deaths caused by cardiovascular disease.

Disorders of blood flow and pressure and disorders of cardiac function are directly and indirectly responsible for many of the diseases that affect the pulmonary and systemic circulation. Disorders of blood flow and pressure include the diseases of the arterial circulation and the venous circulation. Disorders of cardiac function consist of diseases of the pericardium, coronary heart disease, myocardial and endocardial diseases, heart valve disease, cardiac conduction disturbance, heart failure and heart disease in infants and children.

Diseases of the arterial circulation

Hyperlipidaemia Hyperlipidaemia is a general term used to describe an elevation of lipids or fats in the blood. Lipids include cholesterol, phospholipids and triglycerides. Cholesterol is a soft waxy substance that is important in the formation of cell membranes and various hormones. Cholesterol is made by the liver and is also introduced to the body through food. It is transported throughout the systemic circulation by transport proteins called **lipoproteins**.

Low density lipoprotein (LDL) is the major cholesterol carrier in the blood. LDL transports cholesterol to the tissues of the body. LDL is also known as the 'bad' cholesterol because accumulations of LDL form a **plaque** or thick hard deposit that narrows the arteries and impedes blood flow. LDL cholesterol enters cells via binding with LDL receptors (on the cell surface) that then causes entry via endocytosis. **High density lipoprotein (HDL)** carries about one-quarter to one-third of the cholesterol. Known as the 'good' cholesterol, HDL carries cholesterol away from the arteries and to the liver, where it is eliminated from the body as a component of bile. **Phospholipids** are a type of lipid that are also important for the synthesis of cell membranes.

Triglycerides are another form of fat that is stored in fat cells in the human body. An increase in triglycerides is linked to coronary artery disease.

Trans fat

Trans fats are made by the process of hydrogenation (hydrogen is added to vegetable oil) and are found in many processed foods as they help to extend shelf life. Trans fats are not essential to health and high amounts of these fats in the diet can increase the risk of heart disease as they contribute to the increase in the blood levels of LDL cholesterol. In the UK, the addition of trans fats to food was stopped by many of the major food manufacturers by 2007.

Hypercholesterolaemia Hypercholesterolaemia can be classified as primary, in which the condition develops independent of other causes, and secondary, in which it is associated with other health problems or lifestyle.

Many types of primary cholesterolaemia have a genetic basis. For example, the LDL receptor is deficient or defective in the autosomal dominant genetic disorder known as *familial hypercholesterolaemia*. In this case, cholesterol cannot be taken up by cells and high levels of LDL are seen in the blood. Secondary causes of hypercholesterolaemia include obesity and diabetes mellitus. High-calorie diets increase the production of LDL and cholesterol. Diets that are high in triglycerides and saturated fat increase cholesterol synthesis and suppress LDL receptor activity.

Arteriosclerosis Arteriosclerosis and atherosclerosis are diseases of the arteries. Because these diseases significantly contribute to the development of many other diseases in the cardiovascular system, most notably heart disease, they are discussed first.

In **arteriosclerosis**, artery walls thicken and become hard and inflexible, partly due to calcium deposition. 'Hardening of the arteries' aptly describes this condition, because affected arteries are unable to stretch and rebound in response to the pressure of blood as it is forced through them by contraction of the heart. As a result, arteriosclerosis leads to hypertension. The most common cause of arteriosclerosis is atherosclerosis (discussed next), in which fatty material accumulates within the walls of the artery (Figure 6.8). Arteriosclerosis is also associated with the aging process.

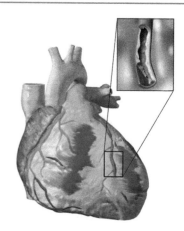

Figure 6.8 An atherosclerotic artery.

Atherosclerosis Atheroslerosis, or a hardening of the arteries, is a multifaceted disease that results from a number of insults that damage the vasculature, and is specifically related to the development of an atheromatous plaque. Hypercholesterolaemia, smoking, hypertension and diabetes mellitus are the key risk factors that initiate the atherosclerotic process. The lesions associated with atherosclerosis are of three types:

- the fatty streak;
- the fibrous atheromatous plaque;
- the complicated lesion.

Fatty streaks are thin, flat discolorations in the vasculature that progressively enlarge and become thicker as they grow in length. Fatty streaks are present in children and increase in number until about the age of 20 years, and then they either remain static or regress.

The **fibrous atheromatous plaque** is the basic lesion of clinical atherosclerosis. It is characterised by the accumulation of intracellular and extracellular lipids and the formation of scar tissue. The lesion begins as a whitish grey lesion thickening of the vessel intima (inner coat of the vessel) that contains a lipid core covered by a fibrous plaque. There is usually disruption of the underlying tunica media with an increase in the number of smooth muscle cells. As the lesion increases in size, the lesion may begin to occlude a vessel, causing a reduction of blood flow (Figure 6.9).

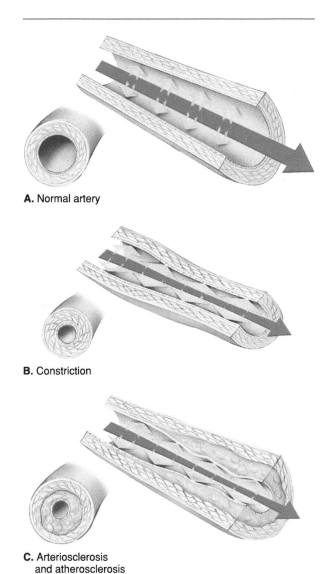

A. Normal artery

B. Constriction

C. Arteriosclerosis and atherosclerosis

Figure 6.9 Blood vessels: (A) normal artery; (B) constriction; (C) arteriosclerosis and atherosclerosis.

The more advanced or **complicated lesions** are characterised by haemorrhage, ulceration and scar tissue deposits. **Thrombosis**, or a clot within a blood vessel, is formed by turbulent blood flow in the region of the plaque and ulceration of the plaque.

Males and people with a history of cardiovascular disease have an increased risk for atherosclerosis. Modifiable risk factors such as hypercholesterolaemia, high blood pressure, diabetes, obesity, physical inactivity, untreated or under-treated hypertension and smoking can be controlled to reduce the risk for atherosclerosis.

A variety of tests are available to confirm the diagnosis of atherosclerosis. The electrocardiogram measures normal and abnormal electrical activity of the heart that may result from atherosclerotic disease. Coronary angiography is a test that is used to visualise the coronary arteries with the use of a contrast media. A CT scan or computerised tomography scan sends X-rays through the body at various angles. The CT scan can directly visualise the heart arteries and measure the amount of calcium deposits in the arteries.

Atherosclerosis is not usually associated with symptoms until the interior of the artery is extensively occluded. Symptoms depend on the location and the severity of the occluded artery. Occlusion of the coronary arteries may result in chest pain and shortness of breath. Blockage of the **carotid arteries** can reduce blood supply to the brain, causing a stroke. A hardening of the arteries in the legs, or **peripheral vascular disease**, leads to pain in the muscles of the leg, especially when walking; however, in severe cases ulceration or **gangrene** of the extremities may result.

Control of blood pressure, reduction of cholesterol and lifestyle changes contribute significantly to the treatment and prevention of consequences that can result from atherosclerosis. Medications commonly prescribed in the treatment of atherosclerosis include antihypertensive and cholesterol lowering medications. Numerous controlled clinical trials confirm the beneficial effects of controlling blood cholesterol levels. Treatment of hypertension reduces the potential for further injury and insult to the arteries.

Peripheral arterial disease Diseases that affect peripheral arteries are similar to those affecting the coronary (heart) or carotid (brain) arteries in that they produce **ischaemia**, a lack of blood and consequently oxygen. Pain, impaired function, infarction and tissue necrosis may then follow. Atherosclerosis is an important cause of peripheral arterial disease. The most commonly affected arteries are the femoral (leg) or popliteal arteries. The disease is seen most commonly in men aged 70–80 years. The risk factors for this disease are the same as those for atherosclerosis, namely heredity and environmental risks.

Inspection of the limbs for signs of ischaemia, such as subcutaneous atrophy, pallor, coolness and absent pulses, provides a preliminary diagnosis. Doppler ultrasound, ultrasound imaging, radionuclide imaging and contrast angiography may also be used to confirm the diagnosis.

The primary symptom of chronic obstructive peripheral artery disease is **intermittent claudication**, or pain with walking. Other signs include a thinning of the skin and subcutaneous tissues of the lower leg. The foot may feel cool to the touch and a lower leg pulse may be faint or absent. When blood flow is significantly reduced, the oxygen and nutritional needs may not be met, and ischaemic pain at rest, ulceration and gangrene may result.

Treatment of peripheral vascular disease is aimed at prevention of further complications in the affected tissues. Walking slowly is usually encouraged because it increases circulation around the clots. Avoidance of injury is important because extremities affected by atherosclerosis are easily injured and slow to heal. Blood thinning agents are used to prevent additional clots from forming. In severe cases, surgical bypass around the clot may be indicated. Removal of the clot may also be considered if the section of the diseased vessel is short.

Raynaud's disease Raynaud's disease is a functional disorder of the arteries caused by **vasospasms**, or intense spasms of the arteries and arterioles in the fingers and toes. Raynaud's disease usually occurs in healthy young women. It is often precipitated by exposure to cold or emotional stress and is usually limited to the fingers (Figure 6.10). The causes

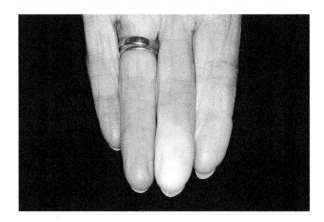

Figure 6.10 Raynaud's disease
(Science Photo Library Ltd/Dr P. Marazzi)

of vessel spasms are unknown, although hyperactivity of the sympathetic nervous system has been suggested.

Symptoms of vasospasm include changes in skin colour, from pallor to cyanosis, accompanied by a sensation of cold, numbness or tingling. The colour changes are most noticeable in the tips of the fingers, later moving to the more distant parts of the fingers and hands. In severe progressive disease, the nails may become brittle and the skin over the affected fingers may thicken. Deprivation of oxygen and nutrients in the affected area may give rise to arthritis, ulceration or, rarely, gangrene of the fingers.

Treatment of Raynaud's disease is aimed at reducing triggers for the symptoms and protecting the hands from trauma. Abstinence from smoking, protection of the hands from cold and avoidance of emotional stress are important. Medications that prevent vasospasm may be used in individuals with frequent symptoms.

Aortic aneurysm Aortic aneurysm refers to dilatation of the aortic lumen. Aneurysms are usually described by their location, size, **morphology** (configuration and structure), and origin. The morphology of an aortic aneurysm is either **fusiform** or **saccular** (Figure 6.11). A **fusiform** aneurysm has a uniform shape, with symmetrical dilatation that involves the circumference of the aortic wall.

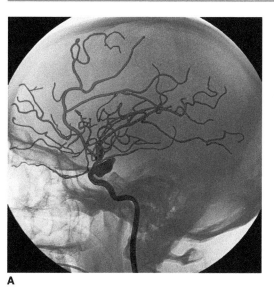
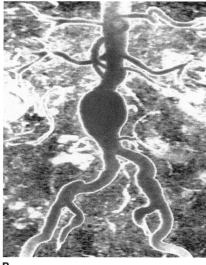

A   **B**

Figure 6.11 Aneurysms: (A) saccular (Simon Fraser/RNC, Newcastle/Photo Researchers, Inc); and (B) fusiform (Zephyr/Photo Researchers, Inc.).

Saccular aneurysms, on the other hand, appear as an out-pouching of only a portion of the aortic wall.

Ultrasound imaging, echocardiography, computed tomography (CT) and magnetic resonance imaging (MRI) scans are often used to diagnose and monitor the progression of an aneurysm.

Aneurysms usually occur in the abdomen below the kidneys (**abdominal aortic aneurysm**) or in the chest cavity (**thoracic aneurysm**). **Cerebral** or brain **aneurysm** is diagnosed less frequently. Regardless of location, the danger of an aneurysm is the tendency to increase in size and rupture, resulting in haemorrhage, possibly in a vital organ such as the heart, brain or abdomen.

Aortic aneurysms typically produce no symptoms and usually develop after age 50 and occur more frequently in men than in women. Atherosclerosis is the most common cause of abdominal aneurysms. Other causes of aortic aneurysms include connective tissue diseases and conditions that cause inflammation of the vessels such as trauma or infections.

Depending on the size and rate of expansion, surgical repair of an aneurysm is at times indicated to prevent rupture. The diseased area of the vessel is removed and replaced with an artificial graft or segment of another blood vessel.

Disorders of arterial pressure

Arterial hypertension Arterial blood pressure is a measure of the force of blood against the arterial walls. In healthy adults, the highest pressure, called the **systolic** pressure, is ideally less than 120 mmHg, and the lowest pressure, called the **diastolic** pressure, is less than 80 mmHg. Blood pressure normally varies throughout the day, increasing with activity and decreasing with rest (Table 6.1).

Hypertension is broadly defined as an arterial pressure greater than 140/90 mmHg in adults on at least three consecutive measures.

Table 6.1 Adult blood pressure guidelines.

Category	Systolic	Diastolic
Optimal	<120	<80
Normal	120–129	80–84
High normal	130–139	85–89
Grade 1 hypertension (mild)	140–159	90–99
Grade 2 hypertension (moderate)	160–179	100–109
Grade 3 hypertension (severe)	≥180	≥110
Isolated systolic hypertension	≥140	<90

Source: European Society of Hypertension & European Society of Cardiology (2003).

Table 6.2 Risk of stroke and heart disease increase with increasing blood pressure.

Blood pressure (mmHg)	Risk
115/75	Normal
135/85	2 times normal
155/95	4 times normal
175/105	8 times normal

Advancing age, sedentary lifestyle, excess weight and excessive dietary salt and alcohol consumption are risk factors for the development of hypertension. Family history of hypertension and African ancestry are also observed risk factors for developing high blood pressure.

Hypertension is the most common cardiovascular disorder and affects about 20% of the adult population worldwide. It is considered one of the major risk factors for heart disease, stroke and kidney disease (Table 6.2). Because of the asymptomatic nature of hypertension, it remains untreated or under-treated in the majority of affected individuals.

Blood pressure measurements obtained by using a sphygmomanometer and stethoscope are important in the diagnosis and follow-up treatment for hypertension. The diagnosis of hypertension using this method is based on the average of at least two or more blood pressure readings taken on at least two separate occasions.

The aetiology of hypertension is divided into two categories: primary and secondary hypertension. Primary hypertension is also called **essential** hypertension; this chronic increase in systolic and diastolic blood pressure occurs without evidence of other disease. Approximately 90–95% of hypertension is classified as primary or essential. In **secondary hypertension**, the elevation in blood pressure results from some other disease, such as kidney disease, or may be related to an endocrine disorder such as a phaeochromocytoma (tumour of the adrenal gland).

Primary hypertension typically does not cause symptoms. When symptoms do occur, they are usually related to the long-term effects of hypertension on the organ systems of the body, including the kidneys, heart, eyes and blood vessels. Hypertension is a major risk factor for the development of atherosclerosis, cardiovascular disease (including heart failure), coronary artery disease, peripheral vascular disease, and cerebrovascular diseases and stroke.

Treatment of primary and secondary hypertension is aimed at reducing blood pressure to less than 140/90 mmHg and preventing organ damage. For individuals with secondary hypertension, control of the disease causing the hypertension may often be curative. Lifestyle modifications such as weight loss, exercise and reduction of salt intake enhance the effectiveness of medication therapy and help reduce further disease risks. The type of medication selected to treat hypertension depends on the stage of hypertension, age, other conditions and patient-specific risk factors.

Pulmonary arterial hypertension Pulmonary arterial hypertension (PAH) is a condition of high blood pressure in the pulmonary artery. The average normal pressure in the pulmonary artery is about 14 mmHg at rest. In PAH, pressures in the pulmonary artery are greater than 25 mmHg at rest and greater than 30 mmHg during exercise.

A number of tests are used to diagnose and assess the severity of PAH. Echocardiography provides information about the severity of the pulmonary hypertension, estimated pulmonary artery pressure and potential causes. An electrocardiogram provides information on cardiac abnormalities. Pulmonary function tests, lung scans and blood tests are useful for identifying secondary causes. Cardiac catheterisation provides a precise measure of the blood pressure in the pulmonary artery.

There are both idiopathic and secondary causes of PAH that cause three general changes in the pulmonary arteries: vasoconstriction, endothelial and/or smooth muscle proliferation, and intimal fibrosis and thrombosis of the pulmonary capillaries or arterioles. **Vasoconstriction** results in a narrowing of the walls of the arteries, which makes the lumen of arteries narrower. As the endothelial cells and smooth muscles proliferate, the walls of the pulmonary artery thicken. Scar tissue forms on

Prevention PLUS!

Sodium intake

Most people from industrialised countries consume more salt (sodium) than their bodies need. Heavy sodium consumption increases blood pressure in some people; a 25-35% reduction in salt intake can reduce the likelihood of heart attack or stroke. You can take action to reduce your blood pressure and decrease likelihood of stroke or heart attack in the following ways:

- *Lose weight*: Weight loss is the single most effective non-drug method to reduce blood pressure
- *Exercise*: Thirty to thirty-five minutes of exercise three times per week can decrease blood pressure, especially when combined with weight loss
- *Limit alcohol consumption*: Alcohol raises blood pressure, even in the absence of hypertensive disease
- *Reduce fat intake and increase vegetable and fruit intake*: A diet high in vitamins and low in fats is associated with lower blood pressure
- *Reduce dietary salt intake*: Keep salt intake below 2400 mg per day, or less than 1 teaspoon (tsp) daily

the walls of the arteries, causing the lumen to narrow. Intimal fibrosis and thrombosis involves the formation of blood clots, causing blockages.

Symptoms of pulmonary arterial hypertension include **dyspnoea** (shortness of breath), fatigue and **syncope** (loss of consciousness, or fainting). As the disease advances, the pumping ability of the heart weakens and symptoms occur at rest.

Without treatment, the prognosis of PAH is poor, with a median survival of less than 3 years. Patients with severe symptoms require aggressive treatment to remove the underlying cause, reduce symptoms and improve quality of life, slow endothelial proliferation and the development of further narrowing of the lumen, and increase the supply of blood and oxygen to the heart. Treatments include medications, oxygen therapy and lung transplantation.

Diseases of the venous circulation

Venous circulation of the lower extremities

The venous systems in the lower extremities consist of the superficial (saphenous) veins and the deep venous channels. Blood from the skin and the subcutaneous tissue accumulates in the superficial veins and is then transported into the deeper venous channels for return to the heart. Venous valves are located along the veins and prevent backflow of blood into the venous system. The leg muscles also assist in moving venous blood from the lower extremities to the heart.

Varicose veins Varicose veins are dilated, distorted veins that usually develop in the superficial veins of the leg, such as the greater saphenous vein. The veins become swollen and painful and appear knotty under the skin. Varicose veins are caused by blood pooling within the veins because of decreased, stagnated blood flow (Figure 6.12).

Varicose veins can be an occupational hazard related to long periods of sitting or standing. Normally, the leg muscle movement moves blood up within the vein from one valve to the next. In the absence of this 'milking action' of the muscles, the blood exerts pressure on the closed valves and thin walls of the veins. The veins dilate to the extent that the valves are no longer competent. The blood collects and becomes stagnant, and the veins become more swollen and painful.

Pregnancy or a tumour in the uterus can also cause varicose veins because pressure on veins causes resistance to blood flow. Heredity and obesity are also associated with varicose veins.

Complications of varicose veins include ulcers and infection, owing to poor circulation, and haemorrhage, caused by weakened vein walls.

Treatment depends on the severity of the symptoms. An elastic bandage or support hose may

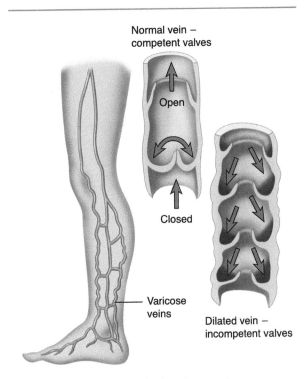

Figure 6.12 Development of varicose veins.

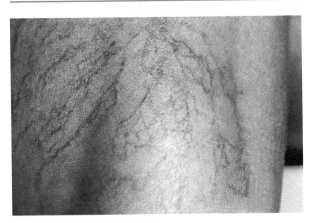

Figure 6.13 Spider veins.
(Courtesy of Jason L. Smith MD)

increase circulation and provide relief from discomfort. Symptoms can be relieved by walking, elevating the legs when seated, and losing weight. A surgical procedure called surgical vein stripping is very successful and involves removing the veins and tying off the remaining open ends. Collateral circulation tends to develop to compensate for the loss of the vein segment.

Spider veins are small, dense networks of veins that appear as red or blue discolorations on the skin. The cause of spider veins is unknown, though there appears to be a genetic link. Spider veins appear in both men and women, but more frequently in women. Female hormones may play a role in their development; puberty, birth control pills, pregnancy or hormone replacement therapy may contribute to them. Spider veins can be treated with laser. The light heats and scars the tiny superficial veins, which closes them off to blood flow (Figure 6.13). Another treatment is **compression sclerotherapy**, in which a strong saline solution is injected into specific sites of the varicose veins. The irritation causes scarring of the inner lining and fuses the veins shut. The procedure is followed by uninterrupted compression for several weeks to prevent re-entry of blood. A daily walking programme during the recovery period is required to activate leg muscle venous pumps.

Chronic venous insufficiency Chronic venous insufficiency (CVI) is a condition of poor venous blood return to the heart. The most common cause of CVI is deep vein **thrombosis**, incompetence of the venous valves and muscles that aid in venous return.

Similar to other diseases, diagnostic screening consists of assessment of medical history, such as smoking, obesity, family history, pregnancy and history of sedentary lifestyle. Additional tests include plethysmography studies and Doppler imaging studies. Outflow plethysmography is a simple tourniquet procedure that requires placing and releasing a tourniquet on the lower extremities. Upon release of the tourniquet, the vein should return to baseline. Doppler imaging studies are used to assess venous flow and the presence of a thrombus.

Signs and symptoms associated with poor blood flow include tissue congestion, oedema, necrosis or skin atrophy and pain upon walking. In advanced disease, venous stasis ulcers may develop.

Risk factors for CVI include advancing age, family history of deep vein thrombosis, sedentary lifestyle, obesity and smoking. The peak incidence of CVI occurs in women aged 40–49 years and men aged 70–79 years.

The treatment of CVI depends on the severity of the disease. Mild cases can be managed with controlled diet and exercise and the use of compression stockings. Compression stockings squeeze the leg and prevent excess blood from flowing backward. Surgical repair of the veins includes repairing the valves, bypassing the incompetent veins and vein stripping (surgical procedure in which the diseased vein is removed). An incision is made below the vein, a flexible instrument is threaded up the vein, and the vein is grasped and removed.

Venous thrombosis A clot, or **venous thrombosis**, can develop in the superficial or the deep veins of the lower extremities. Venous thrombosis is accompanied by an inflammatory response to the vessel wall that results from venous blood stasis, vessel wall injury and increased blood coagulation.

Risk factors for venous thrombosis include conditions that cause venous stasis, hypercoagulability and vascular trauma. Older adults and postsurgical patients are at increased risk for venous thrombosis as immobilisation results in decreased blood flow and venous pooling in the lower extremities.

Venous thrombosis is not associated with symptoms in about 50% of patients. Signs and symptoms of inflammation, such as pain, swelling and deep muscle tenderness, are indications of venous thrombosis.

Early detection and prevention of venous thrombosis is vital to prevent potentially fatal complications such as **emboli**, or distant clots to vital organs such as the lung. Early ambulation after surgery or childbirth, exercising the legs and use of compression stockings are measures that decrease the risk for thrombus formation. Blood thinners are beneficial for patients at high risk. Surgery is performed to remove the thrombus or embolism.

Disorders of cardiac function

Coronary heart disease The coronary circulation supplies the heart with oxygen and nutrients to maintain cardiac function and thus supply the remainder of the body with blood. The body's metabolic needs change rapidly and widely, often requiring rapid adaptation of cardiac function and coronary blood flow. An imbalance in cardiac oxygen demand and supply can cause myocardial ischaemia, cardiac contractile dysfunction, arrhythmias, infarction and death.

A preliminary diagnosis of coronary heart disease (CHD) requires a physical examination, patient medical history and an electrocardiogram (ECG). A patient's medical history is used to identify hereditary and lifestyle risk factors for the disease. The ECG records the heart's electrical activity and can aid in identifying abnormalities in heart rate and rhythm as well as areas of damaged heart tissue. Additional diagnostic tests include echocardiograms, stress tests, nuclear imaging and angiography.

CHD is a disease of reduced coronary blood flow most often due to atherosclerosis. More than 90% of persons with CHD have coronary atherosclerosis. Atherosclerosis can affect the major coronary arteries and their branches. Risk factor categories define major, emerging and underlying conditions that influence the development of atherosclerotic CHD (Table 6.3).

CHD is the leading cause of death worldwide. Approximately 3.8 million men and 3.4 million women worldwide die each year from CHD. The aging world population will have major implications for CHD. By the year 2025, more than 60% of all CHD deaths will be among persons over 65 years

Table 6.3 Risk factor categories for atherosclerotic cardiovascular disease.

Major risk factors	Emerging risk factors
Cigarette smoking	Prothrombotic state
Elevated blood pressure	Proinflammatory state
Elevated LDL cholesterol	Insulin resistance
Low HDL cholesterol	**Underlying risk factors**
Diabetes mellitus	
Metabolic syndrome	High fat diet
	Obesity
	Physical inactivity
	Family history

Source: Adapted from Grundy, S.M. (2007) Cardiovascular and metabolic risk factors: how can we improve outcomes in the high-risk patient. *The American Journal of Medicine*, **120**(9A): S3-S9.

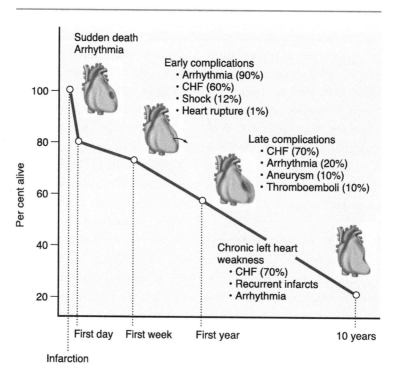

Sudden death
Arrhythmia

Early complications
• Arrhythmia (90%)
• CHF (60%)
• Shock (12%)
• Heart rupture (1%)

Late complications
• CHF (70%)
• Arrhythmia (20%)
• Aneurysm (10%)
• Thromboemboli (10%)

Chronic left heart
weakness
• CHF (70%)
• Recurrent infarcts
• Arrhythmia

Per cent alive

100
80
60
40
20

First day   First week   First year   10 years

Infarction

Figure 6.14 Outcome of myocardial infarction. Of 1-week survivors, 40% have late complications resulting in death; 10-year survival is about 25%. CHF, Congestive heart failure.

of age and more than 40% among persons over 75 years of age.

Symptoms of CHD include chest pain, or **angina pectoris**, which is pain and pressure felt in the chest that results from ischaemia; **palpitations**, or a sensation of a rapid pounding heartbeat; dizziness or fainting; weakness upon exertion or at rest; and shortness of breath. The most devastating sign of CHD is a heart attack, also known as a **myocardial infarction** (Figure 6.14). Crushing pain in the chest, shortness of breath, nausea, pallor, weakness and faintness are among the symptoms of a myocardial infarction.

Treatment of CHD depends on the severity of the disease as well as patient risk factors that may contribute to additional morbidity and mortality. Medications used to treat CHD include blood pressure lowering agents, blood thinners, diuretics (medication that increases excretion of water via the urine), nitrates such as nitroglycerin to stop chest pain and lipid lowering medication. Lifestyle changes, such as a healthy low salt diet and exercise,

are important to prevent further progression of disease.

Angioplasty is a procedure used to open a partly occluded artery (Figure 6.15). The procedure involves inserting a balloon-tipped catheter into the femoral artery, guiding it to the heart and into the narrowed coronary artery. The balloon is expanded to press against the vessel walls and open the lumen. A stent, which is a cylindrical wire mesh of stainless steel or other alloy, surrounds the balloon. Expansion of the balloon forces the mesh into the lining of the vessel, which physically holds the lumen open. Because the vessels commonly become occluded again (re-stenosis) within months or a year, stents are coated with drugs that prevent re-stenosis.

In cases of severe blockage of the coronary arteries, coronary artery bypass surgery may be needed. Coronary artery bypass surgery reroutes blood flow around the clogged arteries to improve blood flow and oxygen supply to the heart. A segment of a healthy blood vessel from another part of the body is attached or grafted from the aorta to the coronary

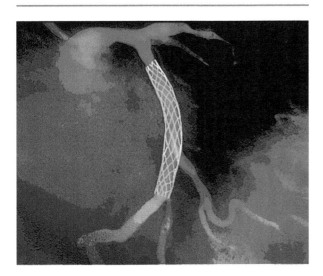

Figure 6.15 Angioplasty procedure. Note stent.
(ISM/Phototake NYC)

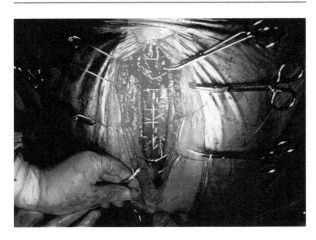

Figure 6.16 Bypass surgery of blocked coronary arteries.
(Antonia Reeve/Photo Researchers, Inc.)

artery below the blocked area. Depending on the number of blocked arteries, one or more grafts may be surgically placed (Figure 6.16).

Myocardial and endocardial diseases

Myocarditis Myocarditis is an inflammatory disease of the heart muscle. Viruses such as the Coxsackie virus, adenovirus and echovirus are the most common infecting viruses. Other potential aetiologies include infections with the human immune deficiency virus (HIV) and various bacterial infections.

Diagnosis of myocarditis can be suggested by clinical symptoms of the disease. An ECG recording provides evidence for conduction disturbances, and echocardiography may show an enlargement or inflammation of the heart muscle. Blood culture tests provide evidence for an infection. Elevations in certain heart muscle enzymes validate evidence for myocardial cell damage.

Myocarditis is often an asymptomatic condition. Patients usually have a history of viral illnesses, fever, chest pain that may feel like a heart attack, shortness of breath and tachycardia, or a rapid heartbeat.

The goal for treatment of myocarditis is prevention of further myocardial damage through patient supportive measures. Bed rest and activity restriction help decrease myocardial work. Antibiotics may be prescribed in cases where an infectious organism has been identified.

Cardiomyopathy Cardiomyopathy is a functional disease of the myocardium. There are three types of myocardial functional impairment: dilated, hypertrophic and restrictive cardiomyopathy (Figure 6.17). **Dilated cardiomyopathy** is the most common form and is characterised by dilatation of the ventricle, contractile dysfunction and symptoms of congestive heart failure. Ventricular hypertrophy is the

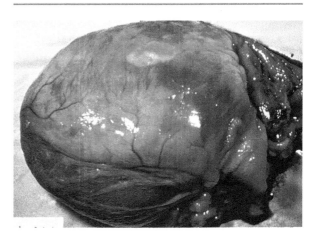

Figure 6.17 Cardiomyopathy.

dominant feature of **hypertrophic cardiomyopathy**. **Restrictive cardiomyopathy** is the least common form and is associated with reduced heart filling pressures and endocardial scarring in the ventricle.

Dilated cardiomyopathy may result from infections, myocarditis, toxic agents, metabolic disorders, genetic disorders and immune disorders. Often the cause is designated as **idiopathic dilated cardiomyopathy** as the aetiology is unknown. The symptoms of dilated cardiomyopathy include dyspnoea on exertion, orthopnoea, weakness, fatigue, ascites (accumulation of fluid in the abdomen) and peripheral oedema. Treatment is aimed at relieving the symptoms with medications, rest and surgical transplantation in severe cases.

Evidence for excessive ventricular growth is diagnostic for hypertrophic cardiomyopathy. Hypertrophic cardiomyopathy is a disease of young adulthood and is the most common cause of sudden cardiac death in the young. The aetiology is often unknown, although genetic mutations are identified in a small number of cases. The treatment of hypertrophic cardiomyopathy includes medications and surgery. The goal of medication therapy is to decrease symptoms of the disorder and to prevent sudden cardiac death. Surgery consists of incision to the ventricular septum and removal of parts of the diseased tissue.

Restrictive cardiomyopathy is distinguished by restricted ventricular filling owing to excessive rigidity of the ventricular walls. This condition is endemic in parts of Africa, India, South and Central America and Asia. The most common cause is a condition called **amyloidosis**, a group of diseases in which one or more organ systems in the body accumulate deposits of abnormal proteins. Symptoms of restrictive cardiomyopathy include dyspnoea, orthopnoea, peripheral oedema, ascites, weakness and fatigue.

Diseases of the endocardium

Infective endocarditis Infective endocarditis is a microbial infection that affects the endocardial endothelium and the heart valves. It occurs in adults and children with predisposing conditions. Rheumatic heart disease, valvular disease, degenerative heart

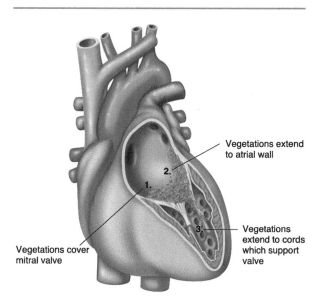

Figure 6.18 Bacterial endocarditis.

disease, congenital heart disease and intravenous drug abuse increase the risk for endocarditis.

Many species of bacteria and fungi cause the majority of cases of infectious endocarditis. Acute forms of this disease involve the formation of nodules or **vegetations** that consist of the infectious organisms and cellular debris enmeshed in a fibrous clot. Typical lesions of endocarditis are shown in Figure 6.18. As fragments of the vegetations break apart, they enter the bloodstream to form emboli which can travel to the brain, kidney, lung or other vital organs, causing a variety of symptoms. The emboli can lodge in small blood vessels of the skin or other organs and cause the blood vessels to rupture.

Symptoms of infective endocarditis include fever, chills, a change in the sound or character of an existing heart murmur and evidence for embolisation of the vegetative lesions. A blood culture test provides a definitive diagnosis of the causative organism and directs antimicrobial treatment. Echocardiograms are useful to detect any underlying valve disease and vegetations.

Immediate and extensive antimicrobial treatment is necessary to eliminate the causative microorganism. Surgical interventions are indicated in cases where the heart is severely damaged by the infection.

Rheumatic heart disease Rheumatic heart disease is a sequela of infection by group A haemolytic streptococci of skin, throat or ear, although the organisms are no longer present when the disease presents itself. Approximately 2 weeks after the streptococcal infection, rheumatic fever develops, characterised by fever, inflamed and painful joints, and sometimes a rash.

Rheumatic fever is an **autoimmune disease** that results from a reaction between streptococcal antigens and the patient's own antibodies against them. All parts of the heart may be affected, and this frequently includes the mitral valve. Blood clots deposit on the inflamed valves, forming nodular structures called vegetations along the edge of the cusps. The normally flexible cusps thicken and adhere to each other. Later, fibrous tissue develops, which has a tendency to contract.

If the adhesions of the cusps seriously narrow the valve opening, the mitral valve becomes stenotic. If sufficiently damaged, the cusps may not be able to meet properly, resulting in stenosis of the heart valves.

The incidence of rheumatic fever is highest among children and young adults. Prompt treatment of the streptococcal infection with antibiotics can prevent rheumatic fever and its complications. One consequence of rheumatic fever is the need for mitral valve surgery later in life.

Valvular heart disease

Valves maintain unidirectional flow of blood through the heart. Valve disorders include stenosis and valvular insufficiency. **Stenosis** refers to a narrowing of the valves opening and failure of the valve to open normally. **Valvular insufficiency** or **regurgitation** refers to a valve that allows backward flow of blood within the heart. Stenotic valves produce distension of the heart chamber that empties blood through the diseased valve and impaired filling of the chamber that receives the blood. Incompetent valves produce distension and strain the chamber ejecting blood through the diseased valve.

Mitral stenosis In **mitral stenosis**, the mitral valve opening is narrow, and the cusps that form the valve, normally flexible flaps, become rigid and fuse together. A deep funnel shape develops, increasing resistance to blood flow from the left atrium to the left ventricle. As back-pressure develops in the left atrium, the left atrial wall hypertrophies. The right side of the heart is also affected (Figure 6.19). Pressure within the heart makes it difficult for the pulmonary veins to deliver blood to the left atrium, leading to increased pressure within the veins. As the congestion increases in the veins, fluid from the blood leaks out into the tissue spaces of the lungs, causing pulmonary oedema. Poor circulation causes cyanosis because an inadequate amount of oxygen is reaching the tissues. The back-up of blood and congestion cause the heart to become exhausted and may lead to congestive heart failure. Another complication of a valve defect is the increased risk for a thrombus (blood clot) to form on the valve. If the thrombus becomes detached, it travels as an embolism and may occlude a blood vessel supplying the brain, kidney or other vital organ.

The predominant cause of mitral stenosis is rheumatic fever, which can cause inflammation of the valve leaflets. The leaflets may further stick together and/or form rigid scar tissue. Rheumatic fever most often occurs in children aged 5–15 years; however, symptoms of mitral stenosis may not be seen for a number of years.

Stenotic valves may be widened to restore blood flow with valvuloplasty, a surgical technique similar to angioplasty. A complication of the surgery may be a leaky valve, in which case the valve may be surgically replaced with metal alloy or pig valve.

Mitral regurgitation In mitral insufficiency, also called mitral regurgitation, the valve is unable to close completely, which allows blood to leak back into the atrium each time the ventricle contracts. As the volume of blood and pressure in the left atrium increases, blood pressure increases in other vessels, including the vessels (pulmonary veins) leading from the lungs to the heart, resulting in lung congestion. The insufficiency is exacerbated by sclerosis and retraction of the valve cusps.

Another cause of regurgitation is the failure of specialised valve muscles in the ventricle, called

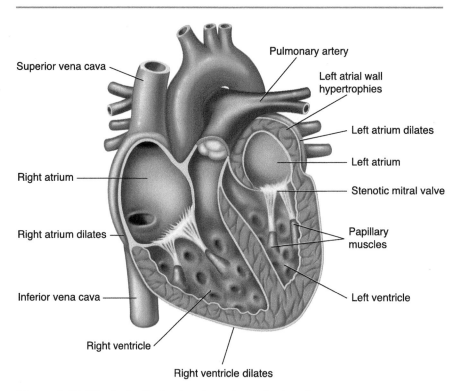

Superior vena cava

Pulmonary artery

Left atrial wall
hypertrophies

Left atrium dilates

Left atrium

Right atrium

Stenotic mitral valve

Right atrium dilates

Papillary
muscles

Inferior vena cava

Left ventricle

Right ventricle

Right ventricle dilates

Figure 6.19 Effect of mitral valve stenosis on the heart.

papillary muscles. These muscles attach to the underside of the cusps by means of small cords (chordae tendinae) that normally prevent the cusps from flipping up into the atria when the ventricles contract. If the papillary muscles fail to contract, the cusps open upward toward the atria under the force of expelled ventricular blood. This failure is commonly called mitral valve prolapse (MVP).

Most individuals with MVP are asymptomatic and lead normal lives. Those who have moderate or more severe cases of MVP take antibiotics such as amoxicillin to prevent bacteria from colonising the defective valves. If the prolapse becomes severe, it may be corrected with surgical reconstruction or replacement.

Aortic stenosis Aortic stenosis, the narrowing of the valve leading into the aorta, occurs more often in men than in women and most frequently in men over 50 years old. It may result from rheumatic fever, a congenital defect or arteriosclerosis. Aortic stenosis is characterised by rigid cusps that adhere together and deposits of hard, calcified material which give a warty appearance to the valve. Because the left ventricle pumps blood through this narrowed valve into the aorta, this chamber hypertrophies. Even with enlarged ventricles, inadequate blood flow to the brain persists and can cause **syncope** (fainting). This valve defect, like others, can be corrected surgically.

Aortic regurgitation In aortic regurgitation, the valve does not close properly. With each relaxation of the left ventricle, blood flows back in from the aorta. Backflow of blood causes the ventricle to dilate, become exhausted and eventually fail. This condition can result from inflammation within the heart, endocarditis or a dilated aorta.

Symptoms of aortic regurgitation have a gradual onset. As the valve disease progresses, backflow of blood in the left ventricle increases, diastolic blood pressure falls, and the left ventricle enlarges. Most persons with aortic regurgitation remain asymptomatic for a number of years. The only sign for a number of years is a heart murmur. With advanced disease, symptoms of heart failure, such as dyspnoea, or shortness of breath, on exertion and at rest, occur.

Valvular defects are usually detected through cardiac auscultation (heart sound) heard via a stethoscope. Diagnosis is confirmed by a number of tests, including echocardiography, cardiac catheterisation, or phonocardiogram. A phonocardiogram is a device that records heart sounds. An ECG tracing is usually collected simultaneously to correlate the sounds to ventricular and atrial contractions.

Cardiac conduction disorders

Cardiac arrhythmias Abnormal heart rhythms, or **arrhythmias**, develop from irregularity in impulse generation and impulse conduction. Electrical impulses from the heart's pacemakers stimulate contraction of the atria and the ventricles. Many forms of heart disease can disrupt the normal contraction and relaxation cycle of the atria and ventricles.

Cardiac arrhythmias are commonly divided into two categories: supraventricular and ventricular. The **supraventricular arrhythmias** include those that are generated by electrical abnormalities in the sinoatrial (SA) node, atria, atrioventricular (AV) node and junctional tissue in the heart. The **ventricular arrhythmias** include those that are generated in the ventricular conduction system and in the ventricle. Because the ventricles are the pumping chambers of the heart, ventricular arrhythmias are the most serious as they can be life-threatening.

Disorders of cardiac rhythm can range from a sustained rapid heart rate of greater than 100 beats per minute, or **tachycardia**, to an abnormally slow heart rate of less than 50 beats per minute, or **bradycardia**. An interruption of the flow of impulses through the conduction system of the heart can lead to **heart block**. Heart block results when impulses are blocked, causing the atria and ventricles to contract independently of one another. The most serious effect of some forms of heart block is a slowing of the heart rate to the extent that circulation to vital organs such as the brain is blocked. An **ectopic pacemaker** is an excitable focus outside of the normally functioning pacemaker of the heart. Ectopic foci can cause additional beats (observed as premature contractions) or take over the normal pacemaker activity of the SA node.

Fibrillation is the result of disorganised current flow within the atria, called **atrial fibrillation**, or ventricles, called **ventricular fibrillation**. Fibrillation interrupts the normal contraction of the atria or the ventricles. In ventricular fibrillation, the ventricle quivers and does not contract and carry out effective coordinated contractions. Because no blood is pumped from the heart, ventricular fibrillation is a form of cardiac arrest. Immediate attempts at resuscitation must be made, or death will result.

Cardiac rhythm disturbances cause a wide variety of symptoms, including palpitations, **syncope** or light-headedness, oedema or shortness of breath. The aetiologies of arrhythmias are numerous and include a history of coronary heart disease, heart valve disease, myocardial infarction, hypertension, atherosclerosis, metabolic diseases, smoking and drug abuse.

Medical therapy for the treatment of cardiac arrhythmias includes medications, electrocardioversion and catheter ablation. Antiarrhythmic medications alter the physiological properties of the heart's conduction system. Electrocardioversion is accomplished using an external device or a surgically placed internal pacemaker. A machine called an automated external defibrillator (AED) delivers electrical shocks and is used to re-establish normal heart rhythm (Figure 6.20). Defibrillators are implanted under the skin of the shoulder to resynchronise the heart on a daily basis, similar to a pacemaker device. Catheter ablation is a non-surgical procedure in which a catheter is inserted into the

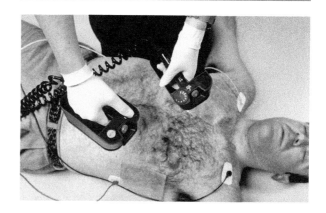

Figure 6.20 Electrocardioversion paddles.

diseased area of the heart. A machine directs energy through the catheter to small areas of the heart that cause the abnormal heart rhythm. This energy severs the connecting pathway of the abnormal rhythm.

CONGESTIVE HEART FAILURE

Congestive heart failure is a condition in which the heart cannot pump enough blood to meet the blood and oxygen needs of other body organs. It is a complication of most forms of heart disease, including coronary and peripheral atherosclerosis. There are nearly 23 million people living with heart failure worldwide.

Diagnostic methods for the diagnosis of heart failure include history and physical examination, laboratory studies, electrocardiography, chest radiography and echocardiography. The patient history includes collecting information on symptoms related to shortness of breath, fatigue and oedema. A complete physical examination includes assessment of heart sounds, heart rate and blood pressure; examination of the neck veins for congestion; and examination of the extremities for oedema. Laboratory tests are used to diagnose anaemia, blood disorders or signs of liver congestion. Echocardiography is useful in assessing the anatomical and functional abnormalities of heart failure, and electrocardiographic studies are useful in diagnosing underlying disorders of cardiac conduction and rhythm. Chest X-rays provide information on the size and shape of the heart and surrounding vasculature. They can also be used to determine the severity of heart failure by revealing the presence of pulmonary oedema.

The manifestations of heart failure depend on the extent of cardiac dysfunction, patient age, concurrent medical illnesses and the extent and rate at which cardiac performance becomes impaired. The severity of impairment ranges from mild, in which symptoms manifest clinically only during stress, to the most advanced form, in which the heart is unable to sustain life without external support. Mild symptoms of heart failure include ankle swelling and shortness of breath with exertion. Severe signs and symptoms include shortness of breath at rest, fatigue and limb weakness, neck vein swelling, rales (wet, crackly lung noises), pulmonary oedema (fluid in the lungs), cyanosis and abnormal heart sounds.

The goals of treatment for heart failure are aimed at relieving the symptoms, improving quality of life and halting the progression of cardiac dysfunction. Treatment includes correction of the underlying causes, medications, restriction of salt and water intake and modification of activities and lifestyle that are consistent with the functional limitations of the patient. Medication management of heart failure is complex and includes diuretics, medications that improve cardiac output, antihypertensives, antiarrhythmics and medications that slow the heart rate and allow the heart muscle to relax and fill with blood. In severe cases, restriction of activity with bed rest often facilitates temporary improvement of heart function.

SHOCK

Shock is a life-threatening condition in which blood pressure drops too low to sustain life. Any condition that reduces the heart's ability to pump effectively or decreases venous return can cause shock. This low blood pressure results in an inadequate blood supply to the cells of the body. The cells can be quickly and irreversibly damaged and die. Major causes of shock include cardiogenic, hypovolaemic, anaphylactic, septic and neurogenic shock. See Table 6.4 for types and aetiology.

Table 6.4 Types of shock and aetiology.

Type of shock	Aetiology
Cardiogenic	Cardiac arrhythmias Myocardial infarction
Hypovolaemic	Haemorrhage Trauma Surgery Extensive burns
Anaphylactic	Allergic reaction
Septic	Toxins released by a bacterial infection
Neurogenic	Damage to the central nervous system

Untreated shock is usually fatal. The prognosis depends on the underlying cause, pre-existing illnesses, the time between onset and diagnosis, and rapidity of response to therapy.

HEART DISEASE IN INFANTS AND CHILDREN

Fetal and perinatal circulation

Fetal circulation is anatomically different from postnatal circulation (Figure 6.21). Before birth, oxygenated blood flows through the placenta from the umbilical vein. The fetal lungs are entirely bypassed either by direct passage from the inferior vena cava to the right atrium through the foramen ovale to the left atrium, or from the right ventricle through the pulmonary artery through the ductus arteriosus to the aorta.

The umbilical vein connects to the fetal venous system, which returns blood to the fetal right atrium via the inferior vena cava. From the inferior vena cava, blood flows into the right atrium and then moves through the foramen ovale into the left atrium. It then passes into the left ventricle and is pumped into the ascending aorta to perfuse the heart and upper extremities. At the same time, venous blood from the heart and upper extremities returns to the right side of the heart by way of the superior vena cava, moves into the right ventricle and is pumped into the pulmonary artery. Blood that is ejected into the pulmonary artery is diverted through the ductus arteriosus into the descending aorta. This blood perfuses the lower extremities.

When a baby takes its first breath after birth, the newly expanded lungs initiate a switch from placental to pulmonary oxygenation of the blood. Cord clamping and removal of the placental circulation cause an increase in left ventricular pressure. The decrease in right atrial pressure and decrease in left atrial pressure produce a closure of the foramen ovale. The newly expanded lungs favour the flow from the right heart via the pulmonary artery to the lungs as opposed to the ductus arteriosus. Closure of both the foramen ovale and the ductus arteriosus leads to the establishment of the postnatal circulation.

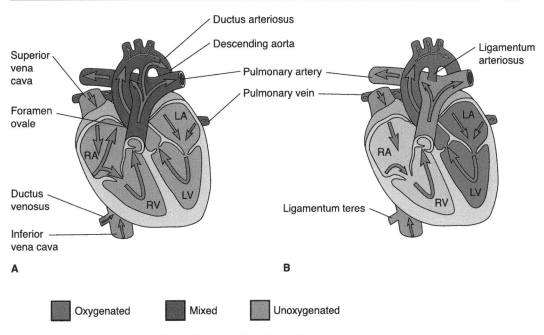

Figure 6.21 (A) Fetal circulation; (B) postnatal circulation.

Congenital heart disease

The embryological development of the heart is complex, and many errors can occur during development. Genetic, environmental and chromosomal changes may alter the development of the heart. Infants born to parents with a history of congenital heart disease are at a higher risk. Infants born with chromosomal abnormalities such as Down's syndrome or Turner syndrome have an increased risk for congenital heart disease. Maternal diabetes, congenital rubella, maternal alcoholism and treatment with anticonvulsant drugs are also associated with congenital heart disease.

Approximately 6 babies in 1000 births in the UK have some form of congenital heart disease. Owing to advances in technology and early recognition of congenital heart disease, approximately 85% of infants born with congenital heart disease can be expected to survive into adulthood. Congenital defects can affect almost any of the cardiac structures or circulatory blood vessels.

Congenital heart disease is divided into aetiologies that cause cyanosis, or blue babies, and those that do not cause cyanosis. For cyanosis to occur, deoxygenated blood must bypass the lungs and enter the systemic circulation.

Cyanotic heart disease

Tetralogy of Fallot Tetralogy of Fallot is one of the most serious of the congenital heart defects and consists of four abnormalities: (1) ventricular septal defect; (2) narrowing of the pulmonary outflow channel, including pulmonary valve stenosis, or a decrease in the size of the pulmonary trunk; (3) misplaced aorta that crosses the interventricular septum; and (4) hypertrophy of the right ventricle (Figure 6.22).

Maternal factors during pregnancy that are associated with tetralogy of Fallot include a history of rubella, poor nutrition, overuse of alcohol, history of diabetes and maternal age over 40. Heredity may also play a role, as parents with a history of tetralogy of Fallot have a greater risk of having a child with this disease. Children with genetic disorders such as Down's syndrome often have congenital heart defects, including tetralogy of Fallot.

Symptoms of this condition include difficulty feeding, failure to gain weight, poor development, cyanosis that becomes more pronounced during feeding, crying or defaecation, fainting, sudden death, clubbing of the fingers and squatting during episodes of cyanosis.

Surgical repair is often advised for all children born with this defect. More than one surgical procedure is required to increase blood flow to the lungs, patch the ventricular septal defect, open the narrowed pulmonary valve, and close any abnormal connections between the aorta and pulmonary artery.

Transposition of the great arteries In this condition, the aorta and the pulmonary artery connect

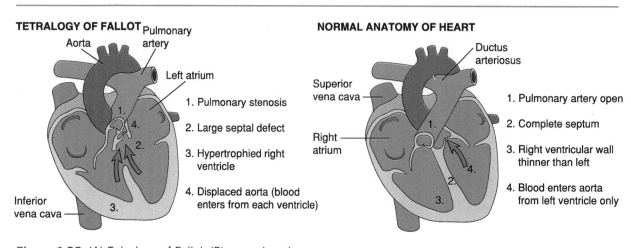

Figure 6.22 (A) Tetralogy of Fallot; (B) normal anatomy.

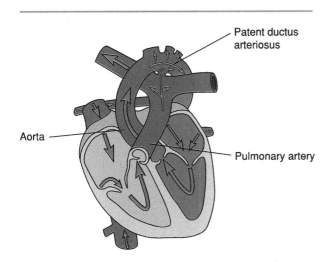

Figure 6.23 Transposition of the great arteries.

to the wrong ventricle. The pulmonary artery is attached to the left ventricle, and the aorta is attached to the right ventricle; thus blood flow in the lungs and in the body occurs independently. Deoxygenated blood returns to the right heart and is pumped to the aorta, which pumps blood to the

systemic circulation. The left heart receives blood from the lungs and then pumps the blood back to the lungs (Figure 6.23).

Symptoms include cyanosis, shortness of breath, poor feeding and clubbing of the fingers. If diagnosed prior to birth, prostaglandins are administered to maintain a patent ductus arteriosus and allow mixing of oxygenated and deoxygenated blood to occur. Corrective surgery within the first 2–3 weeks of life is essential for long-term survival. An arterial switch procedure corrects both systemic and pulmonary blood flow.

Non-cyanotic congenital heart disease

Septal defects Septal defects may occur between the two atria, an atrial septal defect (ASD), or between the ventricles, a ventricular septal defect (VSD). Often these defects can be detected by the presence of a heart murmur on physical examination. In both conditions, blood in the right heart will be a mixture of deoxygenated blood and oxygenated blood that has traversed the left side of the heart (Figure 6.24).

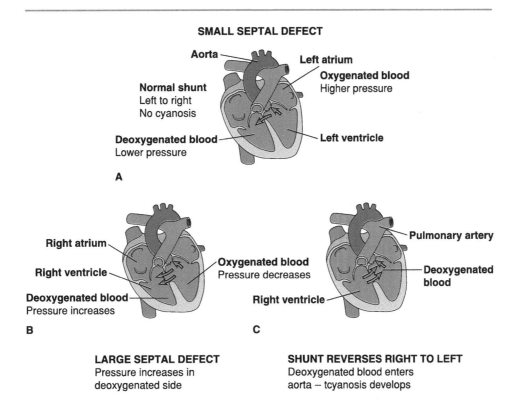

Figure 6.24 Effects of septal defects: (A) normal shunt; no cyanosis; (B) increased pressure in right ventricle; (C) shunt reversal; cyanosis develops.

Small ASDs may not cause any symptoms. Large ASDs can lead to significant overload and enlargement of the right ventricle. Large ASDs require surgical repair.

A VSD causes increased blood flow to the lungs, which can eventually cause severe pulmonary hypertension. In this condition, oxygenated blood is shunted from the left ventricle to the right ventricle, which contains deoxygenated blood. This results in increased pressures in the lungs. As pressure continues to build, the right ventricle shunts unoxygenated blood to the left ventricle, leading to cyanosis. Large VSDs require surgical correction.

Patent ductus arteriosus (PDA) The ductus arteriosus serves as a fetal connection between the pulmonary artery and the aorta. In the fetal circulation, this allows blood to bypass the non-functional fetal lungs. At birth the ductus arteriosus normally closes. If the ductus remains open, blood intended for the body flows from the aorta to the lungs, overloading the pulmonary artery. Persistent increases in pulmonary arterial pressures can result in heart failure (Figure 6.25).

It is more common in premature infants but does occur in full-term infants. Premature babies with PDA are more vulnerable to its effects. PDA is twice as common in girls as in boys.

A patent ductus can be treated medically with anti-inflammatory medications to close the PDA and with antibiotics to prevent endocarditis. If medication therapy fails, a transcatheter device procedure or surgery may be performed to close the PDA.

Coarctation of the aorta Coarctation of the aorta is a congenital narrowing of the aorta that can occur anywhere along its length (Figure 6.26). Most commonly it occurs near the ductus arteriosus. A severe coarctation causes increases in resistance to the left ventricle and can eventually lead to heart failure.

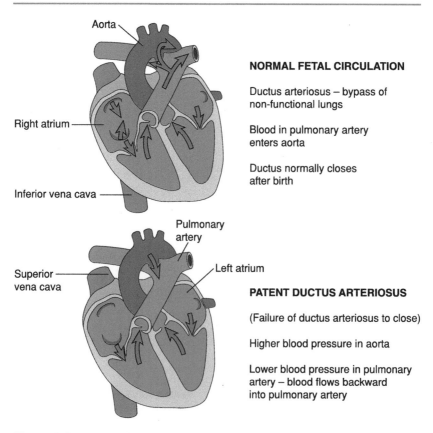

NORMAL FETAL CIRCULATION

Ductus arteriosus – bypass of non-functional lungs

Blood in pulmonary artery enters aorta

Ductus normally closes after birth

PATENT DUCTUS ARTERIOSUS

(Failure of ductus arteriosus to close)

Higher blood pressure in aorta

Lower blood pressure in pulmonary artery – blood flows backward into pulmonary artery

Figure 6.25 Patent ductus arteriosus.

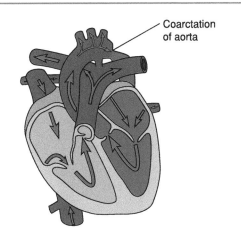

Figure 6.26 Coarctation of the aorta.

Aortic coarctation occurs in approximately 1 out of 10 000 live births. It is often diagnosed in childhood, especially in cases where the narrowing is severe.

In severe cases, symptoms are observed in infancy and include dizziness, shortness of breath and cold legs. A harsh murmur heard on the back with the stethoscope along with X-ray scans, echocardiography and Doppler ultrasound provide a definitive diagnosis for this condition.

Surgery is often recommended to enlarge the narrowing of the aorta. The coarctation of the aorta is surgically corrected by cutting the narrowed segment of the aorta and rejoining the healthy ends.

AGE-RELATED DISEASE

Worldwide, the population of individuals older than 65 years is projected to increase to 973 million (12%) by the year 2030 and comprise about 20% of the population in 2050.

Cardiovascular disease is the most frequent diagnosis in older adults and the leading cause of death in both men and women older than 65 years. In older adults, cardiovascular disease differs from that in younger people. With age, systolic blood pressure and left ventricular mass progressively increase, and ventricular filling, heart rate and cardiac output, exercise capacity and reflex responses of heart rate decrease. Cellular, enzymatic and molecular changes in the arterial vessels lead to arterial dilatation, thickening of the arterial intima and vascular stiffness. With age, the cardiovascular system is less able to respond to increases in workload and stress; therefore, thresholds for symptoms of cardiovascular disease become more common with age.

Resources

Centers for Disease Control: *www.cdc.gov*

World Health Organization: *www.who.int/ mediacentre/factsheets/fs317/en/index.html*

American Heart Association: *www.americanheart.org*

National Institutes of Health: *www.nhlbi.nih.gov.guidelines/cholesterol/ atglance.htm*

DISEASES AT A GLANCE Cardiac system

DISEASE	AETIOLOGY	SIGNS AND SYMPTOMS	DIAGNOSIS	TREATMENT	PREVENTION	LIFESPAN
Hypercholesterolaemia	Genetic, lifestyle, obesity and diabetes, diet high in saturated fat	Elevated serum cholesterol	Blood test	Change in dietary habits, low fat diet, cholesterol lowering medication	Healthy lifestyle, diet and exercise, weight loss, low fat diet	Can occur at any age
Atherosclerosis	Genetic, lifestyle, obesity and diabetes, diet high in saturated fat	Occlusion of an artery. Symptoms depend on location of occlusion	ECG, coronary angiography, blood tests, CT scan	Weight loss, exercise, control blood pressure with antihypertensives, reduce cholesterol with cholesterol lowering medication	Healthy lifestyle, diet and exercise, weight loss, low fat diet	Occurs in adults, older adults
Peripheral artery disease	Genetic, lifestyle, obesity and diabetes, diet high in saturated fat	Intermittent claudication, thinning of the skin of the lower leg, ulceration of the skin, gangrene can occur in advanced stages of this disease	Physical examination for ischaemia, skin atrophy, pallor, absent pulses, Doppler ultrasound	Weight loss, exercise, control blood pressure with antihypertensives, reduce cholesterol with cholesterol lowering medication	Healthy lifestyle, diet and exercise, weight loss, low fat diet	Occurs in adults, older adults
Raynaud's disease	Unknown	Changes in skin colour from pallor to cyanosis, sensation of cold, numbness, or tingling	Physical examination	Abstinence from cigarette smoking, protection of the hands from cold, medications that prevent vasospasm	Abstinence from cigarette smoking, protection of the hands from cold, medications that prevent vasospasm	Most often occurs in healthy young women
Aortic aneurysm	Atherosclerosis, connective tissue disease, infections, trauma, inflammation	Usually asymptomatic until rupture	Physical examination, ultrasound, echocardiography, CT scan, MRI	Surgery to repair aneurysm, control of blood pressure and atherosclerosis	Healthy lifestyle; control of hypertension, diabetes and hypercholesterolaemia	Usually develops after the age of 50 years
Arterial hypertension	Older age, sedentary lifestyle, overweight, excessive dietary salt intake, family history	Elevated blood pressure	Blood pressure measurement via sphygmomanometer	Blood pressure lowering medication, diet, weight loss and exercise	Healthy lifestyle with proper diet and exercise; control of diabetes, hypercholesterolaemia, weight loss	Incidence of high blood pressure increases with age
Pulmonary arterial hypertension	Aetiology unknown in many cases, ventricular septal defect, patent ductus arteriosus	Asymptomatic	Echocardiography, pulmonary function test, lung scan, cardiac catheterisation	Medications to lower pressure, oxygen, lung transplant	Unknown as aetiology often unknown, surgical correction of ventricular septal defect and patent ductus arteriosus	Can occur at any age
Varicose veins	Long periods of standing, pregnancy	Swollen veins of the legs, knotty appearance under the skin	Physical examination of the legs	Elastic bandages, support hose, walking, elevating the legs, surgical vein stripping, compression sclerotherapy	Weight loss, walking, elevation of the legs after long periods of standing	Occurs mostly in adults

DISEASES AT A GLANCE Cardiac system (continued)

DISEASE	AETIOLOGY	SIGNS AND SYMPTOMS	DIAGNOSIS	TREATMENT	PREVENTION	LIFESPAN
Chronic venous insufficiency	Deep vein thrombosis, obesity, smoking, pregnancy, sedentary lifestyle	Tissue congestion, oedema, necrosis or skin atrophy, pain with walking	Outflow plethysmography, Doppler imaging studies	Diet, exercise, compression stockings, surgical bypass procedure	Weight loss, control of atherosclerosis and hypercholesterolaemia, diabetes, exercise, healthy eating	Peak incidence is between the ages of 40 and 49 years in women and 70 and 79 years in men
Venous thrombosis	Hypercoagulability, vascular trauma, surgery, immobilisation	No symptoms in about 50% of individuals. Symptoms of inflammation such as pain, swelling, deep muscle tenderness	Doppler imaging, physical examination	Blood thinning medication, surgery to remove the thrombus	Early ambulation following surgery or childbirth, compression stockings	Can occur at any age, more common in adults and older adults
Coronary heart disease	Atherosclerosis, high blood pressure, diabetes, obesity, inactivity	Angina pectoris, palpitations, myocardial infarction	Physical examination, ECG, stress test, nuclear imaging, angiography	Angioplasty, coronary artery bypass surgery, blood pressure lowering medication, blood thinners, diuretics, nitrates to stop chest pain, cholesterol lowering medication, diet, exercise	Control of atherosclerosis; diet, exercise, weight loss if overweight or obese	Occurs in adults and older adults
Myocarditis	Coxsackie virus, adenovirus, echovirus, HIV	Fever, chest pain, shortness of breath, tachycardia	Echocardiography, ECG, physical examination	Bed rest to prevent further myocardial damage, treatment of the viral infection	Unknown	Can occur at any age
Dilated cardiomyopathy	Infections, myocarditis, metabolic disorders, genetic disorders, immune disorders	Dyspnoea, orthopnoea, weakness, fatigue, ascites and peripheral oedema	Echocardiography, ECG, physical examination	Medications to treat symptoms, rest, heart transplant if severe	Unknown	Can occur at any age
Hypertrophic (A) cardiomyopathy	Unknown	Excessive ventricular growth	Echocardiography, ECG, physical examination	Medications to treat symptoms and prevent sudden cardiac death	Unknown	Usually a disease of young adulthood. Most common cause of sudden cardiac death in the young
Restrictive cardiomyopathy	Endemic in parts of Africa, India, South and Central America and Asia; amyloidosis	Dyspnoea, orthopnoea, peripheral oedema, weakness, fatigue	Echocardiography, ECG, physical examination	Medications to treat symptoms	Unknown	Can occur at any age

DISEASES AT A GLANCE Cardiac system (continued)

DISEASE	AETIOLOGY	SIGNS AND SYMPTOMS	DIAGNOSIS	TREATMENT	PREVENTION	LIFESPAN
Infective endocarditis	Rheumatic heart disease, valvular disease, degenerative heart disease, congenital heart disease, intravenous drug abuse, bacterial infections	Fever, chills, change in sound of an existing murmur, vegetative lesion on the heart valves	Blood cultures, echocardiography, ECG, body temperature, blood cultures to identify bacterium	Antimicrobial therapy, surgery in severe cases to remove vegetations	Prompt treatment of bacterial infections, prophylactic antimicrobial therapy	Can occur at any age
Rheumatic heart disease	Infection with group A haemolytic streptococci	Fever, inflammation of the joints, rash	Blood cultures, ECG, echocardiography	Antimicrobial therapy	Prompt treatment of bacterial infections, prophylactic antimicrobial therapy	Incidence is highest among children and young adults
Valvular heart disease						
Mitral stenosis	Rheumatic fever	Increased pressure in the heart, congestion of the veins, cyanosis, congestive heart failure	ECG, echocardiography, phonocardiogram, cardiac catheterisation	Valvuloplasty, surgical valve replacement	Prompt treatment of bacterial infections, prophylactic antimicrobial therapy, treatment of cardiac symptoms	Can occur at any age
Mitral regurgitation	Mitral valve prolapse	Usually no symptoms	ECG, echocardiography, phonocardiogram, cardiac catheterisation	Surgery to replace valve	Prophylactic antimicrobial therapy prevents bacteria from colonising defective valve	Can occur at any age
Aortic stenosis	Rheumatic fever, congenital defect, arteriosclerosis	Hypertrophy of the left ventricle, calcified deposits on the valve	ECG, echocardiography, phonocardiogram, cardiac catheterisation	Surgery to replace valve	Prophylactic antimicrobial therapy prevents bacteria from colonising defective valve	Occurs more frequently in men over 50 years of age than women
Aortic regurgitation	Endocarditis, dilated aorta	Dilatation of the ventricle. Backflow of blood into the left ventricle, decreased diastolic pressure, symptoms of heart failure	ECG, blood pressure check, echocardiography, phonocardiogram, cardiac catheterisation	Surgery to replace valve	Unknown	Can occur at any age

DISEASES AT A GLANCE Cardiac system (continued)

DISEASE	AETIOLOGY	SIGNS AND SYMPTOMS	DIAGNOSIS	TREATMENT	PREVENTION	LIFESPAN
Cardiac arrhythmias						
Supraventricular	Abnormalities in the SA node, AV node, and junctional tissue of the heart, myocardial infarction, hypertension, atherosclerosis, metabolic disease, smoking and drug abuse	Tachycardia, bradycardia, heart block, syncope, oedema, shortness of breath	ECG, blood pressure check, echocardiography, phonocardiogram, cardiac catheterisation	Antiarrhythmic medications	Prevention of heart disease	Can occur at any age, most commonly occurs in adults and older adults as a consequence of heart disease
Ventricular	Generated by abnormalities in the ventricular conduction system and in the ventricle, myocardial infarction, hypertension, atherosclerosis, metabolic disease, smoking and drug abuse	Tachycardia, bradycardia, heart block, syncope, oedema, shortness of breath	ECG, blood pressure check, echocardiography, phonocardiogram, cardiac catheterisation	Antiarrhythmic medications	Prevention of heart disease	Can occur at any age, most commonly occurs in adults and older adults as a consequence of heart disease
Congestive heart failure	Complication of most forms of heart disease	Shortness of breath, fatigue, oedema	Physical examination, ECG, X-ray, echocardiography, blood pressure	Medication therapy includes diuretics, antihypertensives, antiarrhythmic medications, medications that improve cardiac output, bed rest	Treatment of underlying heart disease	Can occur at any age; most commonly occurs in adults and older adults
Shock	Heart disease, haemorrhage, trauma, surgery, allergic reaction, release of bacterial toxins, damage to the central nervous system	Drop in blood pressure too low to sustain life	Physical examination, medical history	Rapid administration of fluids to increase blood pressure, medication to increase heart rate	Fluid replacement during surgery, prompt treatment of severe bacterial infections, prompt treatment of allergic reactions, blood transfusion in cases of severe blood loss	Can occur at any age
Congenital heart disease						
Tetralogy of Fallot	Maternal history of rubella, overuse of alcohol, maternal history of diabetes or poor prenatal nutrition. Infants born with Down's syndrome	Difficulty feeding, failure to gain weight, poor development, cyanosis, fainting, sudden death	ECG, blood pressure check, echocardiography, phonocardiogram, cardiac catheterisation	Corrective surgery	Unknown	Occurs in infants

DISEASES AT A GLANCE Cardiac system (continued)

DISEASE	AETIOLOGY	SIGNS AND SYMPTOMS	DIAGNOSIS	TREATMENT	PREVENTION	LIFESPAN
Transposition of the great arteries	Unknown	Cyanosis, shortness of breath, poor feeding	ECG, blood pressure check, echocardiography, phonocardiogram, cardiac catheterisation	Administration of prostaglandins at birth to maintain patent ductus arteriosus until corrective surgery can be achieved	Unknown	Occurs in infants
Septal defects	Unknown	Heart murmur, a ventriculoseptal defect causes increased blood flow to the lungs	ECG, blood pressure check, echocardiography, phonocardiogram, cardiac catheterisation	Large defects require surgical correction	Unknown	Occurs in infants; small defects may persist unnoticed through adulthood
Patent ductus arteriosus	Unknown	Initially asymptomatic; increased pressure in the lungs can lead to pulmonary hypertension	ECG, blood pressure check, echocardiography, phonocardiogram, cardiac catheterisation	Antibiotics to prevent endocarditis, anti-inflammatory medication to close the patent ductus	Unknown	More common in premature infants
Coarctation of the aorta	Unknown	Increased pressure in the left ventricle, symptoms of heart failure in severe narrowing	ECG, blood pressure check, echocardiography, phonocardiogram, cardiac catheterisation, Doppler ultrasound	Surgical correction	Unknown	Diagnosed and corrected in infancy

INTERACTIVE EXERCISES

Cases for critical thinking

1. The paramedics are called to a 59-year-old male who is experiencing severe chest pain while playing golf. What type(s) of heart or vascular disease should be considered in this patient?

2. A 65-year-old female goes to her GP with shortness of breath, feeling of faintness, dizziness and productive cough, all of which have persisted over the past 2 months. Upon examination, the GP records a blood pressure of 90/50 mmHg, congestion in the lungs and abnormal heart sounds. What type of heart diseases should be considered in this patient?

3. A 30-year-old obese female complains of pain with walking. The patient has a history of smoking cigarettes and is a 'borderline diabetic'. Explain the role of cardiovascular risk factors for cardiovascular diseases for this patient.

Multiple choice

1. Syncope is _____
   a. hypertension   b. shortness of breath
   c. light-headedness d. fluid retention

2. Diastole is the _____
   a. filling phase of the heart
   b. contracting phase of the heart
   c. alternation between relaxation and excitation of the heart
   d. impulse of the heart

3. The major cholesterol carrier in the blood is

   _____
   a. HDL   b. triglycerides
   c. blood   d. LDL

4. Blockage of the _____ can reduce blood supply to the brain, causing a stroke.
   a. pulmonary artery b. carotid artery
   c. aorta   d. coronary artery

5. The most common cause of an aortic aneurysm is

   _____
   a. atherosclerosis   b. hypertension
   c. enlarged artery   d. embolism

6. A procedure involving insertion of a balloon-tipped catheter into the femoral artery to the heart is called a(n)_____
   a. defibrillator
   b. angioplasty

   c. transcatheter procedure
   d. echocardiography

7. The mitral valve is located _____
   a. between the right atrium and the right ventricle
   b. between the left atrium and the left ventricle
   c. in the atria
   d. in the ventricle

8. The pacemaker of the heart is the

   _____
   a. atrioventricular valve
   b. His-Purkinje fibres
   c. ventricle
   d. sinoatrial node

9. An inflammatory disease of the heart muscle is

   _____
   a. myocarditis
   b. pericardial disease
   c. cardiomyopathy
   d. coronary heart disease

10. Rheumatic heart disease is also known as a(n) _____ disease because it results from a reaction between bacterial antigens and the patient's antibodies.
    a. haemolytic   b. vegetative
    c. autoimmune   d. tricuspid valve

True or false

_____ 1.   Infants born with chromosomal abnormalities have a higher risk for congenital heart disease.

_____ 2.   Salt and water restriction is one form of treatment for congestive heart failure.

_____ 3.   An interruption of the flow of impulses through the conduction system is called bradycardia.

_____ 4.   In ventricular fibrillation, the heart quivers and is unable to maintain cardiac output.

_____ 5.   In mitral valve stenosis, delivery of blood via the pulmonary veins to the left atrium is impaired.

_____ 6.   Cardiomyopathy is a structural disease of the heart.

_____ 7.   The most common cause of infective endocarditis is a bacterial infection.

_____ 8.   The basic lesion of clinical atherosclerosis is a fatty streak.

_____ 9.   Intact aortic aneurysms typically cause symptoms.

_____ 10. Hypertension is broadly defined as an arterial pressure greater than 120/80 mmHg.

Fill-ins

1. The most common cause of chronic venous insufficiency is deep vein _____.

2. More than 90% of patients with coronary heart disease have _____.

3. _____ is associated with reduced heart filling pressure and endocardial scarring.

4. _____ refers to a narrowing of the valves.

5. The predominant cause of mitral stenosis is _____.

6. Backflow of blood in aortic regurgitation causes the _____ to dilate.

7. An _____ is an excitable focus outside of the normally functioning pacemaker of the heart.

8. A machine called an _____ delivers electrical shocks and is used to re-establish normal heart rhythm.

9. Two forms of cyanotic congenital heart disease are _____ and _____.

10. The _____ arteries provide the heart muscle with blood and oxygen.

Labelling exercise

Use the blank lines below to label the following image.

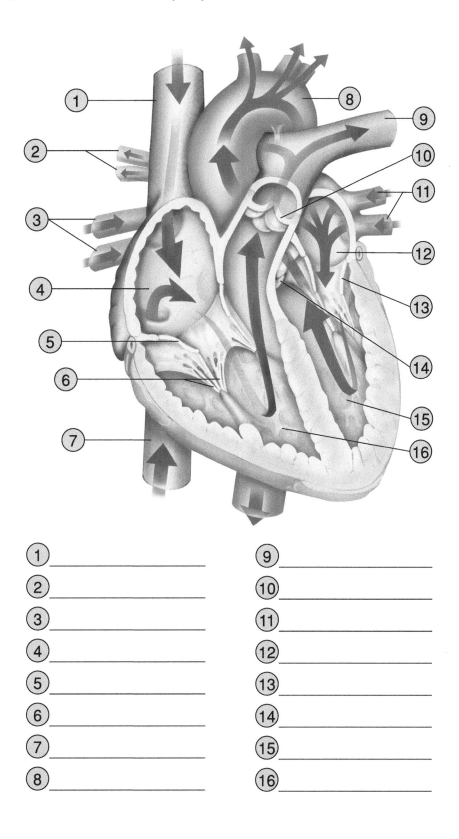

1 _____

2 _____

3 _____

4 _____

5 _____

6 _____

7 _____

8 _____

9 _____

10 _____

11 _____

12 _____

13 _____

14 _____

15 _____

16 _____

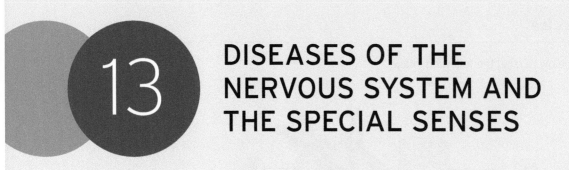

13

DISEASES OF THE NERVOUS SYSTEM AND THE SPECIAL SENSES

Photomicrograph of a neurofibrillary tangle.
(© O.J. Staats/Custom Medical Stock Photo)

Fact or fiction ?

Benign brain tumours are not very serious and therefore are not cause for concern.

Fiction: Benign tumours tend to grow and crowd out precious cranial space and, thus, apply pressure or restrict blood flow to particular brain regions. If these benign growths are inoperable or uncontrolled, they will kill the victim. Malignant brain tumours may be lethal, but they may also be surgically removed or reduced with medication or radiation. All brain tumours require attention and may be lethal if left untreated. Treatment with surgery, medication or radiation is most successful for slowly growing, encapsulated tumours.

Learning objectives

After studying this chapter, you should be able to:

+ Recognise the basic structure and functions of the nervous system and major sensory elements

+ Describe the aetiology, signs and symptoms, diagnostic tests and treatment of different types of headache

+ Describe the aetiology, signs and symptoms, diagnostic tests and treatment of infectious diseases of the nervous system

+ Describe degenerative diseases of the central nervous system, including multiple sclerosis, Parkinson's disease and amyotrophic lateral sclerosis

+ Discuss inherited and congenital diseases of the nervous system

+ Describe the effects of trauma on the brain and sensory organs

+ Discuss the aetiology, signs and symptoms, diagnostic tests and treatment of seizure disorders

+ Discuss the aetiology, signs and symptoms, diagnostic tests and treatment of CVA (stroke) or related cerebrovascular disorders

+ Discuss the definitions, the purpose and the physiology of pain

  + Describe the aetiology, signs and symptoms, diagnostic tests and treatment of selected eye and ear diseases

Disease chronicle

Death to a killer

Not so long ago, your great-grandparent or grandparent may have suffered from this tragic disease or feared it within his or her community. Your parents' generation began to break free from the grip of this disease, and for today's generation this disease has been nearly eradicated. What is this devastating killer disease? Poliomyelitis. Poliomyelitis thrived around the world until the 1950s, especially impacting on the post-war 'baby boom' generation. By 1955, Dr Jonas Salk and Dr Albert Sabin had formulated vaccines that put this disease on the shelf. How was that incredible feat accomplished?

Dr Jonas Salk's vaccine consisted of inactivated poliovirus injected intramuscularly, which stimulated production of antibodies against the polio virus. With the institution of large scale immunisation programmes, cases of polio dropped immediately. Dr Albert Sabin developed an oral vaccine more convenient to administer, particularly to large groups, and it is extremely effective. The Sabin vaccine is taken orally and stimulates the production of antibodies within the digestive system, where the viruses reside. Unlike the Salk vaccine, the Sabin vaccine destroys the viruses in the digestive system, thus preventing transmission and eliminating carriers. Many researchers believe, however, that the Salk vaccine is the better choice because it employs killed virus and ensures that the vaccine itself will not transmit polio, especially secondarily to compromised patients such as those with HIV.

The World Health Organization projects that in the near future polio will be eradicated worldwide. Between 1988 and 1998, polio declined 85% worldwide, and today, polio has been eliminated from much of the world. In 2003, only 700 cases of polio were found in the world, and three-quarters of these cases were in Nigeria, India and Pakistan, where undervaccination has enabled numerous outbreaks to occur. Clearly, it remains important to continue immunisation, both locally and globally, to end this devastating disease.

STRUCTURAL ORGANISATION OF THE NERVOUS SYSTEM

The nervous system monitors the external and internal environment of the body and, along with the endocrine system, controls many of the body's functions, like breathing rate and alertness.

The basic organisation of the nervous system includes two major divisions: the central nervous system (CNS) and the peripheral nervous system (PNS). The CNS is composed of the brain and spinal cord. It integrates information and controls the PNS. The PNS comprises all those nerves outside the CNS, beginning with the 12 pairs of cranial nerves and 31 pairs of spinal nerves. The nerves carry information to and from the CNS. Nerves consist of motor nerves, which carry information to muscles and glands, and sensory nerves, which carry sensory information from sense receptors to the CNS.

Certain organs are highly specialised for gathering sensory input; these are called organs of the special senses and include the eyes, ears and nose. Diseases of the eye and ear will be discussed in this chapter; diseases of the nose were described in Chapter 8.

The basic unit of the nervous system is the **neuron**, or nerve cell. The neuron consists of a cell body with attached filamentous extensions called dendrites that carry information toward the cell body, and a filamentous axon that carries information away from the cell body. A neuron is shown in Figure 13.1. Receptors attached to sensory neurons are capable of detecting environmental changes and transmitting messages to the brain or spinal cord (e.g. touch or pain). Motor neurons convey messages from the CNS out to muscles, causing contraction, or to glands, triggering secretion. The axons of sensory and motor neurons are insulated by a lipoprotein covering called **myelin** that forms a sheath, which insulates and protects the neuron. Deterioration of this sheath decreases the impulse velocity and impairs function. When the myelin degeneration becomes profuse it characteristically causes a misfiring, or incomplete impulses as in multiple sclerosis.

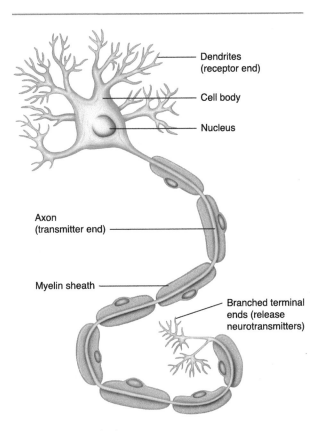

Figure 13.1 Typical neuron.

The brain

Three membranous coverings, called the **meninges**, protect the delicate nerve tissue of both the brain and spinal cord. The innermost covering is the pia mater, the middle layer is the arachnoid, and the toughest outermost covering is the dura mater. Meningitis is a potentially life-threatening disease caused by an inflammation of these coverings.

The brain has three major anatomical areas: the cerebrum, cerebellum and brainstem. The largest portion of the brain is the cerebrum, comprised of two cerebral hemispheres. The cerebral surface is highly convoluted with many elevations (gyri) and depressions (sulci). The outer surface of the brain, the cortex, consists of grey matter, where nerve cell bodies are concentrated. The inner area consists mostly of white matter, the nerve fibre tracts. Deep within the interior of the white matter are clusters of nerve cell bodies known as **basal ganglia**, also called basal nuclei, which help control position and subconscious movements. It is the basal ganglia (also grey matter) that are defective in Parkinson's disease, because they fail to produce sufficient quantities of the neurotransmitter dopamine.

Within the brain are four cavities called ventricles, where **cerebrospinal fluid** (CSF) is formed. These ventricles all interconnect and are continuous with the central canal of the spinal cord. CSF is derived from plasma and flows out of the ventricles through small openings to circulate over the brain and spinal cord, forming a watery, protective cushion. CSF is reabsorbed into the venous sinuses of the dura mater, and new fluid is formed. Obstruction of CSF circulation results in hydrocephalus, a condition commonly called 'water on the brain' in the newborn.

The cerebellum controls voluntary movements, such as riding a bicycle. The brainstem is called the 'vitals centre' because it regulates heart and breathing rates. These three major brain areas will be examined as part of the CNS along with the spinal cord.

The spinal cord

The spinal cord is housed within the vertebral column and is continuous with the brainstem (Figure 13.2). Numerous tracts of nerve fibres within the spinal cord ascend to and descend from the brain, carrying messages to and from muscles, organs and glands.

The autonomic nervous system

One division of the PNS is the autonomic nervous system (ANS). This system controls internal functioning of the body. The ANS houses the sympathetic and the parasympathetic nervous systems, which often work antagonistically to each other. The **hypothalamus**, located within the brain, controls certain activities of the ANS and is known as the centre for homeostasis. Homeostasis is the foundation of all fundamental principles in the study of physiology. The ANS controls arterial blood pressure, heart rate, gastrointestinal functions, sweating, temperature regulation and many other involuntary

actions. Whereas some peripheral nerves affect skeletal or voluntary muscle, the ANS acts on smooth or involuntary muscle and cardiac muscle. Diseases of the digestive system such as stress ulcers, regional enteritis and ulcerative colitis (Chapter 9) are influenced by the ANS. As mentioned earlier, the overall function of the nervous system is to monitor and regulate the various body systems. This monitoring allows the body to adjust to the surrounding environment both internally and externally, and much of this is done by the ANS.

The sensory nervous system

Sensations detected by receptors and carried by sensory neurons from specialised organs such as the eye and ear, as well as in skin, muscles, tendons and internal organs, are transmitted to the CNS. The spinal cord receives simple sensations and directs simple reflex responses, as when one touches a hot stove and quickly withdraws the hand. Complex sensory information must travel to specialised parts of the brain. Impulses reaching the brainstem and cerebellum bring about many unconscious automatic actions, but sensory information involving thought processes must reach the highest area of the brain, the cerebral cortex.

The cerebral cortex has specialised areas to receive sensory information from all parts of the body, such as the feet, the hands and the abdomen. Visual impulses are transmitted to the posterior part of the brain, whereas olfactory and auditory impulses are received in the lateral parts. Association areas of the brain interpret deeper meaning of the sensations, and many of the sensory messages are integrated and stored as memory. Creative thought becomes possible through use of sensory input.

The motor nervous system

Just as the cerebral cortex has areas specialised for the reception of sensory information, it also has areas that govern motor activity. The primary motor cortex is the frontal lobe that controls discrete movements of skeletal muscles. Because the nerve fibres cross over in the medulla or spinal cord,

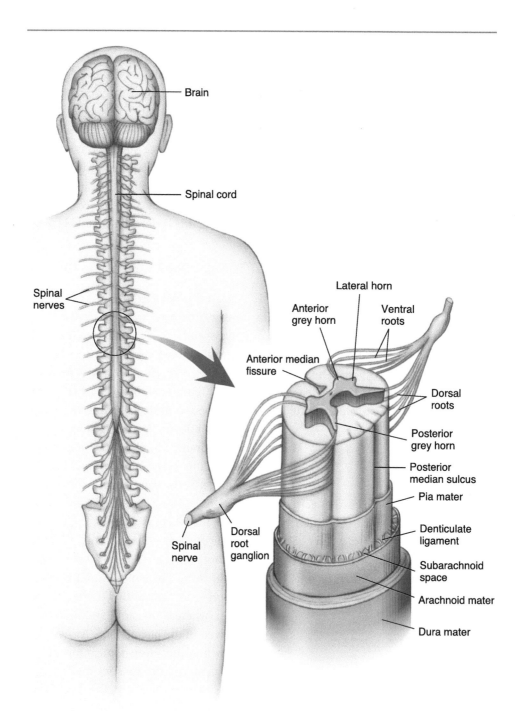

Figure 13.2 The brain, spinal cord and spinal nerves. An expanded view of the spinal cord is shown.

stimulation on one side of the cerebral cortex affects particular muscles on the opposite side of the body.

Anterior to the primary motor cortex is the premotor cortex, which controls coordinated movements of muscles. This process is accomplished by stimulating groups of muscles that work together. The speech area is located here and is usually on the left side, especially in right-handed people. Specialised areas of the brain are shown in Figure 13.3.

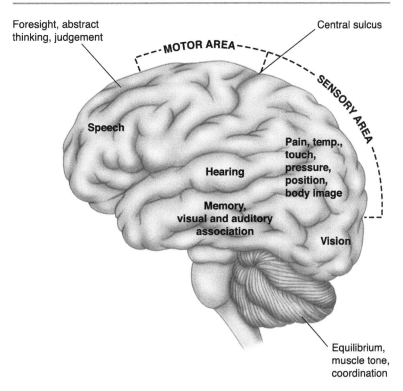

Figure 13.3 Specialised areas of the brain.

DIAGNOSTIC PROCEDURES FOR THE NERVOUS SYSTEM

Neurological laboratory tests include CSF examination obtained by a lumbar puncture, as previously described. Angiography allows visualisation of the cerebral circulation through the injection of radioopaque material. Computerised tomography (CT) scans are particularly valuable for diagnosing pathological conditions such as tumours, haemorrhages, haematomas and hydrocephalus. **Electromyelography (EMG)** is a radiographic process by which the spinal cord and spinal subarachnoid space are viewed and photographed after injection of contrast medium into the lumbar subarachnoid space. Myelography is used to identify spinal lesions caused by trauma or disease, such as amyotrophic lateral sclerosis (ALS). **Electroencephalography (EEG)** records the electrical activity of the brain (brain waves). It is used to diagnose lesions or tumours, and seizures, in impaired consciousness. Magnetic resonance imaging (MRI) uses magnetic fields in conjunction with a computer to view and record tissue characteristics at different planes. MRI is excellent for visualising brain soft tissue, spinal cord, white matter diseases, tumours and haemorrhages. Where a disease is idiopathic or without cure, the diagnosis is directed at relief of symptoms, as in Parkinson's disease.

For the eye, ophthalmoscopy is used for routine eye examinations. This may determine cataracts when viewing through the slit-lighted feature of the scope. Tonometry procedures are used for glaucoma determination. Audio examinations with tuning fork and electronic audio signals help discover tone quality and hearing loss.

DISEASES OF THE NERVOUS SYSTEM

Common headache

Moderate to severe head pain characterises the common headache. Tension or inflammation of muscles in the head, eyes, neck and shoulders may cause the common headache. Other causes include dilatation or constriction of cerebral blood vessels, allergies, chemical fumes, extreme temperatures and constipation. Simple unintended actions like coughing and laughter may trigger a headache, as may an intracranial mass of tumour or lesion. Nausea, vomiting and sensitivity to noise and light may accompany the common headache and more severe cases.

Common household treatments are rest and NSAIDs (non-steroidal anti-inflammatory drugs) such as aspirin or ibuprofen. Resting in a dark, quiet room and applying a cold compress may be beneficial for many sufferers, especially if time and space are available. Two of the more intense and episodic forms of headache are the cluster headache and the migraine.

Cluster headache

Cluster headache affects 1–4 per 1000 individuals, and men, especially middle-aged men, are five times more likely to be affected than women. The cluster headache occurs suddenly, producing severe, sharp and stabbing pain particularly near one eye or temporal area. The headaches are caused by blood vessel abnormalities and may occur two to three times per day for weeks, or may occur intermittently over a span of 1–3 months, subside, and recur months or years later. The pain may develop at any time but usually occurs at night and tends to last from 30 minutes to several hours. The pain is so severe that many individuals cannot lie down or be idle and may pace about. In contrast with migraine, however, light intensity, sounds or strange odours do not elicit nausea or vomiting.

Often there is no family history of cluster headache, although this condition tends to run in families. As of this writing, genetic factors have not been determined. Alcohol and nicotine tend to trigger these painful headaches, along with stress, ingestion of specific foods and glare. Treatment requires medications like subcutaneous or intranasal sumatriptan (Imigran); inhalation of 100% oxygen and ergotamine works well, as well as biofeedback and reduction of stress. Ergotamine tartrate is used as a prophylactic agent given in various modes of delivery.

Migraine headache

Migraine headaches are more common in women than in men and usually begin in the teen years or early twenties. The symptoms are throbbing (moderate) pain on one or both sides of the head plus sensitivity to light and noise or certain odours. Because migraines tend to cause nausea and vomiting, they are referred to as a 'sick headache'. Sometimes an aura or premonition precedes the migraine onset. Additional symptoms include numbness, dizziness and visual blurring. The headaches last from a few hours to a few days and may recur once a month or once every few years. A history of the symptoms helps diagnose migraine. Daily or weekly patient logs of activities, especially timing of migraine onset and subsequent events, helps reduce episodes and the need for medication.

Specific causes have not been identified, although there may be a natural abatement in some women when they discontinue birth control pills or attain menopause. The concentration of the neurotransmitter serotonin appears to have a role in the pathogenesis of migraines, and nitric oxide (NO), a vasodilator, may be implicated as well. When NO or serotonin are blocked, migraine pain subsides.

One of the most recently discovered causes related to migraine headache is a developmental or congenital defect in the heart that occurs as much as 25% of the time in those affected. The normal connection between the two atria in a fetal heart, the foramen ovale, happens to remain open (at least partially) instead of slapping shut at the time of birth. This fetal remnant is called a patent foramen ovale (PFO). Surgeons found that when this defect was closed in their adult patients, migraine episodes resolved. Clinical trials are currently scheduled to evaluate this new development.

Heredity is now known to be a primary factor in the case of migraine. It has been documented that a gene on chromosome 1 contributes to sensitivity of sound; on chromosome 5 a gene is recognised as one that allows pulsating headaches and sensitivity to light; and a gene on chromosome 8 is related to vomiting and nausea.

Bed rest and sleep in a dark, quiet room seems to benefit most migraine sufferers. Drug treatment is aimed at prevention and relief of symptoms. NSAIDs may not provide adequate relief, but prescription drugs like opioids and codeine are often effective. Imigran, mentioned previously, helps relieve pain and reduce nausea and sensitivities to light and sound. Cardiac medications like beta blockers (Atenolol) or calcium channel blockers (Diltiazem) help, but the exact mechanism is not fully understood, and tricyclic antidepressants have shown positive results as well.

INFECTIOUS DISEASES OF THE NERVOUS SYSTEM

Certain pathogenic micro-organisms are neurotropic in that the virus or bacterium has an affinity for nervous tissue. Pathogens obtain access to the nervous system by many routes, including wounds or trauma, and systemic infections entering from the thinner paranasal sinuses or mastoid regions.

Meningitis

Meningitis is an acute inflammation of the first two meninges that cover the brain and spinal cord: the pia mater and the arachnoid mater. A contagious disease, it usually affects children and young adults and may have serious complications if not diagnosed and treated early.

There are many forms of meningitis, and some are more contagious than others. The most common bacterial causes are *Haemophilus influenzae*, *Neisseria meningitidis* (also called meningococcus), and *Streptococcus pneumoniae*. However, other bacteria, as well as viruses, cause meningitis. **Enteroviruses** account for most of the cases when the virus is identified; in aseptic meningitis no bacterium is found and thus it is usually considered a viral condition. The infecting organisms can reach the meninges from the middle ear, upper respiratory tract or frontal sinuses; they can also be carried in the blood from the lungs or other infected sites. Healthy children may be carriers of the bacteria and

spread the organisms by sneezing or coughing. Viral or aseptic meningitis is considered the cause in 30% of the cases involving non-immunised individuals, primarily caused by contracted mumps, and it affects males two to five times more frequently than females. This form is normally a mild case of meningitis that may not require specific treatment. Other cases may be caused by the waning poliomyelitis virus and occasionally by herpes simplex, and non-infectious cases may result from lymphoma, brain cancer or leukaemia.

In the UK, the number of bacterial cases of meningitis is about 2300 per year, while viral cases are more common but less severe. Causative agent, the geographical region and accessibility to medical coverage influence prevalence; in addition, some agents become resistant to penicillin (*S. pneumoniae*) and others have been reduced because of the vaccine (Hib) for *Haemophilus influenzae* type B.

The symptoms of meningitis are high fever, chills and a severe headache caused by increased intracranial pressure. A key symptom is a stiff neck that holds the head rigidly. Movement of neck muscles stretches the meninges and increases head pain. Nausea, vomiting and a rash may also be symptomatic. The high fever often causes delirium and convulsions in children, and they may lapse into a coma.

Diagnosis of meningitis is made by performing a **lumbar puncture** (Figure 13.4), in which a hollow needle is inserted into the spinal canal between vertebrae in the lumbar region. This procedure is possible because the spinal cord terminates as a solid structure at or near the first lumbar vertebra, although a sac containing CSF extends down to the sacrum. In addition, a lumbar puncture may reveal the relative pressure of CSF. The infected fluid contains an elevated protein level, numerous polymorphs/leucocytes and infecting agents. When the level of glucose in the CSF is below normal, bacteria may have used the sugar for their own growth and metabolism.

The prognosis depends on the cause of meningitis and a prompt diagnosis and treatment. Treatment with antibiotics like rifampicin, cefotaxime or ceftriaxone is very effective if the meningitis is bacterial.

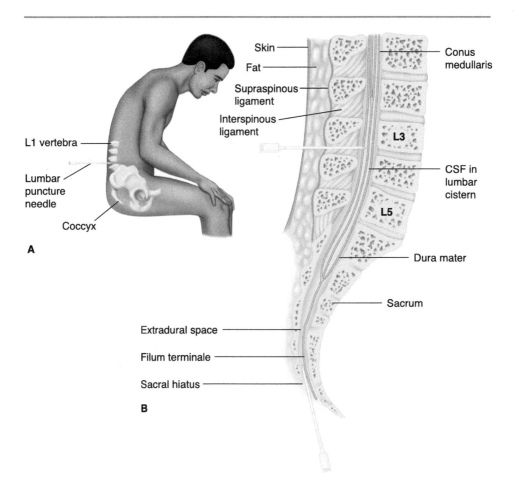

Figure 13.4 (A) Lumbar puncture, also known as spinal tap. (B) Section of the vertebral column showing the spinal cord and membranes. A lumbar puncture needle is shown at L3-4 and in the sacral hiatus.

If not treated, about 15% of those affected suffer permanent brain damage that manifests by sight or hearing loss, paralysis, mental retardation or death. Another complication is blockage of the fourth ventricle by a pyogenic (bacteria) infection, which results in the accumulation of CSF in the brain, a form of **hydrocephalus**. Preventive measures include vaccines like Hib or meningococcal group C conjugate vaccine.

Encephalitis

Encephalitis, an inflammation of the brain and meninges, is caused by several types of viruses. Some of these viruses may be harboured by wild birds and transmitted to humans by mosquitoes, commonly called arboviruses (carried by arthropods, including insects). These cases are mostly seasonal and are represented by regional variations.

Symptoms of encephalitis range from mild to severe, such as headache, sudden fever, stiff neck and drowsiness, to more severe cases that include cerebral dysfunction, disordered thought patterns and seizures in 5% of the cases. Most cases resolve themselves within 1–2 weeks with no specific treatment required except for mild, flu-like symptoms. In serious cases involving extensive brain damage, convalescence is slow and requires prolonged physical rehabilitation. Some nerve damage may cause paralysis, as occurs in 10% of these cases. Personality changes or other emotional disturbances may occur that require therapy.

Diagnosis of encephalitis is made by lumbar puncture. Brain imaging CT or MRI may be used to check for brain swelling. Treatment is essentially aimed at controlling high fever and intracranial pressure, maintaining fluid and electrolyte balance, and carefully monitoring respiratory and kidney function. In individuals generally in good health except for the virus, the prognosis is positive with supportive treatment.

There are many forms of the disease, and they may occur in epidemics. Lethargic encephalitis, or 'sleeping sickness,' is one type of encephalitis characterised by persistent drowsiness and delirium that sometimes results in coma. Secondary encephalitis may develop from viral childhood diseases such as chickenpox, measles and mumps, or herpes. In the case of herpes simplex encephalitis (HSE), type 1 is most common, but type 2 may cause infection in newborns or immunocompromised people like those with HIV or who have received an organ transplant. In the latter case, the patient may be treated with aciclovir or valaciclovir medications.

Prevention depends on control of mosquitoes and deterring contact through use of repellents, clothing and timing of outdoor activities. Other sources may be unavoidable, but early treatment is crucial to reduce neurological severity and deficits or death.

Poliomyelitis

Poliomyelitis, commonly called polio, is an infectious disease of the brain and spinal cord caused by an enterovirus. Motor neurons of the medulla oblongata and pons, which houses the respiratory centre, and the spinal cord are primarily affected. As a result, muscle tissue is not stimulated; it weakens and finally atrophies. If the respiratory muscles are depressed, then an artificial means of respiration is required.

Symptoms of poliomyelitis are stiff neck, fever, headache, sore throat and gastrointestinal disturbances. When diagnosed and treated early, severe damage to the nervous system and paralysis can be prevented. Those who survive paralytic polio may be left with a limp or need a walking aid such as crutches or a wheelchair. Excessive fatigue, muscular

weakness, pain and other difficulties such as muscle atrophy and scoliosis may occur 20–30 years after the onset of the disease. The recurrence of these symptoms is known as post-polio syndrome (PPS). Age seems to be an integral factor, although the exact cause of PPS remains unknown. Additional rest seems to offer some necessary relief from PPS symptoms.

In the 1940s and early 1950s, polio was a highly prevalent disease around the world that crippled or killed thousands, primarily children. This devastating disease has nearly been eradicated worldwide through the development of the Salk and Sabin vaccines (see the Disease chronicle at the start of this chapter).

Rabies

Rabies is an infectious disease of the brain and spinal cord caused by a virus that is transmitted by secretions (saliva, urine) of an infected animal. Rabies is very rare in the UK because of animal and human vaccines in addition to animal control efforts. Rabies can be lethal, and is primarily a disease of warm-blooded animals such as dogs, cats, raccoons, skunks, wolves, foxes and bats, but it can be transmitted to humans through bites or scratches from a rabid animal that licks its fur or feet. The virus may be airborne as a mist from urine in caves and in faecal matter, allowing for transfer to fur, feet or saliva.

The virus passes from the wound site along peripheral nerves to the spinal cord and brain, where it causes acute encephalomyelitis. The incubation period is long, 1 month to perhaps a year, depending on the distance of the wound from the brain or degree of breached surface. Bites on the face, neck and hands are the most serious. The mode of tetanus and rabies transmission to the CNS is illustrated in Figure 13.5.

Symptoms of rabies include fever, pain, mental derangement, rage, convulsions and paralysis. Rabies affects the areas of the brain that control the muscles in the throat required for swallowing and also the muscles used for breathing. As a result, spasms occur within the throat and voice box, causing a painful paralysis. Because of the inability to swallow or clear

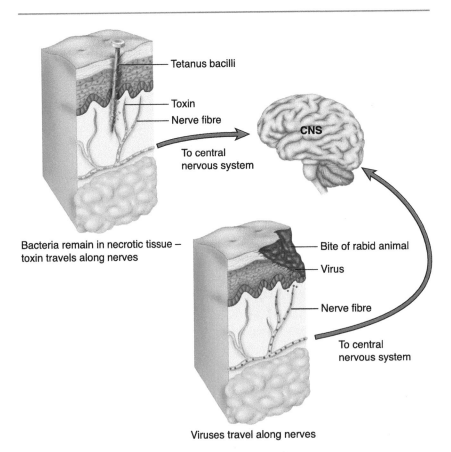

Figure 13.5 Nerve involvement in tetanus and rabies.

the throat effectively, the infected animal or human produces a profuse, sticky saliva and thus tends to 'foam' at the mouth. Hydrophobia is an aversion to water often linked to rabies. The disease is fatal in humans once it reaches the CNS and the symptoms described have developed.

In the case of an animal bite, it is extremely important to know if the animal is rabid, and a detailed investigation of the animal must be made as soon as possible. If rabies is suspected, immunisation and globulin injections are started on the infected person. The victim receives repeated injections of an altered virus to stimulate antibody production and an immune serum to provide a substantial passive immunity. The severity of rabies explains the critical need for the vaccination of dogs and cats against the disease.

Prevention of rabies is achieved by taking a series of three vaccinations over 28 days. The vaccine is required for field workers and medical associates who work with animals and tissues that may carry the rabies virus.

Shingles (herpes zoster)

Shingles is an acute inflammation of sensory neurons caused by the latency effect of the chickenpox virus, herpes zoster. It may even be caused by shingles exposure itself without a reactivation of the chickenpox virus, but that scenario is less common. Shingles is manifested by pain and a rash characterised by small water blisters surrounded by a red area. The lesions follow a sensory nerve, forming a streak toward the midline of the torso, generally across the shoulder, chest or trunk area. The rash is usually confined to one side of the body and does not cross the midline. Blisters fade and the lesions dry up and become encrusted. The encrusted areas cause severe itching and pain and may result in scarring; this after-effect is called **post-herpetic neuralgia** and is caused by the release of substance P (pain agent). The optic nerve can be affected, causing severe conjunctivitis. If not properly treated, ulcerations can form on the cornea, especially from zoster keratitis, and cause scarring or blindness.

Shingles can develop from exposure to a person with shingles in the infectious stage. It may also develop from exposure to chickenpox, which has an incubation period of about 2 weeks. It sometimes accompanies other diseases, such as pneumonia or tuberculosis. Shingles may also result from trauma or reaction to certain drug injections.

Treatment of shingles is directed toward relieving the pain and itchiness. Dry ice pads and lotions such as calamine may provide relief. Glucocorticoids may also be prescribed to suppress the inflammatory reaction, and antiviral agents like aciclovir (Zovirax) are used. Two-thirds of cases of shingles occur in those over the age of 50, and one half are in those aged 85 or more. Repeat occurrences are mostly found in immunocompromised patients.

Prevention includes immunisation against chickenpox.

Reye's syndrome

Reye's syndrome is a potentially devastating neurological illness that sometimes develops in children after a viral infection. Viruses associated with Reye's syndrome include Epstein–Barr, influenza B and varicella, the group which causes chickenpox. Use of aspirin during these infections is associated with Reye's syndrome. The actual cause of the disease is unknown.

Manifestations of Reye's syndrome include persistent vomiting, often a rash and lethargy about 1 week after a viral infection. Neurological dysfunction can progress from confusion to seizures to coma. The encephalopathy includes cerebral swelling with elevated intracranial pressure.

Management is geared toward lowering intracranial pressure and monitoring of vital signs, blood gases and blood pH. The outcome is very satisfactory when diagnosed and treated early, with a recovery rate of 85–90%.

Tetanus

Tetanus is an acute infectious disease, commonly called 'lockjaw', characterised by rigid, contracted muscles that are unable to relax. Tetanus is caused by the tetanus toxin, which is produced by a rod-like tetanus bacillus that lives in the intestines of animals and human beings. The organisms are excreted in the faecal material and persist as spores indefinitely in the soil. The bacilli are prevalent in rural areas and in garden soil fertiliser containing manure, especially from horse farms or race tracks. In developing countries neonatal tetanus kills about 250 000 per year and is called 'the silent death' because the infants die before the birth is recorded.

A laceration, puncture or animal bite introduces the bacterium deep into the tissues, where it flourishes in the absence of oxygen. Thus, deep wounds with ragged, lacerated tissue contaminated with faecal material (manure or contaminated soils) are the most dangerous type.

Tetanus has an incubation period ranging from 1 week to a few weeks. The toxin travels slowly, so the distance from the wound to the spinal cord is significant. The tetanus toxin (see Figure 13.5) anchors to motor nerve cells and stimulates them, which in turn stimulate muscles. Muscles become rigid, and painful spasms and convulsions develop. The jaw muscles are often the first to be affected (hence the name *lockjaw*, also called **trismus**). Because these muscles cannot relax, the mouth clamps tightly closed. The neck is stiff, and swallowing becomes difficult. If the muscles of respiration are affected, asphyxiation occurs. Death can result from even a minor wound if the condition is not treated.

Treatment includes a thorough cleansing of the wound and removal of dead tissue and any foreign substance. Immediate immunisation to inactivate the toxin before it reaches the spinal cord is crucial. The type of immunisation administered depends on the patient's history. If the patient has had no previous immunisation, tetanus antitoxin is given.

If 5 years have elapsed since the previous tetanus injection, the person receives a booster injection of **tetanus toxoid** to increase the antitoxin level.

Additional treatment includes the administration of antibiotics such as metronidazole or benzylpenicillin to prevent secondary infections. Sedatives may be used to decrease the frequency of convulsions. Oxygen under high pressure is also used because the bacillus is anaerobic; that is, it thrives in the absence of oxygen.

Tetanus may be prevented by adequate immunisation. Tetanus toxoid, which stimulates antibody formation, should be given to infants and small children at prescribed times. This inoculation may be done in combination with the diphtheria toxoid and pertussis vaccine (the latter prevents whooping cough).

Abscesses of the brain

Pyogenic organisms such as streptococci, staphylococci, amoebae and *E. coli* can travel to the brain from other infected areas and cause a brain abscess. Infections of the middle ear, skull bones or sinuses, including the mastoid, as well as pneumonia and endocarditis, are potential sources for brain abscess. Figure 13.6 shows abscesses of the brain.

The symptoms of brain abscess may be misleading, because the symptoms may include fever and headache, which can suggest a tumour. Analysis of

Prevention PLUS!

Reye's syndrome

Reye's syndrome (RS) appeared in the 1950s and virtually disappeared by the 1980s. It has been suggested that the disappearance of RS is related to the recognition of metabolic inborn errors that parallel RS in various clinical manners. RS may be misdiagnosed because of mitochondrial dysfunction that allows various metabolites (e.g. liver enzymes and ammonia) that cause RS-type symptoms and conditions to increase. However, prescribing paracetamol instead of aspirin will prevent this syndrome.

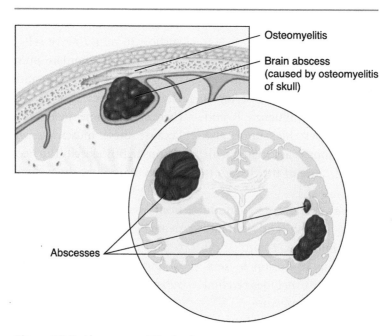

Figure 13.6 Abscesses of the brain.

CSF shows increased pressure and the presence of neutrophils and lymphocytes, indicating infection.

Once the diagnosis of a brain abscess has been made, the abscess must be opened surgically and drained, and the patient must be treated with penicillin-like antibiotics. Brain abscesses are not as common today in the developed world because most infections are held in check by antibiotics. Prevention may be unavoidable owing to accidental trauma situations, but monitoring current infectious situations helps prevent the spread of any disease.

DEGENERATIVE NEURAL DISEASES

Some diseases of the nervous system involve the degeneration of nerves and brain tissue. Abnormalities in muscle and sensory function often result from degeneration of nervous tissue. For example, note that Alzheimer's disease is also discussed in Chapter 14, although it, too, can be considered a type of neurodegenerative disease. Therefore, the description of Alzheimer's in this section focuses on the degenerative aspects of nervous tissue.

Alzheimer's disease

The most common cause of **dementia** (a syndrome of brain abnormalities) in the elderly is Alzheimer's disease (AD), a progressive degenerative brain disease. The incidence of AD rises with age, and the prevalence doubles about every 5 years. Those aged 60–64 have a prevalence of at least 1%, while that number rises to 30–40% for those individuals older than age 85.

The root cause of Alzheimer's disease is genetic, although most cases seem to appear in a random or sporadic manner. Familial cases, or those linked within families, account for about 5–10% of the cases. Chromosomes 1, 10, 12, 14, 19 and 21 have shown genes which affect protein production for specific enzymes or structural components within nerve cells. In the neuron, a support scaffolding of microtubules helps the cell maintain its integrity and to be functionally sound. The directional protein making these microtubules may be corrupted by a malformed compound known as the tau protein. This corruption causes a malformation of microtubules that normally form the linear feature of a neuron and results in a contracted mass known as neurofibrillary tangles. These tangles are not unique to Alzheimer's disease but do indicate a significant breakdown of functioning. These elements are apparent upon autopsy inspection, which is required to confirm a diagnosis of Alzheimer's disease.

Although autopsy is the confirming manner for this devastating disease, a combination of clinical assessment, modern imaging methods and family history can accurately diagnose AD in 80–90% of cases. Within 5–10 years of onset, the person tends to become disabled, immobile and muted; the person usually dies of pneumonia.

Multiple sclerosis

Multiple sclerosis (MS) is a chronic, progressive, degenerative disorder of the CNS. It usually affects young adults between the ages of 20 and 40. The frequency of occurrence is rare, at about 0.1%, and MS currently afflicts about 1 million worldwide.

At first, the disease manifests itself by muscle impairment, beginning with a loss of balance and coordination. Tingling and numbness ensue and are accompanied by a shaking tremor and muscular weakness. Walking is reduced to a shuffle or a cane is used, and occasionally a wheelchair or a more permanent assistance is required. Speech becomes difficult, and urinary bladder dysfunction often develops.

Vision may suddenly become impaired, and double vision frequently occurs. Lesions on the optic nerve can lead to blindness. The individual acquires **nystagmus**, an involuntary, rapid movement of the eyeball. Emotional changes are common owing to less independence and functional control. Signs and symptoms of MS vacillate between periods of remission and exacerbation and proceed at different rates as the disease progresses.

The disease is difficult to diagnose in the early stages, as many disorders of the nervous system have similar symptoms. Diagnosis is based on the specific tissue changes that accompany MS.

The degeneration of nervous tissue in MS involves the breaking up or erosion of the neuronal (myelin) sheath because of chronic inflammation. The nerve tracts do not degenerate in a regular pattern or to the same degree. Therefore, patchy areas of demyelination appear and become sclerotic. A myelin sheath protects the neuron and acts as an insulator to ensure the direction and velocity of the nerve impulse transmission. Any degradation of myelin impairs nerve conduction. MRI demonstrates plaques of demyelinated nerve fibres.

The disease takes one of three potential directions once established: relapsing–remitting involves about 85% of those affected, where flare-up episodes of worsening conditions are followed by partial or complete recovery periods; primary progressive is exhibited by a slow, gradual deterioration at variable rates of speed with minor plateaus of improvement, and involves about 10% of patients; secondary progressive, or progressive–relapsing, involves about 5% of patients and is characterised by steadily progressing deterioration and acute relapses with or without recovery.

The cause of MS is still uncertain, and although it is considered an autoimmune disease, it has been attributed to various viruses or immunological reactions to a virus, bacteria or trauma and heredity. To date, there is no specific treatment for MS that works effectively for long periods. Physical therapy enables the person to use the muscles that are controllable. Muscle relaxants help reduce spasticity, and steroids are often helpful. Some success has been found with beta interferon, and exercising in a pool of cold water seems to be beneficial for some individuals. Psychological counselling is advantageous in dealing with the emotional changes brought about by the disease.

Amyotrophic lateral sclerosis

Amyotrophic lateral sclerosis (ALS), also known as Lou Gehrig's disease, is a chronic, terminal neurological disease noted by a progressive loss of motor neurons and supportive astrocytes. ALS occurs late in life, most commonly in those in their 50s and 60s, and is slightly more common in men than in women. The prevalence of ALS is 2–3 per 100 000 people.

ALS is characterised by disturbances in motility and atrophy of muscles of the hands, forearms and legs because of degeneration of neurons in the ventral horn of the spinal cord. Also affected are certain cranial nerves, particularly the trigeminal (V), facial nerves (VII) and hypoglossal (XI), which impair muscles of the mouth and throat. Swallowing and tongue movements are affected, and speech becomes difficult or impossible.

The cause of ALS is not known. It is diagnosed by an electromyogram (EMG), which shows a reduction in the number of motor units active with muscle contraction. Motor units are motor neurons and their connection to a host of muscle fibres. Also observed are **fasciculations**, the spontaneous, uncontrolled discharges of motor neurons seen as irregular twitching.

ALS requires early education of the patient and the patient's family so that a proper management system may be provided to anticipate and prevent certain hazards. Specifically, the prevention of upper airway obstruction and pathological aspiration – drawing of vomitus or mucus into the respiratory tract – is the main focus. Aspiration can occur from weakened respiratory musculature and ineffective cough. Death usually occurs within 3–5 years after onset of symptoms and generally results from pulmonary failure. However, as the renowned British scientist Stephen Hawking attests, survivorship of ALS does vary.

Prevention of ALS is uncertain because 90% of the cases are indeterminate as to origin, while 10% have an autosomal dominant gene on chromosome 21.

Parkinson's disease

Parkinson's disease (PD) is a degenerative disease that affects muscle control and coordination. PD normally strikes at midlife, about age 45. Approximately 0.2% of the UK population are affected with PD, with 10 000 people diagnosed every year. More men than women are affected, and as the cause of Parkinson's disease is still unknown, environmental factors, particularly undetected viruses, are suspected.

A very small percentage of PD cases are hereditary as either autosomal dominant or recessive genes. The resultant cause is related to a loss of cells and the neurotransmitter dopamine in the substantia nigra of the basal nucleus within the core of the brain. Dopamine suppresses undesired movements that skeletal muscles may be instructed to do but are normally held in check or dormant. Therefore, when dopamine is not present, the unrestrained signals call for an uncoordinated 'shaky' tremor.

Symptoms are progressive and include tremor, rigid muscles and loss of normal reflexes. The tremors are called 'tremors at rest', meaning they occur while the patient is inactive and subside when the muscles are put into motion. A mask-like facial expression is noticed along with faltering gait and mental depression in approximately 10–15% of patients.

In the earlier stages, physical therapy and exercise help maintain flexibility, motility and mental well-being. Relaxation is particularly important for PD patients because stressful situations worsen the condition. Figure 13.7 summarises possible effects of PD.

Treatment includes the administration of levadopamine (L-dopa), a form of dopamine that passes the blood–brain barrier and is similar to the natural form. The drug does not stop the degeneration, but it restores dopamine levels in the brain and reduces symptom severity. Other similar drugs like pergolide and co-careldopa (Sinemet) may be used, as well as anticholinergic medications like orphenadrine for treatment.

In later stages, physical therapy, including heat and massage, helps reduce muscle cramps and relieve tension headaches caused by the rigidity of neck muscles. Psychological support is needed while learning to cope with the disability. In terminal stages, an increased risk for suicide has been noted.

Deep brain stimulation with electrodes implanted into the thalamus has become an additional tool for controlling tremors. The patient may turn on/off the implanted pulse generator by passing a magnet over

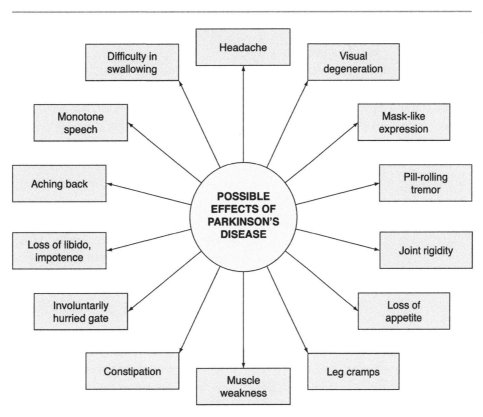

Figure 13.7 Summary of Parkinson's disease effects.

it. The small, pacemaker-like device is implanted under the collar bone. Normally, a constant trickle of charge is sent to the thalamus to interrupt tremor-causing signals, similar to surgical techniques that destroy part of the thalamus to limit involuntary movements.

Another future treatment being suggested is a sort of 'brain transplant', in which dopamine-producing neural tissue from a mouse or pig is implanted in the brain to replenish the missing dopamine. Most PD patients are unaware of the initial agent(s) that bring about this disorder, and prevention is not an option in hereditary cases. Pesticides are suspected causative agents.

Essential tremor

This disorder is often confused with Parkinson's disease even though it usually becomes symptomatic in adolescence. Like PD, essential tremor progresses with the passage of time; at rest the problem abates. Moving or shaking of the head and hands and a halting or quivering voice are characteristic of this condition. There is a familial pattern, but the genetics are not clear. Drugs like beta blockers, known for heart regulation, tranquillisers like Valium and botox injections help approximately 40% of the patients, and a noticeable improvement occurs in about 60% of the patients receiving brain implant devices. Still, some of those afflicted choose to leave the disease untreated until it interferes with the basic routines of living.

Prevention is uncertain and there may be familial links, but these associations are not clearly identified at this time.

Huntington's disease (Huntington's chorea)

Huntington's chorea is a progressive degenerative disease of the brain that results in the loss of muscle control. *Chorea* refers to involuntary and ceaseless, rapid, jerky movements. The disease affects both the mind and body. Physical disabilities include speech loss and a difficulty in swallowing, coupled with involuntary jerking, twisting motions and muscle

spasms. Personality changes include carelessness, poor judgement and impaired memory, ultimately deteriorating to total mental incompetence.

World prevalence is about 5 per 100 000 people. Huntington's disease is an inherited disease, but symptoms may not appear until middle age (ages 30–50). If either parent has the disease, the children have a 50% chance of inheriting it because it is an autosomal dominant trait (see Chapter 5 for a discussion of genetic transmission). The responsible gene has been identified on chromosome 4. The abnormality causes the neurotransmitter dopamine to be produced in excess, and insufficiencies of acetylcholine underlie the dementia and abnormal muscle activity. To reduce dopamine action, the drug tetrabenazine can be used. Given its genetic component, prevention is not an option. There is no cure for Huntington's chorea. When desired, carriers can be identified with gene testing. Following onset, death normally occurs 15–20 years afterward, with a progressive deterioration.

CONVULSIONS

A convulsion is a sudden, intense series of uncontrollable muscular contractions and relaxations. Causes of convulsions include accumulation of waste products in the blood, such as occurs in uraemia, toxaemia of pregnancy, drug poisoning or withdrawal from alcohol. Infectious diseases of the brain, such as meningitis and encephalitis, and high fevers, especially in young children, are frequently accompanied by convulsions. The basis for convulsions is abnormal electrical discharges in the brain, which stimulates muscles to contract abnormally.

Epilepsy

Epilepsy is a group of uncontrolled cerebral discharges that recurs at random intervals. The seizures associated with **epilepsy** are a form of convulsion. Brain impulses are temporarily disturbed, with resultant involuntary convulsive movements. Epilepsy can be acquired as a result of injury to the brain, including birth trauma, a penetrating wound or depressed skull fracture. A tumour can irritate the brain, causing abnormal electrical discharges to be released. Alcoholism can also lead to the development of epilepsy. Most cases of epilepsy are idiopathic, but a predisposition to epilepsy may be inherited.

Epilepsy is one of the more common, yet controllable, neurological disorders, with European studies showing that 40–70 adults per 100 000 have a first unprovoked seizure. Childhood prevalence is rather higher, especially under 10 years old, and involves proportionally more boys than girls.

Epilepsy may manifest itself mildly, particularly in children. Loss of consciousness may last only a few seconds, during which time the child appears in a state of shock or absent-mindedness (amnesia). Some muscular twitching may be noticed around the eyes and mouth, and the child's head may sway rhythmically, but the child may not fall to the floor. This form of epileptic seizure is known as absence (or petit mal) and usually disappears by the late teens or early twenties.

Major seizures, called tonic clonic or grand mal, involve a sudden loss of consciousness during which the person falls to the floor. *Tonic* refers to the increased muscle tone or contraction phase, while *clonic* involves alternating contracting and relaxing muscle activities. Absence and tonic forms are considered generalised convulsions and range from mild to severe, with violent shaking and thrashing movements lasting about 1 minute. Hypersalivation causes a foaming at the mouth. The individual tends to lose control of the urinary bladder and sometimes bowels. Sometimes there are repeated seizures, without a recovery period, that may last 30 minutes. This condition is known as status epilepticus.

Individuals sometimes have a warning of an approaching seizure that gives them time to lie down or reach for support. This warning, known as an **aura**, may come as a ringing sound in the ears, a tingling sensation in the fingers, spots before the eyes or various odours. The signs described are characteristic of the absence or clonic form of seizure. After a seizure, the person is fatigued, groggy and unaware of what happened. Seizures last for varying lengths of time and appear with varying frequencies.

Epileptic seizures may take different forms. The International Classification of Epileptic Seizures, adopted by the World Health Organization, classifies seizures into four categories:

1. Partial seizures begin locally and may or may not involve a larger area of brain tissue.
2. Generalised seizures are bilaterally symmetrical and without local onset.
3. Unilateral seizures generally involve only one side of the brain.
4. Unclassified epileptic seizures are less defined in origin and degree.

Diagnosis of epilepsy can be made on the results of an electroencephalogram (EEG), a recording of brain waves. X-ray films are also used to identify any brain lesions. Family histories of epilepsy are very important in diagnosing the condition. The diagnosis of epilepsy and the seizure type has become more accurate with new techniques for imaging the brain. CT scans, using X-rays, and MRI, using magnetic fields, visualise brain anatomy.

Medication is very effective in controlling epilepsy, particularly anticonvulsant drugs, such as carbamazepine. Alcohol must be avoided with anticonvulsant medication. Molecular neurobiology research is providing new information on how nerve cells control electrical activity, thus making development of more effective antiepileptic drugs possible. It is now known which drugs are best for treating the various kinds of seizures. Assistance or treatment during a seizure is directed toward preventing self-injury. Finally, epilepsy does not appear to interfere with mental prowess or creative talents for those afflicted. A consistent medication regimen usually prevents epileptic episodes.

DEVELOPMENTAL ERRORS OR MALFORMATIONS

Spina bifida

Spina bifida, a neural tube defect (NTD), is a developmental error in which one or more vertebrae fail to fuse, leaving an opening or weakness in the vertebral column. The consequences of spina bifida depend on the extent of the opening and the degree to which the vertebral column, usually in the lumbar area, is exposed and the involvement of the spinal cord. One form of spina bifida, spina bifida occulta (hidden), may not be apparent at birth. In this mildest case, a slight dimpling of the skin and tuft of hair over the vertebral defect indicates the site of the lesion.

Lesions of spina bifida occulta show internal weakness or backbone breaks that can be readily seen on X-ray films. Other malformations, such as hydrocephalus, cleft palate, cleft lip, club foot and **strabismus** (crossed eyes), tend to accompany this developmental error and may occur simultaneously or separately. Any single malformation may point to spina bifida and trigger closer observations of the individual even without noticeable disability. Muscular abnormalities, such as incorrect posture, inability to walk or lack of urinary bladder and bowel control appear later.

A second form of spina bifida noticeable at birth is a **meningocele**. In this condition, meninges protrude through the opening in the vertebra as a sac filled with CSF. The spinal cord is not directly involved in this case.

Meningomyelocele is a serious anomaly in which the nerve elements protrude into the sac and are trapped, thus preventing proper placement and development. The child with this defect may be paralysed, fail to develop, lack sensation and experience mental retardation. The consequences of the defect depend on the region and size of the spinal cord affected. Surgical corrections of the various forms of spina bifida have been very effective. Some procedures are intrauterine, to repair the defect of the fetus, and these new operations look promising. Physical rehabilitation may allow for a more normal lifestyle, depending on severity.

The most severe form of spina bifida is **myelocele**, in which the neural tube itself fails to close and the nerve tissue is totally exposed and disorganised. This condition is usually fatal. The various forms of spina bifida are shown in Figure 13.8.

Hereditary and environmental influences or idiopathic instances are possible causes of spina bifida. Worldwide, the occurrence rate of spina bifida is about 1 per 1000 births, but is higher in

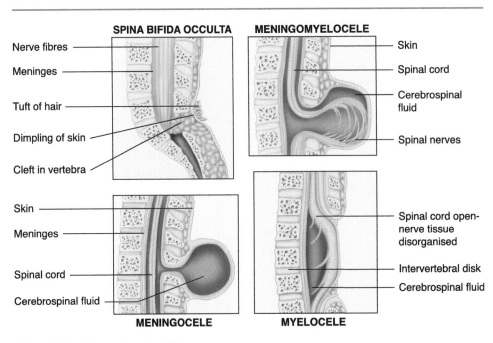

Figure 13.8 Forms of spina bifida.

the UK, at about 2–3 per 1000 births. However, since the introduction of folate into the neonatal care regimen, the number of cases has been cut significantly. Spina bifida and other NTD cases may be detected by ultrasound and elevated blood levels of alpha fetoprotein.

Hydrocephalus

Hydrocephalus is a consequence of excess CSF trapped within the brain. The formation, circulation and absorption of CSF were described earlier in this chapter. In hydrocephalus, this fluid and pressure increases abnormally, causing the ventricles to enlarge and press the brain against the skull, which forces it to enlarge greatly, especially in the case of newborns.

An obstruction in the normal flow of CSF is the usual cause of hydrocephalus. A congenital defect causes stenosis (narrowing) of an opening from the ventricles, or an acquired lesion can block the CSF flow. Meningitis, a tumour or birth trauma may result in acquired hydrocephalus. The error may also be a failure to absorb the fluid into the circulatory system.

There are two types of hydrocephalus: *communicating* and *non-communicating*. In the communicating type, the excess CSF enters the subarachnoid space. In non-communicating hydrocephalus, the increased pressure of the CSF is confined within the ventricles and is not evident in a lumbar puncture (LP).

The head of a child born with hydrocephalus may appear normal at birth, but it will enlarge rapidly in the early months of life as the fluid accumulates. The brain is compressed, the cranial bones are thin, and the sutures of the skull tend to separate under the pressure. A hydrocephalic infant exhibits a prominent forehead, bulging eyes and a facial expression of fright or pain. The scalp is stretched and the veins of the head are prominent. The weight of the excessive fluid in the head makes it impossible for the baby to lift its head. Infant growth is stunted, as is mental development.

There have been cases of self-arrested hydrocephalus in which expansion of the head stops. A balance is reached between production and absorption of the CSF fluid. The cranial sutures knit together and the skull bones thicken. The extent of brain damage before the expansion stops determines the degree of mental retardation.

The number of cases involved is difficult to attain because of causes, ages and matters of degree, especially when tabulated in combination with other diseases. For example, an obvious case at birth is noted, but trauma or a tumour or encephalitis cases may not be accounted for and may simply be considered cerebral oedema. The incidence of hydrocephalus in the UK is approximately 6.46 per 10 000 per year. Success in relieving the excessive CSF can be achieved by placing a shunt between the blocked cerebral ventricles and the jugular vein (Figure 13.9), to the heart or placed into the peritoneal cavity. This connection facilitates the reduction in cranial pressure and allows the fluid to enter the general circulation. Prevention is difficult owing to the uncertainty of events that gradually lead to this crucial disorder.

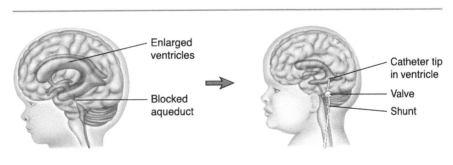

Figure 13.9 Hydrocephalus.

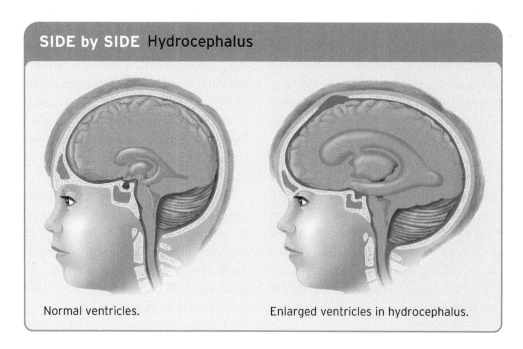

SIDE by SIDE **Hydrocephalus**

Normal ventricles.

Enlarged ventricles in hydrocephalus.

BRAIN INJURY

Cerebral palsy

Cerebral palsy is not a disease but a functional disorder of the brain manifested by motor impairment that may induce varying degrees of mental retardation; it usually becomes apparent before age 3. The assault causing brain damage may be due to injury at or near the time of birth, a maternal infection such as rubella (German measles) or infection of the brain even after birth. Reduced levels of oxygen, primarily caused by reduced blood flow or incompatible blood type or Rhesus (Rh) factor, may cause brain injury. For example, a pinched umbilical cord against the birth canal may shut off blood and starve the fetus of necessary oxygen. With incompatibilities, a Rh⁻ mother may produce antibodies against the blood of a Rh⁺ fetus. The result is excessive destruction of fetal blood cells that causes hyperbilirubinaemia; bilirubin is toxic to the brain and causes damage. Often, cerebral palsy is idiopathic. Cerebral palsy affects 2–4 per 1000 infants in industrialised countries and is 10 times more often found in premature and low birthweight babies.

There are four recognised forms of cerebral palsy: spastic, choreoathetoid, atactic and mixed. However, it is not easy to diagnose a specific type before the infant is at least 18 months old because the signs may be subtle and attributed to immature development. The largest percentage of cerebral palsy type (70%) is the spastic version in which muscles are tense and reflexes are exaggerated. In the athetoid form, constant, purposeless movements are uncontrollable. A continuous tremor or shaking of the hands and feet is common. Cerebral palsy sufferers with the atactic form have poor balance and are prone to fall. Poor muscular coordination and a staggering gait are characteristic of this form of the disorder.

Depending on the area of the brain affected, there may be seizures along with visual or auditory impairment. If the muscles controlling the tongue are affected, speech defects result. Intelligence may be normal, but often there is reduced mental capacity.

Treatment depends on the nature and the severity of the brain injury. Anticonvulsant drugs reduce seizures, and casts or braces may aid walking. In addition, muscle relaxants can relieve spasms along with traction or surgery, which is necessary in some cases. Muscle training is the most important therapy, and the earlier it is started, the more effective it is. Prevention may depend on circumstances such as sterile environment and strict monitoring of fetal status at the time of birth.

STROKE OR CEREBROVASCULAR ACCIDENT

The main cause of cerebral haemorrhage is hypertension. Prolonged hypertension tends to result from atherosclerosis, which leads to arteriosclerosis, explained in Chapter 6. The combination of high blood pressure and hard, brittle blood vessels is a predisposing condition for cerebral haemorrhage. **Aneurysms**, weakened areas in vascular walls, are also susceptible to rupture (Figure 13.10). Surrounding the pituitary gland is the circle of Willis, a major crossroads of cerebral vascularity, vulnerable to weakness, especially aneurysms. If the rupture or leakage occurs here, the collection of blood within the cranial cavity increases and the intracranial pressure increases proportionally to dangerous levels. When this pressure increase is controlled or alleviated early, brain damage and death is unlikely. The pressure relief may come in the form of medication or emergency surgical procedure. Any subsequent haemorrhage into the brain tissue damages the neurons, causing a sudden loss of consciousness. Death can follow, or, if the bleeding stops, varying degrees of brain damage can result. When detected, swift surgical repairs of aneurysms save lives.

Cerebrovascular accident (CVA) is the second leading cause of death in the UK, the first being heart attacks. Prevention includes not smoking, maintaining proper diet and exercise and monitoring blood pressure; some people take an aspirin each day if they are not taking blood thinners like coumarins. CVAs are basically of two varieties; those due to a haemorrhage or to a blood clot. Most CVAs result from the blood clot or occlusion and will be addressed in the next section.

Thrombosis and embolism

Blood clots that block the cerebral arteries cause infarction of brain tissue. **Thromboses** are blood clots that develop on walls of atherosclerotic vessels, particularly in the carotid arteries. These clots take time to form, and some warning may precede the occlusion of the vessel. The person may experience blindness in one eye, difficulty in speaking or a generalised state of confusion. When the cerebral blood vessel is completely blocked, the individual may lose consciousness.

An **embolism** is a travelling clot that may suddenly occlude a blood vessel and cause ischaemia. The embolism is most frequently a clot from the heart, aorta or carotid artery, but it can travel from another part of the body, such as the deep veins of the leg. Consciousness may be lost suddenly. When this event occurs, a thrombolytic drug (alteplase), called a 'clot buster', may be used to dissolve clots and restore blood flow in occluded vessels. However,

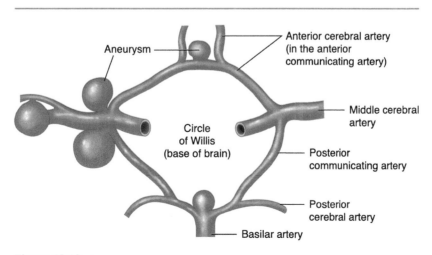

Figure 13.10 Aneurysms.

if this is given in haemorrhagic cases of CVAs, intracranial bleeding and increasing pressure continue and the individual could die. Crucial decisions must be made in acute cases, and because most CVAs are of the ischaemic form, alteplase is a reliable and available agent for the physician.

The site and extent of the brain damage, regardless of its cause, determines the outcome for the patient. Gradually consciousness is regained, but immediately after the **stroke**, speech is often impaired. Loss of speech, or **aphasia**, is normally temporary but may require therapy to assist in a full recovery.

Damage to the motor nerves at the point passing down the spinal cord causes weakness (**paresis**) or paralysis on the side of the body opposite the brain lesion owing to the crossover of nerve tracts in the brainstem. Paralysis on one side of the body is referred to as **hemiplegia**.

Various procedures make it possible to determine the site of blockage in a cerebral blood vessel. Angiography, a process in which radio-opaque material is injected into cerebral arteries, allows X-rays to locate the lesion.

A blockage in a carotid artery can be treated surgically. **Endarterectomy**, the more common procedure, removes the thickened area of the inner vascular lining. Carotid bypass surgery removes the blocked vascular segment, and a graft is inserted to allow blood flow to the brain. Other vascular replacement may be performed in other areas, such as the aorta, to reduce the risk of haemorrhage.

Transient ischaemic attack

Transient ischaemic attacks (TIAs) are caused by brief but critical periods of reduced blood flow in a cerebral artery. TIAs may be thought of as 'mini' strokes resulting from blood clots occluding vessels or vessel spasms that interrupt blood flow and thus impair neurological functioning. The individual may lose feeling in the face or extremity or have tingling sensations for a brief time. Factors influencing the constrictions are similar to CVA, and with prior TIAs there is a tenfold chance of a stroke. Reduced flow may be caused by an atherosclerotic narrowing

of the blood vessel or to small emboli that temporarily lodge in the vessel. The attacks may last less than a minute or two or up to several hours, with the average attack lasting 15 minutes. Manifestations are often abrupt and can include visual disturbances, transient hemiparesis (muscular weakness on one side) or sensory loss on one side. Lips and tongue may become numb, causing slurred speech. Multiple TIAs often precede a complete stroke and may serve as warning of a cerebral vascular disturbance. Further diagnostic testing, such as a cerebral angiogram or CT scan, may be indicated. Prevention of a TIA is uncertain, but their occurrence may alert the person to see a doctor and prevent further damage caused by a full-scale stroke by taking 'blood thinning' medications.

TRAUMATIC DISORDERS

Concussion of the brain

A **concussion** is a transient shaking of the brain resulting from a violent blow to the head or a fall. The person typically loses consciousness and cannot remember the events of the occurrence. Although the brain may not actually be damaged, the whole body is affected; the pulse rate is weak, and when consciousness is regained, the person may experience nausea and dizziness. A severe headache may follow, and the person should be watched closely, since a coma may ensue, and that could be life-threatening.

In the UK, about 8 per 100 000 people every year suffer severe traumatic brain injuries (TBIs), another 18 per 100 000 suffer moderate TBIs, and 250–300 per 100 000 suffer mild TBIs. About 6–10 per 100 000 TBI victims die per year in the UK, and TBI is a leading cause of death for those under the age of 45. There are many causes of TBI, from falling and vehicle accidents to sports injuries.

A person suffering from a concussion should be kept quiet, and drugs that stimulate or depress the nervous system, such as painkillers, are contraindicated. The condition usually corrects itself with time and rest. Prevention is difficult because of the unpredictability of some situations, but vehicular accident-related concussions are down owing to the use of seatbelts and child car seats.

Contusion

In a **contusion**, there is a bruising to brain tissue even though the skin at the site of the trauma may not be broken, as it is in a skull fracture. The brain injury may be on the side of the impact or on the opposite side, where the brain is forced against the skull. Blood from broken blood vessels may accumulate in the brain, causing swelling and pain. The blood clots and necrotic tissue form and could block the flow of CSF, causing a form of hydrocephalus.

Efforts must be made to reduce intracranial pressure, and surgery may be necessary to alleviate pressure and to remove blood clots. Simple pain reduction measures, such as ice packs, may help until professional help arrives. Along with observation, rest will be necessary for full recovery, although some pain medications may be prescribed if needed.

Skull fractures

The most serious complication of a skull fracture is damage to the brain. A fracture at the base of the skull is likely to affect vital centres in the brainstem. The pressure that increases because of accumulation of CSF or blood must be reduced by emergency medical intervention. Another danger of skull fractures is that bacteria may be able to access the brain directly.

Haemorrhages

Haemorrhages can occur in the meninges, causing blood to accumulate between the brain and the skull. A severe injury to the temple can cause an artery just inside the skull to rupture. The blood then flows between the dura mater and the skull; this is known as an **extradural** or **epidural** haemorrhage (Figure 13.11). The increased pressure of the blood causes the patient to lose consciousness. Surgery is required immediately to seal off the

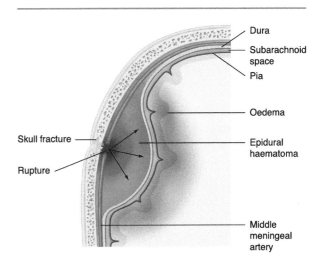

Figure 13.11 Extradural haematoma.

bleeding vessel and remove the blood. No blood would be found in a lumbar puncture because the blood accumulation is outside the dura mater.

A haemorrhage under the dura mater is a **subdural** haemorrhage or haematoma (Figure 13.12), and is caused by a rupture of a cranial vein, or the large venous sinuses of the brain, rather than an artery. This breach may occur from a severe blow to

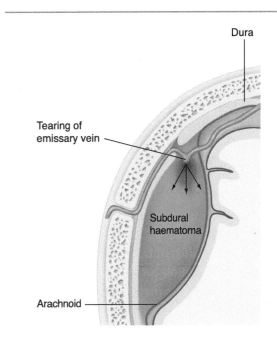

Figure 13.12 Subdural haematoma.

the front or back of the head. The blood clots and CSF accumulates in a cyst-like formation. Intracranial pressure increases, but the cerebral symptoms may not develop for a time. Subdural haemorrhages are sometimes chronic occurrences in cases of alcoholic abuse (owing to falling accidents) and in battered or violently abused individuals.

The surface membrane of the brain may be torn by a skull fracture, causing a **subarachnoid** haemorrhage. Blood flows into the subarachnoid space, where CSF circulates. Blood is found in the CSF with a lumbar puncture. Rupture of an aneurysm can also cause a subarachnoid haemorrhage.

Many haemorrhages are accidental and unpredictable. Therefore, prevention is not easy to project, but prior symptoms may be used as indicators to reduce occurrences.

BRAIN TUMOURS

Tumours of the brain may be malignant or benign. Because benign tumours may grow and compress vital nerve centres, they are considered serious growths. Benign tumours are usually encapsulated, and they can be completely removed surgically. Malignant tumours have extensive roots and are extremely difficult or impossible to remove in their entirety. Most malignant tumours of the brain are metastatic from other organs, especially the lung and breast. Primary malignant tumours of the brain are called **gliomas**, tumours of the glial cells that support nerve tissue rather than growths of the neurons themselves.

Brain tumours manifest themselves in different ways depending on the site and growth rate of the tumour. **Astrocytomas** are basically benign, slow-growing tumours. **Glioblastomas multiforme** are highly malignant, rapidly growing tumours. Brain function is affected by the increased intracranial pressure. Mannitol, corticosteroids and cranial shunts help relieve the pressure symptoms. Blood supply to an area of the brain may be reduced by an infiltrating tumour or by oedema, and this causes dysfunctional activity as well as causing the tissue to become necrotic.

Symptoms of brain tumours typically include a severe headache because of the increased pressure of the tumour. Personality changes, loss of memory or development of poor judgement may give further evidence of a brain tumour. Visual disturbances, double vision or partial blindness often occur, and the ability to speak may be impaired. An upright person may be unsteady while standing or become drowsy. Seizures often develop and may progress into a coma.

Diagnostic measures include MRI and CT scans plus a full array of skull X-rays. Treatment depends on growth type and location. When possible, surgery (see Chapter 4) is followed by radiation and/or chemotherapy. Radiosurgery uses a gamma knife, and the radiation is beamed through designated holes in a helmet that directs the radiation specifically to the target. A limitation of gamma knife surgery is that a special nuclear facility is required for this procedure.

CRANIAL NERVE DISEASE

Trigeminal neuralgia

Any one of the twelve pairs of cranial nerves may be subject to impairment. Individual cranial nerves may be affected by degeneration or unknown causes and is thus involved with various ailments. The fifth (V) cranial nerve, or trigeminal nerve, may become inflamed, causing severe intermittent pain, usually on one side of the face. This condition, known as trigeminal neuralgia or *tic douloureux*, affects 10 people per 100 000 in the UK (Figure 13.13). The cause of *tic douloureux* is often idiopathic but may be caused by stress, tumours compressing the nerve or, in young individuals, may be an indication of multiple sclerosis barring other neurological signs. Those affected are usually age 40 or older and complain of severe pain, especially around the oral cavity (the tongue, lips and gums). This recurring pain may or may not respond readily to pain medication. Anticonvulsive agents like phenytoin or carbamazepine are generally prescribed. In very severe and resistant cases, surgery may be considered.

Sensory distribution

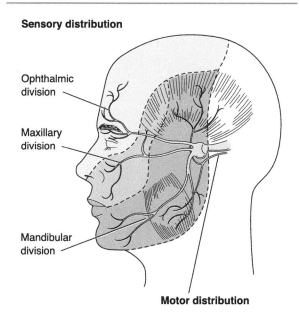

Figure **13.13** Sensory and motor distribution of the trigeminal nerve. There are three sensory divisions: ophthalmic, maxillary and mandibular.

Figure **13.14** Bell's palsy, showing typical drooping of one side of the face.
(NIH/Phototake NYC)

Ablation or microvascular decompression of the nerve as it exits the skull will reduce the pain, as will using glycerol, radiofrequency or even radiation to damage the sensory root elements and give pain relief in a procedure called **rhizotomy**.

Bell's palsy

Bell's palsy involves the inflammation of the seventh (VII) cranial nerve, or facial nerve. The aetiology is usually unknown, but viruses, autoimmunity and vascular ischaemia are probable factors. This nerve may also be traumatised, compressed or invaded by pathogens. Because the seventh cranial nerve innervates facial muscles and salivary glands, attacks cause sagging of the facial muscles on one side of the face and a watery eye. The person may drool and have slurred speech (Figure 13.14). In these cases, massage or heat treatment may help. Recovery may take weeks. The occurrence of Bell's palsy is about 25 per 100 000 in the UK.

Some corticoid medications such as prednisone or antiviral agents (aciclovir) are given if herpes simplex 1 (HSV1) is suspected. Therefore, relief of symptoms may not always be quick or simple. Bell's palsy is rare in children. Usually it strikes between ages 25 and 50. If the situation fails to be resolved, a facial contracture develops. The prognosis is generally good, although complete healing may take many months to a year.

PAIN

Pain and pain perception are integral parts of nervous system function. In this section, we will discuss the following:

- Definition of pain
- The function or purpose of pain
- Types and characteristics of pain
- The physiology of pain
- Pain assessment
- Pain management
- Other methods of pain control

Pain means different things to different individuals. Pain includes a major degree of perception and is therefore subjective. This symptom requires a level of threshold and therefore acts as a gauge of tolerance, plus learned behaviours, that rely on past experience and culture. Threshold accounts for the initial level of pain that an individual acknowledges, while tolerance suggests the point at which the same individual requires treatment in dealing with the pain. Thus, pain may be thought of as an individualistic occurrence.

In neurophysiology, pain is described as a result of some form of tissue damage. However, this simple definition does not account for emotional pain or pain resulting from some functional disorders. When physical breakdowns or lesions are apparent, it is easier to ascertain an accompanying pain criterion. Functional disparities are not always found or determined through superficial observation (e.g. a microscope), but many forms of psychogenic pain are well recognised and treated.

Regardless of definition, perception or understanding, pain is a sensation of hurt or a strong discomfort, typically from some form of noxious stimulus. Therefore, pain is caused by injury or disease and is transmitted throughout the body to associated cortical areas in the brain for interpretation and prospective recourse.

Pain does have a purpose and function. Its primary purpose is to warn the person of an abnormal state, like inflammation, infection, body trauma or injury. Second, it is a signal not to pursue any activity that causes additional pain and thus may cause any more damage. This pause will assist the healing process by allowing the body to rest and conserve resources for recovery and homeostasis. Pain is considered the most common cause that forces individuals to the doctor's surgery.

There is a rare alternative to pain sensation, known as 'congenital insensitivity to pain', found in individuals who are born without a sense of pain. In these cases, the nervous system is not equipped to instruct the person about injurious conditions or accidents and may allow continual walking on broken limbs or permit advanced infections to go untreated. There is a natural reluctance to pain, but without it life may be less safe.

Categories and characteristics of pain

Various categories of pain usually refer to origination or duration. The pain origin includes areas such as cutaneous (skin), somatic (body), visceral (organ), neuropathic or referred (redirected site). Somatic pain involves blood vessels, nerves, muscles and joints (e.g. sprained ankle), while cutaneous pain may emanate from a pinprick or sunburn. Visceral pain may be diffuse or poorly localised. In the case of appendicitis, pain is referred to the surface of the right lower quadrant of the abdomen, even though the problem is internal (see Table 13.1).

Neuropathic pain may not be caused by a commonly held noxious agent but tends to be delayed and induce a generalised burning sensation and occasionally stabbing pain, as found in the legs of some diabetics.

Pain duration is acute (immediate) or chronic. Acute pain has a relatively short time of activity (e.g. within 6 months), whereas chronic pain exceeds the 6-month time frame and may last for years. Severity and specific descriptions, like pounding, throbbing, and sharp or dull, help to qualify the situation as well.

Pain importance may be ascribed to the fact that pain receptors (**nociceptors**) are the most abundant sensory receptor in the skin; there are as many as 1300 per square inch. Compared to touch or thermal receptors, pain reception is scattered around to ensure basic protection and homeostatic balance. Nociceptors consist of free nerve ending elements

Table 13.1 Body regional pain.

Body region	Pain manifestations
Cranial	Headache - common, migraine Oral - toothache Facial - Bell's palsy
Cervical - neck	Whiplash - may become chronic pain
Torso	Chest - heart pain, lung Abdominal - gastric (e.g. ulcer) Appendix, gallbladder - stones Lumbar - lower back, pinched nerve Pelvic - ovary, urinary bladder
Extremities - limbs	Muscle and joint pain (e.g. arthritis)

(not encapsulated) attached to a sensory neuron. Pain receptors are found in the viscera, or internal organs, as well, as noted by gas pains or gastric burning sensations, and in the muscles and joints.

The physiology of pain and the pain theory concept

The most commonly supported theory by which pain is exhibited is called the gate control theory. The physiological process begins with an afferent nociceptor that responds to the stimulus of pain. This information then travels along a neuronal fibre as an impulse. There are differences in the size or diameter of the neuronal fibres. They can be insulated with myelin or unmyelinated and this causes a variance in the conduction velocity of their impulse. The largest diameter fibre type is the A-beta form, which responds to light touch in the skin and therefore normally does not cause a pain response. The small diameter myelinated A-delta and unmyelinated C fibres are found in nerves of the skin and deeper somatic (body) and visceral structures. These fibres are missing in individuals with congenital insensitivity to pain. Some designated areas, like the cornea, have only A-delta and C fibre neurons because they respond maximally only to intense and painful stimuli. For the most part, afferent nociceptors respond to heat and intense mechanical stimuli (e.g. pinching and noxious or irritating chemicals). When these fibres are blocked from responding, then no pain sensation is expressed.

The gate control theory holds that pain impulses are transmitted from specialised nociceptors within the skin, muscle or joints to the spinal cord. These impulses are carried by large A and small C fibres to a specialised area within the superior horn of the spinal cord known as the substantia gelatinosa. This area acts as a gate that regulates transmission for impulses to the CNS. Stimulation of the larger fibres (A) causes cells within the substantia gelatinosa to 'close the gate' and therefore diminish pain perception. The smaller fibre elements (C) do the reverse and thus enhance pain perception. Depending on the degree of opening and closing, the CNS regulates

pain output. Similarly, the thalamus, functioning as a relay station, tends to delegate or transmit some pain activity and alternately inhibit other pain transmission. The quick-acting myelinated large nerve fibres (A) tend to carry impulses for well localised, sharp pain, while the unmyelinated C fibres carry sensations more slowly, as in a diffuse burning or aching feeling (Figure 13.15). Note that amplified or continual outside impulses interfere with pain input, as when we bang our head against a wall or pound our fist; the force of the activity delays or diverts the pain sensation.

Another concept, known as the nociceptor pain process, extends the gate control theory. It consists of four primary features: transduction, transmission, perception of pain and modulation; these will be discussed here. These features parallel physiological nerve conduction operations.

In transduction, the nociceptors distinguish among the various stimuli as to noxious or harmful versus innocuous inputs. Transduction also converts the noxious stimuli into sensory nerve ending impulses to the spinal cord and describes how pain is perceived by the body. Transmission is the movement of the transduced stimuli into impulses that ascend up the spinal cord to the brainstem and thalamus. From here the dispatched impulse proceeds to the proper cortical lobe or area (e.g. parietal lobe) for pain interpretation. Some impulses may be challenged or blocked from relay as well. Perception of pain means the sensation has become a conscious feeling. The overall perception and response process is not well understood, especially among different individuals. Again the reminder here is that pain is an individual-type sensation. Modulation is the manipulation that the brain imposes on signals to modify or inhibit pain impulses. In this case, the brain naturally releases compounds that produce relief (analgesia) called **endorphins** and **enkephalins**. These compounds are often referred to in the case of marathon runners who feel a sense of euphoria miles into a race. Both of the prevailing concepts of pain attempt to incorporate basic neurological processes or principles with a means to envision a mechanism for interpretation and control.

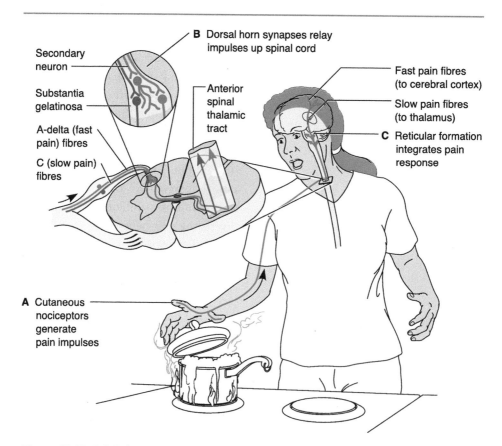

Figure 13.15 (A) Cutaneous nociceptors generate pain impulses that travel via A-delta and C fibres to the spinal cord's dorsal horn. (B) Secondary neurons in the dorsal horn pass impulses across the spinal cord to the anterior spinothalamic tract. (C) Slow pain impulses ascend to the thalamus, while fast pain impulses ascend to the cerebral cortex. The reticular formation in the brainstem integrates the emotional, cognitive and autonomic responses to pain.

Pain assessment and management

The most reliable indicator of the presence and degree of pain is reported by the person experiencing it. Pain must also be assessed. During the assessment process, there are a variety of considerations: language barriers, children and developmental stage, and those with hearing limitations or who are intubated. A variety of tools are used to assess pain. These tools include simple pictorial or numeric scales or mnemonics that can help convey vital information from the patient to the healthcare assistant or clinician (Figure 13.16). Culture, age and past experience with pain can also influence assessment findings.

Chronic pain causes fatigue and interferes with the routines of working, eating, sleeping and concentrating. In the case of cancer, chronic pain may become the central concern. The cancer may become secondary to pain for some stricken individuals, because it may be exacerbated by treatment and fear. Cancer-related pain can be acute or chronic, but accurate assessment of pain is essential as it influences treatment. Counselling and group therapy may help relieve some anxiety and uncertainty, especially in cases of little or no family support.

Pain management depends on a number of variables, but the focus is to control pain without serious side effects. Over-the-counter and prescription

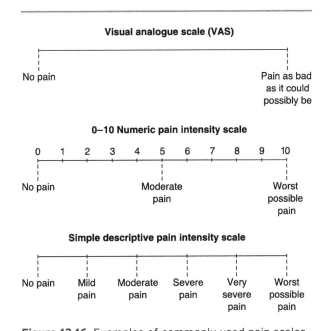

Figure 13.16 Examples of commonly used pain scales.

medications such as opiates are often needed to treat acute or chronic pain. See Table 13.2 for a summary of alternative treatments.

The body has its own endogenous opioid agents, called endorphins or enkephalins, to counteract pain-causing symptoms such as induced by substance P, an agent that is thought to be released from a pain source. However, it is the medication that tends to act on a specific target. Aspirin is a widely used drug; others include NSAIDs, like paracetamol, ibuprofen or naproxen, all of which work to reduce or stop pain primarily in the PNS. Opiates or narcotic-type drugs work best in the CNS by blocking or interfering with pain receptors or pathways (e.g. oxycodone or pethidine). Chronic pain requires stronger remedies like morphine.

Table 13.2 Alternative pain therapies.

Therapy	Methodology/purpose
Acupuncture	Ancient Eastern method may stimulate release of endorphins
Aromatherapy	Oils and scents along with bath or massage
Biofeedback therapy	Electrothermal devices plus training for pain (e.g. migraine)
Heat and cold packs	Pain relief in traumas such as sprains and burns
Humour	Acts as a distraction and comfort, at least temporarily
Hypnosis	Extends pain relief or blocks pain perception
Imagery	Induces relaxation; may induce endorphins and reduce stress
Massage	Promotes muscle relaxation and blood flow for comfort
Music and art	Provide soothing atmosphere in clinics and help to calm patient fears
Relaxation techniques	Reduce muscle tension and increase pain threshold; reflexology is an example
Transcendental meditation (TM)	Solitary introspection for calming relaxation
Transcutaneous electrical nerve stimulation (TENS)	Electrical stimulation through skin patches to interfere with pain release and timing activities
Yoga	Body manipulation, mind relaxation and mind control technique

DISEASES OF THE SPECIAL SENSES: EYE AND EAR

Special senses include the nose for olfaction or sense of smell; the tongue for gustatory or taste sensations; the eyes for vision; and the ears for acoustics or hearing. Diseases related to the nose and nasal cavity were discussed in Chapter 8; diseases of the eye and ear are covered in the sections that follow.

The eye

Our discussion starts with protective coverings of the eye, called eyelids and associate glands, and continues to the eye surface or conjunctiva, the clear area known as the cornea, the photoreceptors and the retina, and the optic nerve (Figure 13.17). The ear disorders will also be covered from the external to the internal components.

Eyelids and associate glands One of the most noticeable lesions found on the eyelid is the common **stye** or **hordeolum**. This reddish tender lump is caused by a local staphylococcus abscess on the upper or lower lid. Smaller styes tend to be external to the lid surface and on the margin, while internal

styes tend to jut toward the eye surface. Sometimes they resolve themselves, but when the lesion is large enough to cause irritation or a reduced field of vision, treatment is required. A warm compress or application of an antibiotic ointment usually resolves the situation. Because of oversight or lack of attention, these common bumps tend to recur, especially in youngsters.

Similar to the stye is a hardened internal lesion called a **chalazion**. This inflammation impacts a deeper oil gland (**meibomian**) and feels tender and irritated. The oil secreted by the meibomian gland is necessary to prevent the watery tear fluid from evaporating. When the oil is absent, a dry eye develops, which causes pain and potential for a coarse sclera and corneal surface or superficial cracks. As in cases of exophthalmia, found in Graves' disease (Chapter 12), eye drops help relieve the dryness. When given extended, albeit untreated, time, the condition may resolve itself, but hot compresses normally help, with a gentle massage, repeated twice daily for best results. If the condition does not improve, vision may be impaired and a corticosteroid injection may be needed or the cyst may need to be lanced to let it drain. Once resolved, the problem seems to subside and, with increased awareness, the occurrence is reduced.

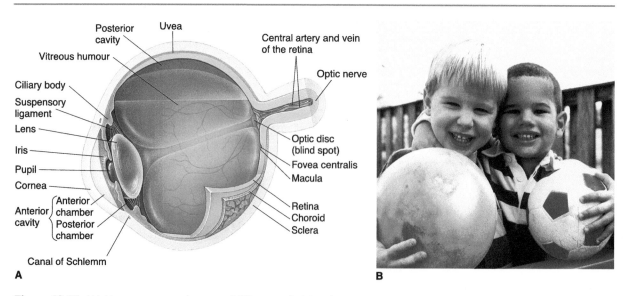

Figure 13.17 (A) Human eye anatomy and (B) normal vision image.
(National Eye Institute)

Blepharitis is a common chronic inflammation, with or without ulcers, often involving both eyelid margins and perhaps becoming bilateral (occurring in both eyes). This bacterially initiated problem resembles seborrhoea of the scalp and eyebrows or perhaps acne rosacea (see Chapter 16). Itching and burning sensations are caused by oozing pus, and a thick crust develops, especially after sleep. The potential for ulceration of the cornea is serious, and treatment is warranted. Antibiotic ointment such as polymyxin B may be used for known microbe types and, if other skin conditions are factors, they should be addressed as well. Preventive measures include good hygiene, with consistency, and proper training to keep hands away from nose, mouth and especially eyes.

Dacryocystitis is an infection and obstruction of the nasolacrimal apparatus for tear production and drainage. Common skin flora like *Staphylococcus aureus* or the beta version of streptococcus and yeast infection (e.g. *Candida albicans*) are all potential sources. Symptoms include swelling, tenderness and pain. If chronic, tearing and pus discharge are cause for surgical relief, and antibiotics may continue, although they may have been unable to dry up the ducting network initially. Spontaneous healing can occur in some patients.

Prevention of common infectious conditions is achieved through hygiene and retraining of old habits, like unnecessary finger and hand contact with the eye. If known allergies are recognised, they must be avoided or eliminated if possible.

Conjunctivitis Conjunctivitis is an inflammation of the conjunctiva, the superficial covering of the visible sclera (white of the eye) and the inner linings of the eyelids. Red, swollen eyes with discharge and some discomfort are the usual symptoms. About 30% of all eye complaints are conjunctivitis, commonly called 'pink eye', yet many cases go unreported, and children are the primary source group.

Various fumes, such as from peeled onions or bathroom cleansers, may initiate an inflammatory or allergic response. However, viruses and various bacteria, including the normal bacterial flora such as *Staphylococcus aureus*, or fungi commonly cause

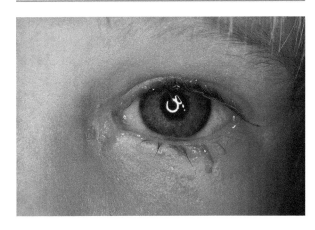

Figure 13.18 Conjunctivitis.
(© Dorling Kindersley)

conjunctivitis. Unfortunately, these viral and bacterial infections are quite contagious, and therefore patients, usually children, are instructed to stay home from school or social activities. Reinfections may occur owing to lack of hygiene and to rubbing or touching the eye unnecessarily. Often the inflammation subsides on its own accord, but it may progress into *inclusion conjunctivitis*, which is caused by particular bacteria (e.g. *Chlamydia trachomatis*) and is longer lasting. For diagnosis and determination of infective agents, ocular swabs are taken to culture and suggest favourable antidotes. Topical antibiotics or eye drops, such as chloramphenicol (even in viral cases, to prevent secondary infection) or antihistamines and cold compresses help control the 'pink eye' (see Figure 13.18).

Chronic conjunctivitis, or **trachoma**, results when the infecting agent invades the conjunctiva. These cases tend to be highly contagious and, when severe, may disrupt the corneal surface and impair vision. The infective agent in this case is *Chlamydia trachomatis*, mentioned previously, the same organism responsible for the STI chlamydia (see Chapter 11). Infected mothers pass on this infection to the newborn. Tetracycline is usually administered to resolve trachoma.

Prevention of conjunctivitis is best achieved by reducing hand to eye contact, disposing of contaminated materials such as contact lenses and beauty products (e.g. mascara), and avoiding known allergic agents or persons with conjunctivitis.

Glaucoma Glaucoma is an insidious, painless disease that typically results from pressure building up in the anterior chamber of the eye or the space in front of the lens. This condition is known as chronic glaucoma and will be discussed here; however, another condition is acute glaucoma, which is accompanied by intense pain and blurriness. In acute cases intraocular pressure must be relieved immediately to reduce pain and to save vision.

The aqueous humour made by the ciliary body apparatus is produced at a fairly constant rate and normally drains away. But in glaucoma, fluid accumulates and increases the pressure within the eye. Pressure exceeding twice the normal intraocular pressure (8–21 mmHg) causes the retina to start losing its ability to distinguish images clearly. This progression of events continues until a partial to total blindness develops. Peripheral vision is severely reduced if the condition is untreated; then it is lost and 'tunnel vision' ensues as the photoreceptors on the retina are destroyed and continue to deteriorate visual quality (eyesight) (Figure 13.19).

A glaucoma gene, *GLCA1*, on chromosome 1 may account for some of the 172 000 new referrals each year, of which about a third become confirmed cases in the UK. Worldwide, glaucoma affects about 66.8 million individuals. Most congenital glaucoma is hereditary, while secondary glaucoma is caused by systemic diseases, such as infections, or drugs like corticosteroids. This disease increases in prevalence over the age of 40. In South East Asia glaucoma is quite common, considering a host of tropical infections and lack of treatment. Individuals with a family history or with diabetes should have frequent eye checkups.

The ophthalmoscope is the primary portable tool used by the ophthalmologist to view the interior of the eyeball for general inspection. However, to diagnose glaucoma, a non-contact ('air-puff') **tonometer** helps to screen for the disease by bouncing a puff of air off the cornea that flattens it slightly and allows a quick register of intraocular pressure. After first using numbing droplets on the eye, a more accurate measurement is done with **applanation tonometry**, which allows the instrument to touch the cornea lightly. The pressure required to indent the corneal surface is measured, and using a slit lamp (magnifying) device allows the ophthalmologist to explore the whole interior of the eye with bright light and obtain a three-dimensional view. In this case, the lighted interior tends to show a cupping of the optic disc, where the optic nerve enters the back of the eye.

Drugs such as timolol reduce fluid production, and pilocarpine promotes aqueous humour flow. Surgery involves piercing the anterior chamber with a laser, which promotes draining and reduction in pressure and improves vision. Prevention is basically genetically determined but includes a healthy diet with adequate intake of vitamin A, and good vision care (e.g. reducing infections via limited hand–eye contact, and wearing eye protection such as sunglasses).

Figure 13.19 Glaucoma visual image reveals tunnel vision.
(National Eye Institute)

Uveitis The uvea is the second layer of the eye known as the vascular or pigmented layer and includes the ciliary body and the coloured part of the eye known as the iris. Inflammation of the uvea may be caused by infectious agents, especially in reduced immune conditions, but uveitis itself has an immunological or neoplastic basis.

Symptoms include pain, redness, photophobia and blurred vision. If the inflammatory attack is in front of the lens (anterior) or behind it (posterior), different approaches are taken to ensure the best outcome. Anterior inflammation accounts for about 90% of the cases and usually lends itself to topical corticosteroids. Posterior uveitis requires systemic (internal) medications or intravitreal (in uvea) corticosteroid therapy, and, if bacterial agents are present, then appropriate antibiotics are used. This primarily immune disorder is related to or accompanies many other conditions or diseases, from psoriasis to Crohn's disease. Prevalence is estimated at 38 per 100 000 in the western world, with approximately 9100 new cases per year in England and Wales.

Light and refractory distortions

Astigmatism Light enters the clear curved cornea. If the cornea is pitted from prior ulceration or is asymmetrical or has thick and thin sections, it transmits light to the lens and retina in irregular wavelengths. Similarly, if the lens is warped or irregular, the transmitted light is uneven. Both scenarios give a blurry or unclear image when the light (image) strikes the retinal surface. This refractory condition is called **astigmatism**. It may be associated with any other eye condition, like myopia, and may affect one eye or both. The objects viewed might be recognisable, but there is always some degree of distortion to the overall image. Corrective lenses, including contact lenses, help but may not fully repair the condition, especially if the irregularities are with the internal lens. Cornea adjustments may be made surgically, or the lens can be replaced. Most individuals tend to ignore the minor deficiency and adjust to it.

Myopia and hyperopia (nearsightedness and farsightedness)

The more common types of eye problems involve distance. An acuity test done by the famous Snellen chart (E letters) allows determination of a 20/20 (normal) or a range from 20/200 to 20/10 reading for different distance levels. Nearsightedness, or myopia, and farsightedness, or hyperopia, as well as astigmatism, described earlier, are outlined in Figure 13.20.

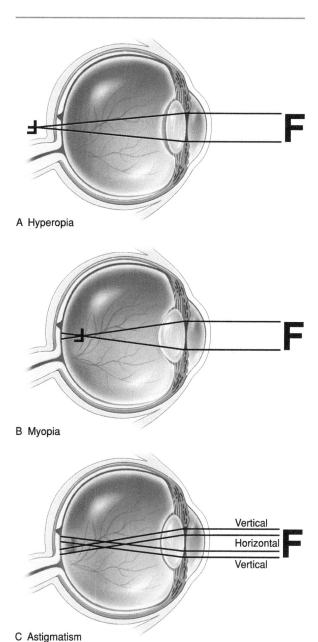

A Hyperopia

B Myopia

C Astigmatism

Figure 13.20 In hyperopia light rays focus behind the retina, making it difficult to focus on objects at close range. In myopia light rays focus in front of the retina, making it difficult to focus on objects that are far away. In astigmatism light rays do not uniformly focus on the eye owing to abnormal curvature of cornea or lens.

Compared to normal vision, myopia or nearsightedness is noticed when close objects are clear and sharp while more distance objects are blurred. The eyeball is longer than normal, so the image falls short (thus the term short/nearsightedness) and does not reach the retina sufficiently, leaving a blurry image. It may be that the lens is too thick and thus the image would fall in front of the retina. To correct myopia, a concave lens is required to stretch incoming light rays to reach the retina and give a clear picture. Approximately 5 million people in the UK have myopia.

In the case of hyperopia (hypermetropia), objects at a distance are clear, but those images close up are blurry. About twice as many people have hypermetropia as have myopia in the UK. The eyeball appears too short, or the lens may be too thin. A convex lens is required to bend the light waves more quickly or shorter to strike the retina in a clearly focused fashion. Contact lenses work well, and laser treatments may shave layers off the cornea or lens to improve sight. LASIK surgery, a type of cornea surgery, holds great promise for long-term relief. LASIK surgery eliminates or reduces use of eyeglasses or contact lenses for most normal activities requiring near- or far-sighted vision. For some tasks, reading glasses may still be required. With either case, astigmatism may be an additional part of the visual correction, and that would require a special lens or glasses to offer a sharper image at the retinal surface. The astigmatism may be in one or both eyes and be of varying degree.

Presbyopia Presbyopia is an age-related and refractive disorder. At about age 45, the crystalline lens of the eye loses its flexibility and causes a reduction in the ability to focus images on the retina. This may happen rather suddenly, but the lens has been growing from birth and continues to grow throughout life, so by the time of death the lens has increased in weight by about four times. This change is a normal modification to the eye caused by aging, and individuals notice the problem when they hold pictures and written material at arm's length to obtain a better view. Optometrists can fit corrective lens like bifocals or trifocals or contact lenses for better vision. Because things continue to change, so must the corrective lenses.

Cataracts Cataracts are the result of a clouding of the lens. There are three types of cataracts that correspond to the three layers of the lens. The outer layer is a clear membrane or capsule, the middle zone is composed of soft clear material called the cortex, and the core is the least flexible site called the nucleus. The cause of cataracts is not known, but they have been attributed to a congenital defect, eye trauma, the effects of toxins and aging. The main symptom is fading and distortion of vision. Additional lighting is useful early on, especially for printed material, and this helps clue the person as to an impending visual impairment.

By age 65, some degree of cataracts and thus impaired vision has occurred in a large portion of the population, increasing in numbers further after age 75. Usually by the eighth decade, cataracts have become more evident or ripe. A routine (general) eye examination, using ophthalmoscopy, normally detects early stages of cataracts. This detection allows planning for treatment if needed or preventative measures to reduce the progression of cataract development, such as avoiding bright light and wearing sunglasses. A new measuring device called an **aberrometer** allows a better record of the status of the eye and assists the preparation of LASIK surgery to match or exceed what glasses or contact lenses do for sight. The patient looks at a pattern of faint red lights, and the machine makes detailed optical measurements as it inspects the interior of the eyeball. This procedure is simple and painless. In the past, treatment was usually non-specific or withheld, and with time the lens was surgically replaced. Outpatient surgery for lens replacement, including lenses for 20/20 vision or bifocals, has become a routine procedure, and vision is restored to normal in patients 95% of the time. Prevention is almost impossible for an age-related condition or in the face of a concurrent disease (e.g. diabetes or syphilis). However, avoiding harmful drugs or chemicals and direct sunlight can postpone this common disorder (see Figure 13.21).

Retinal image defects

Macular degeneration Macular degeneration is the reduction or loss of acute vision. Macular degeneration develops in 10% of the elderly and affects both eyes, affecting only central vision and leaving

Figure 13.21 Cataracts show the whole image as blurry.
(National Eye Institute)

peripheral vision intact. There are two forms of macular degeneration: the atrophic (dry) version, comprising 70+% of the cases, and the exudative (wet, haemorrhagic) type, a more destructive version (see Figure 13.22).

Figure 13.22 Age-related macular degeneration demonstrating loss of central vision.
(National Eye Institute)

Causes for this degeneration are not well understood, but it is known that obstructed blood flow, followed by revascularisation (as occurs in atherosclerosis), compromises the area of the retina responsible for acute vision. Other contributing factors are injury, inflammation, infection and heredity.

Diagnosis is by direct eye examination with ophthalmoscope and fluorescein angiography, which reveal leaking vessels in the subretinal area. There is no cure for the atrophic case, but 5–10% reduction in the exudative condition can be accomplished by using an argon laser to cause photocoagulation.

Diabetic retinopathy About 40% of diabetes type 1 patients will be diagnosed with diabetic retinopathy within 3 years of diagnosis. Depending on the intensity of the diabetes and patient's age, it may be a mild abnormality or a major factor causing loss of eyesight. It is the leading cause of new blindness in adults aged 20–65. In type 2 diabetes, about 20% of cases have diabetic retinopathy at the time of diagnosis. Screening involves dilated pupils and ophthalmoscopy, which may become routine annual events with eye checkups. Special attention must be given to those pregnant or attempting to become pregnant. This monitoring is performed primarily through diabetes control measures, such as blood glucose levels and kidney functioning plus blood pressure measurements. In exudative cases, leakage can be abated by using an argon laser to cause photocoagulation. Prevention is unlikely considering the universal effect over the body that diabetes mellitus presents.

Retinitis pigmentosa Retinitis pigmentosa is a genetic disease either as a recessive or dominant trait on the X chromosome. Other forms may exist, but it is a rare, progressive retinal degeneration that eventually causes blindness. The symptoms of weakened sight start in childhood and slowly encroach peripherally and cause tunnel vision, somewhat like glaucoma. A special electroretinogram that measures the retina and its response to light determines the disease and its status. No particular treatment is known, although some success has been noted with fetal retinal tissue transplant. Retinal detachment is possible here as well, and that causes more complications for treatment.

The optic nerve may be a part of the visual disturbance pattern, and that may be caused by physical strain, such as trauma or pressure (stretching) in the event of exophthalmos, as found in hyperthyroidism. With various toxins (especially heavy metals), low oxygen levels and drugs (including Viagra), the optic nerve is sensitive to many factors injurious to eyesight. Blindness normally develops when light is blocked to the retina as in cataracts and when there is increased intraocular pressure as in glaucoma, optic nerve damage or image failure recognition by the occipital cortex. Regardless of cause, the best way to prevent visual impairment is to practise good hygiene (e.g. avoid unnecessary hand–eye contact), observe safety precautions and seek medical help with any noticeable eye problem.

The ear

Hearing loss is a major problem for those with normal acoustic function, and there are three categories of hearing loss: conductive, mainly a blockage or physical problem; sensory loss owing to inner ear elements being lost or compromised; and neural hearing loss from damage to the auditory nerve (VIII). Age can be a major factor in hearing disabilities, along with the environmental workplace and modern instrumentation, including mobile phones and personal audio devices that put a significant stress on hearing abilities. Almost 9 million people in the UK are deaf or have some hearing loss; that is, about one in seven of the population, particularly the elderly.

Conductive hearing loss is commonly caused by excess ear wax build-up (cerumen impaction), a tumour, or pus build-up in the auditory canal or middle ear from infection (external otitis, otitis media). The middle ear bony ossicles may stiffen as in arthritis, called **otosclerosis**, and a perforated ear drum is a frequent occurrence. All of these situations reduce hearing abilities and require different modes or procedures to correct them. External and middle ear infection are common events, especially in children, and these dysfunctional disorders are now addressed.

External ear The visible part of the external ear is known as the **auricle** or **pinna** and it enhances hearing perception by a small amount (2–4%). It assists hearing by collecting sound waves and funnelling them down the auditory canal and is subject to skin cancer, primarily from sun exposure, and trauma from accidents or athletic activities, e.g. rugby. Skin cancer is treated mainly by surgery. Trauma cases may require surgery as well and to prevent disfigurement (such as a 'cauliflower' appearance). Cosmetically, auricle design or size may be an issue, especially for children when the auricles are extra large or protrude and appear asymmetrical. Infections can occur when pierced ear ring sites are not properly cleaned, and some metals cause allergic reactions. Protecting the ear from severe environmental extremes and using ear plugs for noise reduction are effective preventive measures for reducing hearing loss (see Figure 13.23).

Cerumen impaction Wax is necessary for the soft texture and flexibility of the ear drum. However, cerumen impaction or excess wax build-up may recur, especially in youngsters or the elderly. Upon first appearance of wax building, better hygiene is required. The build-up is usually alleviated by heated water, oil treatment, hydrogen peroxide (3%) or alcohol drops as simple remedies. However, on occasion a suction action or mechanical removal is necessary. It is imperative to have an intact ear drum when performing any treatment, and be sure to dry the ear area completely following treatment. Prevention is possible through routinely checking the ear canal for signs of wax accumulation.

External otitis External otitis, or 'swimmer's ear', is an infection caused by bacteria and fungi. Symptoms and signs include pain, pruritis, fever and (temporarily) hearing loss.

The pathogens responsible for external otitis are found in contaminated swimming pools or beaches. Drying the external ear opening after bathing or swimming and cleaning ear phones,

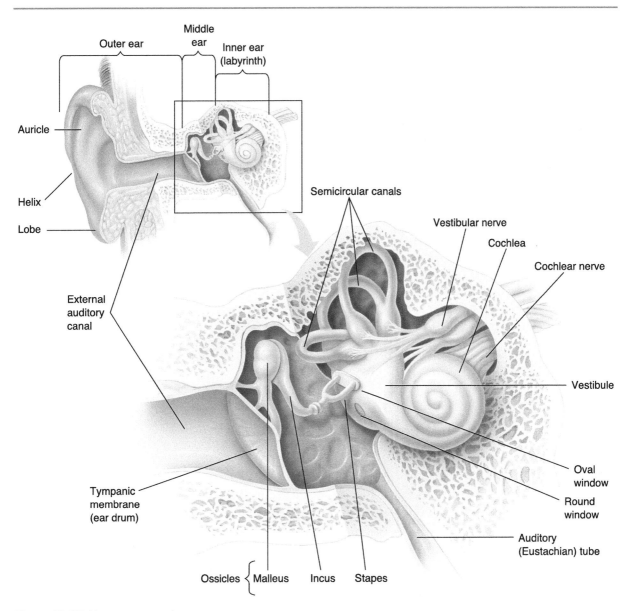

Figure 13.23 Human ear anatomy.

ear plugs and ear muffs can prevent it. Treatment with antibiotics is effective for bacterial infections, but some fungus infections may be more stubborn to control.

Otitis media Acute otitis media is a middle ear infection that affects primarily infants and children because of weak immune systems and perhaps the lack of breastfeeding. Symptoms include pain and oedema, with pus and, left unchecked, the condition may cause perforation of the tympanic membrane (ear drum). Otitis media often follows pneumonia or an upper respiratory tract infection (URTI), such as laryngitis. Most often, bacteria are the cause. Children are more susceptible than adults to middle ear infections because their nearly horizontal auditory tubes prevent adequate drainage. Diagnosis is primarily performed by observation of pus in the ear canal and complaint of earache. Pain can be controlled with analgesics, and swelling is reduced by use of decongestants. To relieve pressure and allow pus to drain, small ear tubes like tiny cylinders are placed through the ear drum (tympanic membrane) to allow air into the middle ear. They are called tympanostomy tubes or myringotomy tubes, or grommets. In recurrent cases, scarring of the ear drum, auditory ossicles and inner ear components can occur. There is potential for invasion of the nearby mastoid area, a honeycombed sinus area, and this penetration results in **mastoiditis**. With mastoiditis comes a fever and the possibility of brain infection or abscess formation because of the relatively thin membrane between the sinus area and the brain vault. In developing countries with inadequate access to healthcare and antibiotics, chronic otitis media and its complications is very common among both adults and children. Penicillin-type antibiotics help, but in some resistant cases, such as those caused by *Pseudomonas aeruginosa*, stronger agents are required.

For chronic otitis media there may be relief. A clinical test study published in 2005, using a device called the EarPopper, had an efficacy (effectiveness) rate of about 85% for those tested. This tool sends a gentle stream of air into the nasal cavity and, as the individual swallows, it forces the Eustachian tube (or auditory tube) open and equalises the pressure within the middle ear. If fluid is present, it may take two treatments per day for a few weeks, but the benefit is that ear surgery is not required. This device is safe, basically pain-free, and can be used by anyone, including children.

Inner ear The inner ear consists of the semicircular canals (which register changes in equilibrium) and the snail-like device called the cochlea. The semicircular canals give a sense of balance and of being upright. In addition, at the base where the three semicircular canals meet and form a connection with the cochlea, stiff ciliated (brush-like) elements attached to neurons line a common chamber. In this same chamber of fluid are grains called **otoliths** that tumble or float down like an hourglass and thereby stimulate the sensory elements to signal the brain about body positioning or orientation (e.g. turned head). Along with the cerebellum and visual cues, the body maintains a normal standing or sitting posture or comprehends body location.

Some infections may interfere with the functioning of semicircular canals. In the case of fever or various drug interactions and electrolyte imbalances, the viscosity of the internal fluid may be altered. Vertigo or dizziness may cause nausea, headache or accidental stumbling or falling. Acute cases of imbalance that may become episodic or longer term vertigo need to be addressed.

The cochlea houses coiled tubes filled with fluid that rushes over miniature hair cells collectively called the **organ of Corti** which triggers signals to the auditory nerve. When the organ of Corti is damaged or lost, the hearing loss is permanent. Loud noises or sounds from heavy equipment, airplanes and loud music or ototoxic drugs like some chemotherapy drugs, and various infective agents leave a scar on the hearing apparatus.

As with sight and age, hearing too has its limitations; this is called **presbycusis**. This condition is the most common cause of sensorineural hearing loss in adults. The actual cause is not known, but the condition tends to run in families and progresses with age. Constant exposure to loud noises gives ample reason to wear devices (ear plugs) to protect the natural hearing mechanism. About 25% of those aged 65–75 have measurable hearing loss, in part due to age, and about half of those over age 75 have presbycusis. Hearing aids help restore some sound, but clarity is somewhat sacrificed.

Neural loss involving the eighth cranial nerve (vestibulocochlear) or auditory nerve has many possibilities. If the nerve is damaged by trauma, high fever, toxins or other agents, the loss may be permanent.

Deafness can have a genetic component, e.g. when a baby is born deaf, and cochlear implants can be used to overcome deafness. Inheritance of deafness may be either dominant or recessive, and over 100 genes have been identified as instrumental in this deficiency. The *connexin-26* mutation has been suggested as a prevalent form of recessive hearing loss. Mitochondrial (cell organelle) disorders and hearing loss also play a significant role in the complex mechanism of auditory challenge. Whatever the circumstance, it is critical to save and protect all areas of the auditory pathway for the melodies of sound; cochlear implants are a viable alternative when hearing is lost.

Ménière's disease The occurrence of **Ménière's disease** is about 1 per 1000 and it usually occurs in the mid to late forties. Primarily considered idiopathic, some cases may be initiated by trauma, tumour or autoimmune diseases that impact the cochlear apparatus whereby fluid and delicate sensory hairs are altered or degenerated. Ménière's disease is characterised by intermittent hearing loss, tinnitus (see below) and episodes of vertigo or dizziness. Therapy is focused on vertigo. Diuretics and restricted salt intake control fluid levels and short-term glucocorticoids reduce inflammatory activity. Surgery may be a later option, but some loss of hearing may occur. Many individuals live with this disease if dizzy spells are reasonably under control.

Tinnitus **Tinnitus** is defined as the perception of ringing, buzzing or roaring sounds from an environment void of sound. The cause or pathophysiology of tinnitus is not well known, perhaps because there are many causes and tinnitus may be just one indication among many of other disease attributes. At least 1% of the UK population have tinnitus, and some have it severely enough that it interferes with daily life. This development may involve either conductive or sensorineural hearing loss. A full examination of the ear, nose and throat is required to discern problems such as infection, trauma or growths, plus family history and any drug regimen. Diagnosis is similar to other ear investigation and begins with the **Weber and Rinne tuning fork** test. Not only are the frequencies or pitch of the sound noted, but more so, whether the limitation is conductive or sensorineural. The stem of the vibrating fork is placed on the skull near the mastoid process (just behind and under the ear), or maybe the teeth, to tell if a sound is louder or softer compared to the sound in air. If the sound is louder in air versus the contacted bone, then it appears to be a sensorineural insufficiency, and if louder by bone contact, it appears to be a conduction defect.

Tinnitus is known to be affected by, or is part of, a hearing loss problem because of excessive loud noise exposure, poor reaction to some medications or various other health concerns. Treatment by the **otolaryngologist** includes hearing aids to overpower the background sounds, sound-masking devices to cancel or reduce the ringing noises, amplifier devices on phones, or electronic equipment to pick up better quality sound, plus medications and relaxing techniques. People with tinnitus should avoid loud sounds and be patient; some may find that lipoflavanoid supplementation is helpful. Lipoflavanoid is a dietary supplement used since the 1960s to specifically improve the microcirculation within the inner ear. Therefore, the flexibility of the sensory hair cells responsible for sound transmission to the brain is maintained and the fluid within the cochlear canals flows easier. Lipoflavanoid improves inner ear health and reduces the intensity of ear ringing found in tinnitus as well as symptoms found in Ménière's syndrome.

All senses make for a more enjoyable life. Any reduced stress promotes better homeostasis, and that means a healthier and better existence. The olfactory sensation, mentioned in Chapter 8, may add pleasure or displeasure to the environment and is necessary for detecting methane gas or rotten odours from spoiled food sources; thus a sense of smell could help prevent illness or save a life. Similarly, the sense of taste (gustatory) is necessary to detect rotten, toxic or pleasurable attributes of our living arena. Taste and smell often diminish with age, disease and drugs like chemotherapy treatments. Zinc supplements seem to offer some relief in the case of reduced gustatory abilities and allow for a more pleasant taste of life.

AGE-RELATED DISEASES

Neurological disease affects individuals at all stages of life. Glaucoma and cataracts are age-related visual problems, as is presbyopia, a lens condition that occurs usually in the mid 40s. In presbyopia, the lens becomes less resilient and remains relatively flat, leaving distance vision intact but impairing near vision. Corrective lenses are very common after age 43–45. Macular degeneration typically comes along with age, as do cataracts and difficulty hearing (called presbycusis). Tinnitus, an ear ringing sensation, normally develops in later years owing to environmental or unknown factors. Cranial nerve dysfunction usually occurs in young and middle-aged adults. Alzheimer's disease (see Chapter 14) is a prominent concern for the elderly. The incidence of dementia and Parkinson's disease increases with age. In trisomy 21 (Down's syndrome), patients who live past age 45 tend to develop dementia.

Finally, with age, the 3-pound brain reduces in weight and size, with concurrent loss of neurons and synapses. Thus, it is understandable that functional losses in hearing, sight and coordination will be experienced in the elderly. Reaction times are reduced, and so is agility, which increases risks for injury.

Resource

National Institutes of Allergy and Infectious Diseases: *www.nei.nih.gov*

DISEASES AT A GLANCE Nervous system and special senses

DISEASE	AETIOLOGY	SIGNS AND SYMPTOMS	DIAGNOSIS	TREATMENT	PREVENTION	LIFESPAN
Glioma, glioblastoma	Idiopathic	Severe headache, personality changes, loss of speech, unsteady movement, seizures, coma	CT scan, MRI	Surgery, chemotherapy, radiation	Uncertain	Any age, usually adult
Meningitis	Bacterial, viral	High fever, chills, severe headache, stiff neck, nausea, vomiting, rash, delirium, convulsions, coma	Lumbar puncture	Antibiotics if bacterial infection	Be aware, avoid contact	Can occur at any age
Encephalitis	Viral	Mild to severe headache, fever, cerebral dysfunction, disordered thought, seizures, persistent drowsiness, delirium, coma	Lumbar puncture	Control fever, control fluid and electrolyte balance, monitor respiratory and kidney function	Depends on circumstance	Can occur at any age
Poliomyelitis	Viral	Stiff neck, fever, headache, sore throat, GI disturbances, paralysis may develop	Physical examination	Supportive; preventive vaccination	Vaccine	Usually younger to early adult
Tetanus	*Clostridium tetani*	Rigidity of muscles, painful spasms and convulsions, stiff neck, difficulty swallowing, clenched jaws	Physical examination, patient history	Antitoxin, symptom relief, preventive vaccination	Vaccine	Can occur at any age
Rabies	Viral	Fever, pain, mental derangement, rage, convulsions, paralysis, profuse sticky saliva, throat muscle spasm produces hydrophobia	Physical examination, history of animal bite	Vaccination before disease develops; fatal once CNS involved	Vaccine, be alert	Can occur at any age
Shingles	Varicella, herpes zoster	Painful rash of small water blisters with red rim, lesions follow a sensory nerve, confined to one side of body, severe itching, scarring	Physical examination	Alleviation of symptoms and pain relief, steroids	Avoid contact, vaccine	Usually 50+
Reye's syndrome	Idiopathic or viral; Epstein-Barr, influenza B, varicella	Persistent vomiting, rash, lethargy about 1 week after a viral infection, may progress to coma; linked with use of aspirin in children under 16 years of age	Patient history, liver enlargement, hypoglycaemia, ammonia in blood	Supportive; close monitoring necessary	Avoid aspirin in children, seek care	Infants, young children
Abscess	Pyogenic bacteria	Fever, headache	Lumbar puncture	Surgical draining of abscess, antibiotics	Quick treatment	Can occur at any age
Multiple sclerosis (MS)	Idiopathic, suspect viral or autoimmune	Muscle impairment, double vision, nystagmus, loss of balance, poor coordination, tingling and numbing sensation, shaking tremor, muscular weakness, emotional changes, remission and exacerbation	Physical examination, patient history, MRI	None effective; physical therapy and muscle relaxants, steroids, counselling	Basically autoimmune and polygenetic	Midlife
Amyotrophic lateral sclerosis (ALS), or Lou Gehrig's disease	Idiopathic	Disturbed motility; fasciculations; atrophy of muscles in hands, forearms and legs; impaired speech and swallowing; death from pulmonary failure in 3-4 years	Electromyelography (EMG)	Supportive	Uncertain	Midlife

DISEASES AT A GLANCE Nervous system and special senses (continued)

DISEASE	AETIOLOGY	SIGNS AND SYMPTOMS	DIAGNOSIS	TREATMENT	PREVENTION	LIFESPAN
Huntington's disease (Huntington's chorea)	Genetic	Involuntary, rapid, jerky movements; speech loss; difficulty swallowing; personality changes; carelessness; poor judgement; impaired memory; mental incompetence	Patient history (inherited disease) and physical examination	No cure; genetic counselling for family	Totally genetic	Age 35+
Convulsion: epilepsy	Trauma, chemical, idiopathic, genetic	Involuntary contractions or series of contractions; a seizure is a sign of illness, not a disease. Petit mal: brief loss of consciousness, 'absence seizure'. Grand mal: often preceded by aura (various sensations), total loss of consciousness, generalised convulsions, hypersalivation; incontinence may occur	Observation of seizure, electroencephalogram (EEG), X-ray, family history, CT scan, MRI	Removal of cause once detected; anticonvulsive drugs	Avoid cranial trauma; use helmet or headgear	Can occur at any age
Spina bifida	Congenital, lack of folate	Opening in vertebral canal. Spina bifida occulta – hidden; meningocele – meninges protrude; meningomyelocele – nerve elements protrude; myelocele – nerve tissue disorganised	Physical examination, CT scan, MRI, EEG	Surgical, physical therapy	Variable, folate supplements	Middle-aged mother
Hydrocephalus	Congenital, idiopathic	Enlarged head develops	Physical examination, CT scan, MRI, lumbar puncture	Implant shunt to drain CSF	Variable to pathogen exposure	Can occur at any age, but more prevalent among newborns
Cerebral palsy	Birth trauma, rubella infection	Seizures, visual or auditory impairment, speech defects. Spastic – muscles tense, reflexes exaggerated. Athetoid – uncontrollable, persistent movements, tremor. Atactic – poor balance, poor muscular coordination, staggering gait	Physical examination	Muscle relaxants, anticonvulsive drugs, casts, braces, traction, surgery, physical therapy	Variable, birth caution	Can occur at any age
Transient ischaemic attacks (TIA), 'mini strokes'	Ischaemia, aneurysm, hypertension	Visual disturbances, transient muscle weakness on one side, sensory loss on one side, slurred speech; attacks last minutes to hours, average 15 minutes	Cerebral angiogram, CT scan	Depends on cause; surgical treatment of blocked vessels	Blood pressure monitoring, uncertain	Usually middle age
Cerebrovascular accident (CVA) stroke, brain attack	Trauma	Severe, sudden headache; muscular weakness or paralysis; disturbance of speech; loss of consciousness	Angiography, CT scan, MRI	Clot-dissolving drugs, surgery, endarterectomy	Uncertain, family history, keep low blood pressure levels	Usually mid life+
Alzheimer's disease	Idiopathic, but genetically connected	Memory loss, moody, indigent	Behavioural, clinical screening	Care facilities, medications	None with long survival	Onset middle age, progressive with time

DISEASES AT A GLANCE Nervous system and special senses (continued)

DISEASE	AETIOLOGY	SIGNS AND SYMPTOMS	DIAGNOSIS	TREATMENT	PREVENTION	LIFESPAN
Special senses: eye						
Conjunctivitis	Viral, bacterial	Inflamed eye surface, oozing	Eye inspection, environment, eye fluids	None or ointment or eye drops	Contagious, avoid contact	Usually young child, but not determined by age
Glaucoma	Poor aqueous fluid drainage	Elevate intraocular pressure, dim vison	Ophthalmoscope and slit-scope	Eye drops	None, 10% genetic	Middle age+
Uveitis	Infectious agents	Eye discharge, pain, low vision	Eye examination	Corticoids	Basically autoimmune	Variable
Astigmatism	Irregular cornea or lens	Blurry vision	Chart examination, eye inspection	Corrective lenses	None	Variable
Cataracts	Cloudy lens	Blurred, dim vision	Ophthalmoscope	Some laser, lens replacement	None, avoid sunlight, STIs	Usually elderly
Macular degeneration	Idiopathic	Central vision lost	Ophthalmoscope	Non-specific	None	Older persons
Diabetic retinopathy	Diabetes	Blurred, cloudy vision to blinded	Ophthalmoscope and fluorescein angiography	Some laser, control diabetes and blood pressure	Perhaps control diabetes	More likely with aging
Retinitis pigmentosa	X chromosome	Weakened sight gradual blindness	Electroretinogram	Non-specific	None	From birth
Special senses: ear						
External otitis	Infection	Discharge, pus	Ear inspection	Antibiotic, cleanse area	Depends, use good hygiene, keep ear canal dry	Can occur at any age
Otitis media	Infection	Internal fluid pressure, fever	Ear inspection	Drain tube, antibiotics	Depends, use good hygiene	Children+
Presbycusis	Increased age	Hard of hearing	Audio testing	Hearing aids	None	Worse with age
Ménière's disease	Idiopathic, trauma, autoimmune?	Vertigo, disorientated, tinnitus	Hearing test and examination	Glucocorticoids, low salt diet	Uncertain	Age 40+
Tinnitus	Idiopathic, may be blood pressure-related, loud sounds	Ringing, roaring internal sounds without real sounds externally	Hearing test	Sound aids, low sound makers for interference	Depends	Usually middle aged, but expected in younger people following loud music performances

INTERACTIVE EXERCISES

Cases for critical thinking

1. John has had a severe headache for the past 12 hours, a fever of 102°F, plus a stiff neck. Following a lumbar puncture, *Streptococcus pneumoniae* was found in culture along with low sugar levels and higher protein values. What disease best explains these findings? What is the prognosis and treatment?

2. At age 78, Karen started rubbing her eyes and constantly cleaning her (old) glasses for a better view. The right eye particularly was not very good, and she hoped the problem, which she first noticed months ago, would finally go away. The vision in the right eye was foggy, dim and not focused. There was essentially no pain. What do the symptoms suggest? What are the prognosis and treatments for this woman?

3. Trevor complained of an earache, and after a recent bout with a bad cold, he was rather irritable. The ear was 'beet red' and felt warm. He could hardly hear on that side, but he knew there was nothing intentionally or accidentally poked into the ear. What disease best explains these symptoms? Give some recommendations for treatment.

Multiple choice

1. What is the infective agent for rabies?

    a. bacterium   b. virus
    c. fungus   d. tick

2. Which of the following may cause epilepsy?

    a. a birth trauma
    b. injury to the brain
    c. a penetrating wound
    d. all of these

3. What functions are controlled by the brainstem?

    a. sensory function   b. muscle action
    c. memory   d. heart rate and breathing

4. What is called an acute inflammation of the first two meninges of the brain and spinal cord, the pia mater and the arachnoid?

    a. thrombophlebitis   b. meningitis
    c. prostatitis   d. encephalitis

5. Which of the following is true of polio?

    a. it is caused by a virus
    b. it affects sensory neurons
    c. it is found in most people by age 80
    d. it was wiped out in 1976

6. Which of the following applies to MS?

    a. it occurs only in males
    b. it occurs primarily in east European cultures
    c. it results from a damaged myelin sheath
    d. it strikes adults age 20 or beyond

7. Within 3-4 hours, what clot buster may be used to treat the most common form of CVA?

    a. aspirin   b. TPA
    c. ATP   d. haemolase

8. What disease has a seizure symptom known as petit mal?

    a. polio   b. MS
    c. epilepsy   d. encephalitis

9. What is the lesion in Parkinson's disease?

    a. no dopamine   b. no myelin
    c. autoimmunity   d. cerebral blood clot

10. Paul, in Year 7, woke one morning to discover a blood-shot right eye and a yellowish mass near the medial corner of his eye. What is the correct diagnosis?

    a. common cold   b. trachoma
    c. conjunctivitis   d. osteitis

True or false

_____ 1.   Rabies is a viral infection.

_____ 2.   The Sabin vaccine works in the digestive tract.

_____ 3.   Oxygen under high pressure is effective in treating rabies.

_____ 4.   Blood is not normally found in cerebrospinal fluid.

_____ 5.   Dopamine deficiency causes epilepsy.

_____ 6.   Transient ischaemic attacks are characterised by loss of consciousness.

_____ 7.   An aura is a flashback of previous contusion events.

_____ 8.   Viral meningitis requires quarantine isolation procedures.

_____ 9.   Excess Dilantin may cause Parkinson's disease.

_____ 10. Conjunctivitis is usually a viral attack in adults.

Fill-ins

1.   _____, commonly called lockjaw, is an infection of nerve tissue caused by the tetanus bacillus that lives in the intestines of animals and human beings.

2.   Amyotrophic lateral sclerosis is diagnosed by _____.

3.   _____ _____ is a chronic, progressive disease of the central nervous system with myelin destruction.

4.   _____ _____, also known as shaking palsy, is a disease of brain degeneration that appears gradually and progresses slowly.

5.   The common drug given to victims of Parkinson's disease is _____.

6.   _____ headaches are severe, are unilateral, involve the periorbital and orbital area, and typically occur in men.

7.   _Tic douloureux_, or _____ _____, causes severe pain elicited from cranial nerve V.

8.   _____ _____ is a unilateral dysfunction of muscles in the face that leaves the person with slurred speech and a watery eye.

9.   _____ is called Lou Gehrig's disease.

10. _____ is the worst form of spina bifida.

Labelling exercise

What processes does each labelled part of the diagram control?

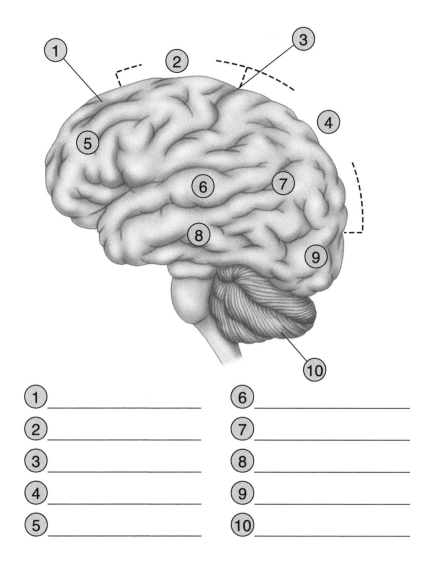

1 _____   6 _____

2 _____   7 _____

3 _____   8 _____

4 _____   9 _____

5 _____   10 _____

Cancer

DNA Synthesis, Mitosis, and Meiosis

Cancer cells divide
when they should not.

SPL/Photo Researchers, Inc.

LEARNING OUTCOMES

LO1 Describe the cellular basis of cancer.

LO2 Compare and contrast benign and malignant tumors.

LO3 List several risk factors for cancer development.

LO4 List the normal functions of cell division.

LO5 Describe the structure and function of chromosomes.

LO6 Outline the process of DNA replication.

LO7 Describe the events that occur during interphase of the cell cycle.

LO8 Diagram two chromosomes as they proceed through mitosis of the cell cycle.

LO9 Describe the process of cytokinesis in animal and plant cells.

LO10 Describe how the cell cycle is regulated and how dysregulation can lead to tumor formation.

LO11 Explain how genes and environment both impact cancer risk.

LO12 Discuss the various methods of cancer detection and treatment.

LO13 Explain what types of cells undergo meiosis, the end result of this process, and how meiosis increases genetic diversity.

LO14 Diagram four chromosomes from a diploid organism undergoing meiosis.

LO15 Explain the significance of crossing over and random alignment in terms of genetic diversity.

Nicole's early college career was similar to that of most students. She enjoyed her independence and the wide variety of courses required for her double major in biology and psychology. She worried about her grades and finding ways to balance her coursework with her social life. She also tried to find time for lifting weights in the school's athletic center and snowboarding at a local ski hill. Some weekends, to take a break from school, she would ride the bus home to see her family.

Managing to get schoolwork done, see friends and family, and still have time left to exercise had been difficult, but possible, for Nicole during her first two years at school. That changed drastically during her third year of school.

One morning in October of her junior year, Nicole began having severe pains in her abdomen. The first time this happened, she was just beginning an experiment in her cell biology laboratory. Hunched over and sweating, she barely managed to make it through her two-hour biology lab. Over the next few days, the pain intensified so much that she was unable to walk from her apartment to her classes without stopping several times to rest.

Later that week, as she was preparing to leave for class, the pain was so severe that she had to lie down in the hallway of her apartment. When her roommate got home a few minutes later, she took Nicole to the student health center for an emergency visit. The physician at the health center first determined that Nicole's appendix had not burst and then made an appointment for Nicole to see a gynecologist the next day.

After hearing Nicole's symptoms, the gynecologist pressed on her abdomen and felt what he

Nicole got sick during her junior year of college.

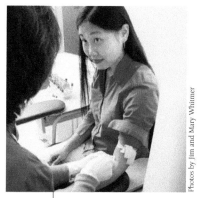
She had to undergo some procedures to see if she had cancer.

She wants to understand why she got cancer.

thought was a mass on her right ovary. He used a noninvasive procedure called ultrasound to try to get an image of her ovary. This procedure requires the use of high-frequency sound waves. These waves, which cannot be heard by humans, bounce off tissues and produce a pattern of echoes that can be used to create a picture called a sonogram. Healthy tissues, fluid-filled cysts, and tumors all look different on a sonogram.

Nicole's sonogram convinced her gynecologist that she had a large growth on her ovary. He told her that he suspected this growth was a *cyst,* or fluid-filled sac. Her gynecologist told her that cysts often go away without treatment, but this one seemed to be quite large and should be surgically removed.

Even though the idea of having an operation was scary for Nicole, she was relieved to know that the pain would stop. Her gynecologist also assured her that she had nothing to worry about because cysts are not cancerous. A week after the abdominal pain began, Nicole's gynecologist removed the cyst and her completely engulfed right ovary through an incision just below her navel.

After the operation, Nicole's gynecologist assured her that the remaining ovary would compensate for the missing ovary by ovulating (producing an egg cell) every month. He added that he would have to monitor her remaining ovary carefully to see that it did not become cystic or, even worse, cancerous. She could not afford to lose another ovary if she wanted to have children someday.

Monitoring her remaining ovary involved monthly visits to her gynecologist's office, where Nicole had her blood drawn and analyzed. The blood was tested for the level of a protein called CA125, which is produced by ovarian cells. Higher-than-normal CA125 levels usually indicate that the ovarian cells have increased in size or number and are thus associated with the presence of an ovarian tumor.

Nicole went to her scheduled checkups for five months after the original surgery. The day after her March checkup, Nicole received a message from her doctor asking that she come to see him the next day. Because she needed to study for an upcoming exam, Nicole tried to push aside her concerns about the appointment. By the time she arrived at her gynecologist's office, she had convinced herself that nothing serious could be wrong. She thought a mistake had probably been made and that he just wanted to perform another blood test.

The minute her gynecologist entered the exam room, Nicole could tell by his demeanor that something was wrong. As he started speaking to her, she began to feel very anxious—when he said that she might have a tumor on her remaining ovary, she could not believe her ears. When she heard the words *cancer* and *biopsy,* Nicole felt as though she was being pulled underwater. She could see that her doctor was still talking, but she could not hear or understand him. She felt too nauseated to think clearly, so she excused herself from the exam room, took the bus home, and immediately called her parents.

After speaking with her parents, Nicole realized that she had many questions to ask her doctor. She did not understand how it was possible for such a young woman to have lost one ovary to a cyst and then possibly to have a tumor on the other ovary. She wondered how this tumor would be treated and what her prognosis would be. Before seeing her gynecologist again, Nicole decided to do some research in order to make a list of questions for her doctor.

1 What Is Cancer?

Cancer is a disease that begins when a single cell replicates itself although it should not. **Cell division** is the process a cell undergoes to make copies of itself. This process is normally regulated so that a cell divides only when more cells are required and when conditions are favorable for division. A cancerous cell is a rebellious cell that divides without being given the go-ahead.

Tumors Can Be Cancerous

Unregulated cell division leads to a pileup of cells that form a lump or **tumor.** A tumor is a mass of cells; it has no apparent function in the body. Tumors that stay in one place and do not affect surrounding structures are said to be **benign.** Some benign tumors remain harmless; others become cancerous. Tumors that invade surrounding tissues are **malignant** or cancerous. The cells of a malignant tumor can break away and start new cancers at distant locations through a process called **metastasis** (**Figure 1**).

Cancer cells can travel virtually anywhere in the body via the lymphatic and circulatory systems. The lymphatic system collects fluids, or lymph, lost from blood vessels. The lymph is then returned to the blood vessels, thus allowing

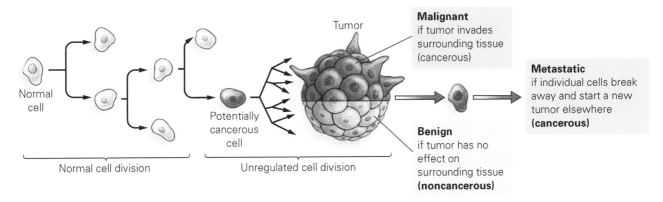

Figure 1 What is cancer? A tumor is a clump of cells with no function. Tumors may remain benign, or they can invade surrounding tissues and become malignant. Tumor cells may move, or metastasize, to other locations in the body. Malignant and metastatic tumors are cancerous.

cancer cells access to the bloodstream. Lymph nodes are structures that filter the lost fluids. When a cancer patient is undergoing surgery, the surgeon will often remove a few lymph nodes to see if any cancer cells are in the nodes. If cancer cells appear in the nodes, then some cells have left the original tumor and are moving through the bloodstream. If this has happened, cancerous cells likely have metastasized to other locations in the body.

When cancer cells metastasize, they can gain access not only to the **circulatory system,** which includes blood vessels to transport the blood, but also to the heart, which pumps the blood. Once inside a blood vessel, cancer cells can drift virtually anywhere in the body.

Cancer cells differ from normal cells in three ways: (1) They divide when they should not; (2) they invade surrounding tissues; and (3) they can move to other locations in the body. All tissues that undergo cell division are susceptible to becoming cancerous. However, there are ways to increase or decrease the probability of getting cancer.

Risk Factors for Cancer

Certain exposures and behaviors, called **risk factors,** increase a person's risk of obtaining a disease. General risk factors for virtually all cancers include tobacco use, a high-fat and low-fiber diet, lack of exercise, obesity, excess alcohol consumption, and increasing age. **Table 1** outlines other risk factors that are linked to particular cancers.

Tobacco Use. The use of tobacco of any type, whether via cigarettes, cigars, pipes, or chewing tobacco, increases your risk of many cancers. While smoking is the cause of 90% of all lung cancers, it is also the cause of about one-third of all cancer deaths. Cigar smokers have increased rates of lung, larynx, esophagus, and mouth cancers. Chewing tobacco increases the risk of cancers of the mouth, gums, and cheeks. People who do not smoke but who are exposed to secondhand smoke have increased lung cancer rates.

Tobacco smoke contains more than 20 known cancer-causing substances called **carcinogens.** For a substance to be considered carcinogenic, exposure to the substance must be correlated with an increased risk of cancer. Examples of carcinogens include cigarette smoke, radiation, ultraviolet light, asbestos, and some viruses.

The carcinogens that are inhaled during smoking come into contact with cells deep inside the lungs. Chemicals present in cigarettes and cigarette smoke have been shown to increase cell division, inhibit a cell's ability to repair damaged DNA, and prevent cells from dying when they should.

Stop & Stretch 1 In addition to dividing uncontrollably, cancer cells also fail to undergo a type of programmed cell death called *apoptosis,* during which a cell uses specialized chemicals to kill itself. Why do you think it is useful that our own cells can "commit suicide" in certain situations?

Chemicals in cigarette smoke also disrupt the transport of substances across cell membranes and alter many of the enzyme reactions that occur within cells. They have also been shown to increase the generation of *free radicals,* which remove electrons from other molecules. The removal of electrons from DNA or other molecules causes damage to these molecules—damage that, over time, may lead to cancer. Cigarette smoking provides so many different opportunities for DNA damage and cell damage that tumor formation and metastasis are quite likely for smokers. In fact, people who smoke cigarettes increase their odds of developing almost every cancer.

TABLE 1

Cancer risk. Risk factors and detection methods for particular cancers are given.

Cancer Location	Risk Factors	Detection	Comments
Ovary Oviduct Ovary	• Smoking • Mutation to *BRCA2* gene • Advanced age • Oral contraceptive use and pregnancy decrease risk	• Blood test for elevated CA125 level • Rectovaginal exam	Fifth leading cause of death among women in the United States
Breast	• Smoking • Mutation to *BRCA1* gene • High-fat, low-fiber diet • Use of oral contraceptives may slightly increase risk	• Monthly self-exams, look and feel for lumps or changes in contour • Mammogram	• Only 5% of breast cancers are due to *BRCA1* mutations • Second-highest cause of cancer-related deaths • 1% of breast cancer occurs in males
Cervix Uterus Cervix Vagina	• Smoking • Exposure to sexually transmitted human papilloma virus (HPV)	• Annual Pap smear tests for the presence of precancerous cells	• Precancerous cells can be removed by laser surgery or cryotherapy (freezing) before they become cancerous
Skin	• Smoking • Fair skin • Exposure to ultraviolet light from the sun or tanning beds	• Monthly self-exams, look for growths that change in size or shape	• Skin cancer is the most common of all cancers; usually curable if caught early
Blood (leukemia)	• Exposure to high-energy radiation such as that produced by atomic bomb explosions in Japan during World War II	• A sample of blood is examined under a microscope	• Cancerous white blood cells cannot fight infection efficiently; people with leukemia often succumb to infections

(continued)

TABLE 1 *(continued)*

Cancer risk. Risk factors and detection methods for particular cancers are given.

Cancer Location	Risk Factors	Detection	Comments
Lung	• Smoking • Exposure to secondhand smoke • Asbestos inhalation	• X-ray	• Lung cancer is the most common cause of death from cancer, and the best prevention is to quit, or never start, smoking
Colon and rectum Small intestine Colon	• Smoking • Polyps in the colon • Advanced age • High-fat, low-fiber diet	• Change in bowel habits • Colonoscopy is an examination of the rectum and colon using a lighted instrument	• Benign buds called polyps can grow in the colon; removal prevents them from mutating and becoming cancerous
Prostate Bladder Prostate Rectum	• Smoking • Advanced age • High-fat, low-fiber diet	• Blood test for elevated level of prostate-specific antigen (PSA) • Physical exam by physician, via rectum	• More common in African American men than Asian, white, or Native American men
Testicle Testicle Scrotum	• Abnormal testicular development	• Monthly self-exam, inspect for lumps and changes in contour	• Testicular cancer accounts for only 1% of all cancers in men but is the most common form of cancer found in males between the ages of 15 and 35

A High-Fat, Low-Fiber Diet. Cancer risk may also be influenced by diet. The American Cancer Society recommends eating at least 5 servings of fruits and vegetables every day as well as 6 servings of food from other plant sources, such as breads, cereals, grains, rice, pasta, or beans. Plant foods are low in fat and high in fiber. A diet high in fat and low in fiber is associated with increased risk of cancer. Fruits and vegetables are also rich in *antioxidants*. These substances help to neutralize the electrical charge on free radicals and thereby prevent the free radicals from taking electrons from other molecules, including DNA. There is some evidence that antioxidants may help prevent certain cancers by minimizing the number of free radicals that may damage the DNA in our cells.

Lack of Exercise. Regular exercise decreases the risk of most cancers, partly because exercise keeps the immune system functioning effectively. The immune system helps destroy cancer cells when it can recognize them as foreign to the host body. Unfortunately, since cancer cells are actually your own body's cells run amok, the immune system cannot always differentiate between normal cells and cancer cells.

Obesity. Exercise also helps prevent obesity, which is associated with increased risk for many cancers, including cancers of the breast, uterus, ovary, colon, gallbladder, and prostate. Because fatty tissues can store hormones, the abundance of fatty tissue has been hypothesized to increase the odds of hormone-sensitive cancers such as breast, uterine, ovarian, and prostate cancer.

Excess Alcohol Consumption. Drinking alcohol is associated with increased risk of some types of cancer. Men who want to decrease their cancer risk should have no more than two alcoholic drinks a day, and women one or none. People who both drink and smoke increase their odds of cancer in a multiplicative rather than additive manner. In other words, if one type of cancer occurs in 10% of smokers and in 2% of drinkers, someone who smokes and drinks multiplies chances of developing cancer to a rate that is closer to 20% than 12%. The risk factor percentages are multiplied rather than added.

Increasing Age. As you age, your immune system weakens, and its ability to distinguish between cancer cells and normal cells decreases. This weakening is part of the reason many cancers are far more likely in elderly people. Additional factors that help explain the higher cancer risk with increasing age include cumulative damage. If we are all exposed to carcinogens during our lifetime, then the longer we are alive, the greater the probability that some of those carcinogens will mutate genes involved in regulating the cell cycle. Also, because multiple mutations are necessary for a cancer to develop, it often takes many years to progress from the initial mutation to a tumor and then to full-blown cancer. Scientists estimate that most cancers large enough to be detected have been growing for at least five years and are composed of close to one billion cells.

Nicole's cancer affected ovarian tissue. Why might ovarian cells be more likely to become cancerous than some other types of cells? Cells that divide frequently are more prone to cancer than those that don't divide often. When an egg cell is released from the ovary during ovulation, the tissue of the ovary becomes perforated. Cells near the perforation site undergo cell division to heal the damaged surface of the ovary. For Nicole, these cell divisions may have become uncontrolled, leading to the growth of a tumor.

2 Passing Genes and Chromosomes to Daughter Cells

Most cell division does not lead to cancer. Cell division produces new cells to heal wounds, replace damaged cells, and help organisms grow and reproduce themselves. Each of us begins life as a single fertilized egg cell that undergoes millions of rounds of cell division to produce all the cells that comprise the tissues and organs of our bodies.

(a) Amoeba

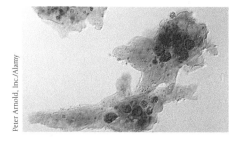

Peter Arnold, Inc./Alamy

(b) English ivy

rossco/Shutterstock

Figure 2 Asexual reproduction.
(a) This single-celled amoeba divides by copying its DNA and producing offspring that are genetically identical to the original, parent amoeba. (b) Some multicellular organisms, such as this English ivy plant, can reproduce asexually from cuttings.

(a) Uncondensed DNA

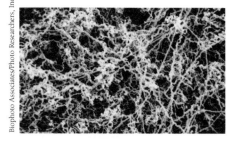

Biophoto Associates/Photo Researchers, Inc.

(b) DNA condensed into chromosomes

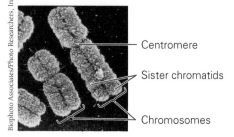

Biophoto Associates/Photo Researchers, Inc.

Centromere

Sister chromatids

Chromosomes

Some organisms reproduce by producing exact copies of themselves via cell division. Reproduction of this type, called **asexual reproduction,** does not require genetic input from two parents and results in offspring that are genetically identical to the original parent cell. Single-celled organisms, such as bacteria and amoeba, reproduce in this manner (**Figure 2a**). Some multicellular organisms can reproduce asexually also. For example, most plants can grow from clippings of the stem, leaves, or roots and thereby reproduce asexually (**Figure 2b**). Organisms whose reproduction requires genetic information from two parents undergo **sexual reproduction.** Humans reproduce sexually when sperm and egg cells combine their genetic information at fertilization.

Genes and Chromosomes

Whether reproducing sexually or asexually, all dividing cells must first make a copy of their genetic material, the **DNA (deoxyribonucleic acid).** The DNA carries the instructions, called **genes,** for building all of the proteins that cells require. The DNA in the nucleus is wrapped around proteins to produce structures called **chromosomes.** Chromosomes can carry hundreds of genes along their length. Different organisms have different numbers of chromosomes in their cells. For example, dogs have 78 chromosomes in each cell, humans have 46, and dandelions have 24.

Chromosomes are in an uncondensed, string-like form prior to cell division (**Figure 3a**). Before cell division occurs, the DNA in each chromosome is condensed (compressed) in a short, linear form (**Figure 3b**). Condensed linear chromosomes are easier to maneuver during cell division and are less likely to become tangled or broken than are the uncondensed and string-like structures. When a chromosome is replicated, a copy is produced that carries the same genes. The copied chromosomes are called **sister chromatids,** and each sister chromatid is composed of one DNA molecule. Sister chromatids are attached to each other at a region toward the middle of the replicated chromosome, called the **centromere.**

The DNA molecule itself is double stranded and can be likened to a twisted rope ladder. The backbone or "handrails" of each strand are composed of alternating sugar and phosphate groups. Across the width or "rungs" of the DNA helix are the nitrogenous bases, paired together via hydrogen bonds such that adenine (A) makes a base pair with thymine (T), and guanine (G) makes a base pair with cytosine (C).

You also learned that two of the people credited with determining DNA structure are James Watson and Francis Crick. Watson and Crick reported their hypothesis about the structure of the DNA molecule in a 1953 paper for the journal *Nature*. Although they did not go so far as to propose a detailed model for how the DNA molecule was replicated, they did say, "It has not escaped our notice that the specific pairing we have postulated immediately suggests a copying mechanism for the genetic material." The copying mechanism that Watson and Crick referred to is also called *DNA replication*.

Figure 3 DNA condenses during cell division. (a) DNA in its replicated but uncondensed form prior to cell division. (b) During cell division, each copy of DNA is wrapped neatly around many small proteins, forming the condensed structure of a chromosome. After DNA replication, two identical sister chromatids are produced and joined to each other at the centromere.

DNA Replication

During the process of **DNA replication** that precedes cell division, the double-stranded DNA molecule is copied, first by splitting the molecule in half up the middle of the helix. New nucleotides are added to each side of the original parent molecule, maintaining the A-to-T and G-to-C base pairings. This process results in two daughter DNA molecules, each composed of one strand of parental nucleotides and one newly synthesized strand (**Figure 4a**). Because each newly formed DNA molecule consists of one-half conserved parental DNA and one-half new daughter DNA, this method of DNA replication is referred to as *semiconservative replication*.

Replicating the DNA requires an enzyme that assists in DNA synthesis. This enzyme, called **DNA polymerase,** moves along the length of the unwound helix and helps bind incoming nucleotides to each other on the newly forming daughter strand (**Figure 4b**). When free nucleotides floating in the nucleus have an affinity for each other (A for T and G for C), they bind to each other across the width of the helix. Nucleotides that bind to each other are said to be *complementary* to each other.

(a) DNA replication   **(b) The DNA polymerase enzyme facilitates replication.**

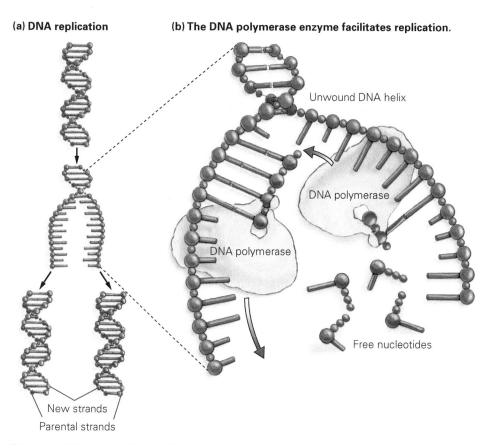

Unwound DNA helix

DNA polymerase

DNA polymerase

Free nucleotides

New strands
Parental strands

Figure 4 DNA replication. (a) DNA replication results in the production of two identical daughter DNA molecules from one parent molecule. Each daughter DNA molecule contains half of the parental DNA and half of the newly synthesized DNA.

Visualize This: Assume another round of replication were to occur with the incoming nucleotides still being purple in color. How many total DNA molecules would be produced, and what proportion of each DNA molecule would be purple?

(b) The DNA polymerase enzyme moves along the unwound helix, tying together adjacent nucleotides on the newly forming daughter DNA strand. Free nucleotides have three phosphate groups, two of which are cleaved to provide energy for this reaction before the nucleotide is added to the growing chain.

Figure 5 Unduplicated and duplicated chromosomes. An unreplicated chromosome is composed of one double-stranded DNA molecule. A replicated chromosome is X-shaped and composed of two identical double-stranded DNA molecules. Each DNA molecule of the duplicated chromosome is a copy of the original chromosome and is called a sister chromatid. In this illustration, the letters A, b, and C represent different genes along the length of the chromosome.

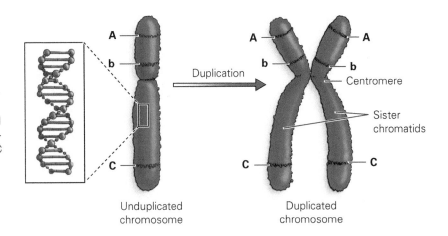

Unduplicated chromosome

Duplicated chromosome

The DNA polymerase enzyme catalyzes the formation of the covalent bond between nucleotides along the length of the helix. The paired nitrogenous bases are joined across the width of the backbone by hydrogen bonding, and the DNA polymerase advances along the parental DNA strand to the next unpaired nucleotide. When an entire chromosome has been replicated, the newly synthesized copies are identical to each other. They are attached at the centromere as sister chromatids (**Figure 5**).

Stop & Stretch 2 DNA replication is not entirely analogous to photocopying. Explain how it differs.

3 The Cell Cycle and Mitosis

After a cell's DNA has been replicated, the cell is ready to divide. Mitosis is one way in which this division occurs. **Mitosis** is an asexual division that produces daughter nuclei that are exact copies of the parent nuclei. Mitosis is part of the cell cycle, or life cycle, of non-sex cells called **somatic cells.**

For cells that divide by mitosis, the cell cycle includes three steps: (1) **interphase,** when the DNA replicates; (2) *mitosis,* when the copied chromosomes split and move into the daughter nuclei; and (3) **cytokinesis,** when the cytoplasm of the parent cell splits (**Figure 6a**). As you will see, interphase and mitosis are further divided into steps as well.

Interphase

A normal cell spends most of its time in interphase (**Figure 6b**). During this phase of the cell cycle, the cell performs its typical functions and produces the proteins required for the cell to do its particular job. For example, during interphase, a muscle cell would be producing proteins required for muscle contraction, and a blood cell would be producing proteins required to transport oxygen. Different cell types spend varying amounts of time in interphase. Cells that frequently divide, like skin cells, spend less time in interphase than do those that seldom divide, such as some nerve cells. A cell that will divide also begins preparations for division during interphase. Interphase can be separated into three phases: G_1, S, and G_2.

During the G_1 (first gap or growth) phase, most of the cell's organelles duplicate. Consequently, the cell grows larger during this phase. During the

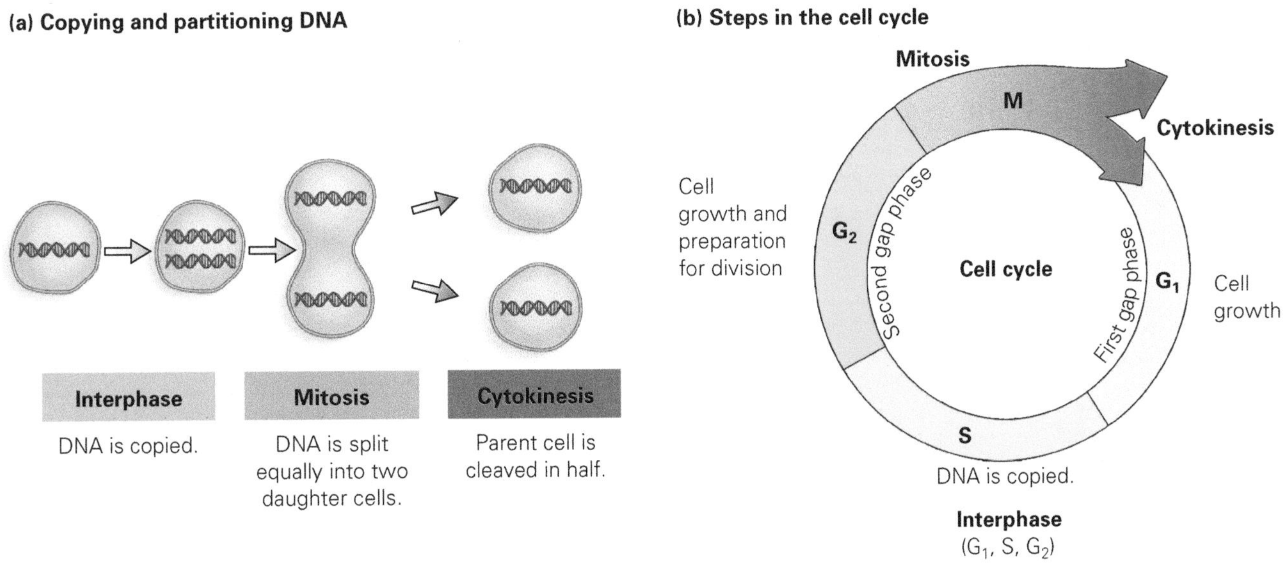

(a) Copying and partitioning DNA

Interphase	Mitosis	Cytokinesis
DNA is copied.	DNA is split equally into two daughter cells.	Parent cell is cleaved in half.

(b) Steps in the cell cycle

Figure 6 The cell cycle. (a) During interphase, the DNA is copied. Separation of the DNA into two daughter nuclei occurs during mitosis. Cytokinesis is the division of the cytoplasm, creating 2 daughter cells. (b) During interphase, there are two stages when the cell grows in preparation for cell division, G_1 and G_2 stages, and one stage where the DNA replicates, the S stage. The chromosomes are separated and two daughter cells are formed during the M phase.

S (synthesis) phase, the DNA in the chromosomes replicates. During the G_2 (second gap) phase of the cell cycle, proteins are synthesized that will help drive mitosis to completion. The cell continues to grow and prepare for the division of chromosomes that will take place during mitosis.

Mitosis

The movement of chromosomes into new cells occurs during mitosis. Mitosis takes place in all cells with a nucleus, although some of the specifics of cell division differ among kingdoms. Whether these phases occur in an animal or a plant, the outcome of mitosis and the next phase, cytokinesis, is the same: the production of genetically identical daughter cells. To achieve this outcome, the sister chromatids of a replicated chromosome are pulled apart, and one copy of each is placed into each newly forming nucleus. Mitosis is accomplished during 4 stages: prophase, metaphase, anaphase, and telophase. **Figure 7** (on the next page) summarizes the cell cycle in animal cells. The four stages of mitosis are nearly identical in plant cells.

During **prophase,** the replicated chromosomes condense, allowing them to move around in the cell without becoming entangled. Protein structures called **microtubules** also form and grow, ultimately radiating out from opposite ends, or **poles,** of the dividing cell. The growth of microtubules helps the cell to expand. Motor proteins attached to microtubules also help pull the chromosomes around during cell division. The membrane that surrounds the nucleus, called the **nuclear envelope,** breaks down so that the microtubules can gain access to the replicated chromosomes. At the poles of each dividing animal cell, structures called **centrioles** physically anchor one end of each forming microtubule. Plant cells do not contain centrioles, but microtubules in these cells do remain anchored at a pole.

During **metaphase,** the replicated chromosomes are aligned across the middle, or equator, of each cell. To do this, the microtubules, which are

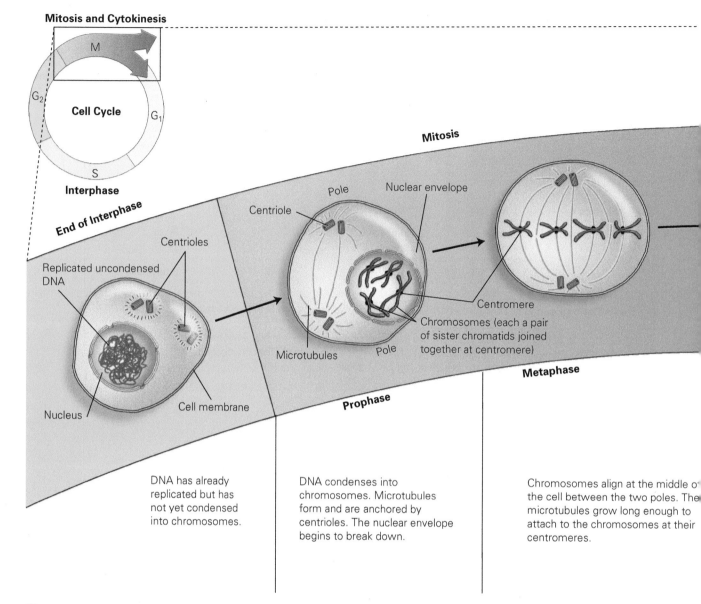

Figure 7 Cell division in animal cells. This diagram illustrates how cell division proceeds from interphase through mitosis and cytokinesis.

attached to each chromosome at the centromere, line up the chromosomes in single file across the middle of the cell.

During **anaphase,** the centromere splits, and the microtubules shorten to pull each sister chromatid of a chromosome to opposite poles of the cell.

In the last stage of mitosis, **telophase,** the nuclear envelopes re-form around the newly produced daughter nuclei, and the chromosomes revert to their uncondensed form.

Stop & Stretch 3 How does the similarity in the process of mitosis between animals and plants support the idea that all organisms share a common ancestor?

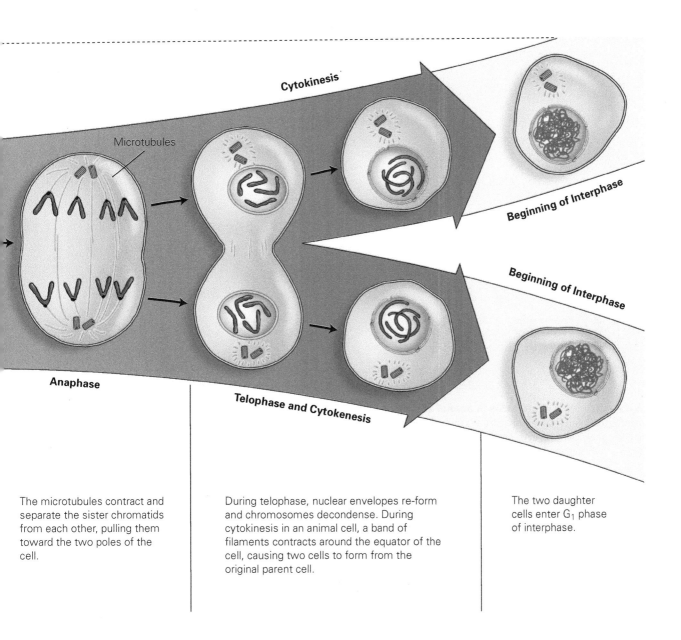

Microtubules

Cytokinesis

Anaphase

Telophase and Cytokenesis

Beginning of Interphase

Beginning of Interphase

The microtubules contract and separate the sister chromatids from each other, pulling them toward the two poles of the cell.

During telophase, nuclear envelopes re-form and chromosomes decondense. During cytokinesis in an animal cell, a band of filaments contracts around the equator of the cell, causing two cells to form from the original parent cell.

The two daughter cells enter G_1 phase of interphase.

Cytokinesis

Cytokinesis divides the cytoplasm, and daughter cells are produced. During cytokinesis in animal cells, a band of proteins encircles the cell at the equator and divides the cytoplasm. This band of proteins contracts to pinch apart the two nuclei and surrounding cytoplasm, creating two daughter cells from the original parent cell. Cytokinesis in plant cells requires that cells build a new **cell wall,** an inflexible structure surrounding the plant cells. **Figure 8** (on the next page) shows the difference between cytokinesis in animal and plant cells. During telophase of mitosis in a plant cell, membrane-bound vesicles from the Golgi apparatus deliver the materials required for building the cell wall to the center of the cell. The materials include a tough, fibrous carbohydrate called **cellulose** as well as some proteins. The membranes surrounding the vesicles gather in the center of the cell to form a structure called a **cell plate.** The cell plate and cell wall grow across the width of the cell

(a) Cytokinesis in an animal cell

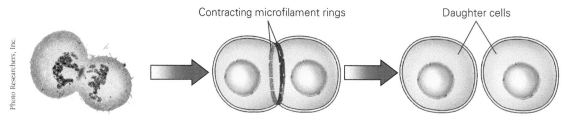

Contracting microfilament rings

Daughter cells

(b) Cytokinesis in a plant cell

Forming cell wall   Parent cell wall

Vesicles with cell wall material

Forming cell plate

New cell wall

Daughter cells

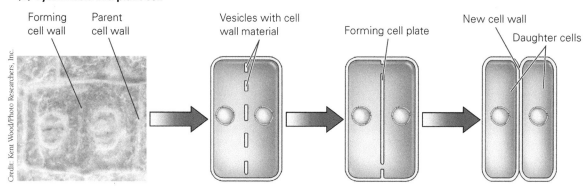

Figure 8 A comparison of cytokinesis in animal and plant cells. (a) Animal cells produce a band of filaments that divide the cell in half. (b) Plant cells undergoing mitosis must do so within the confines of a rigid cell wall. During cytokinesis, plant cells form a cell plate that grows down the middle of the parent cell and eventually forms a new cell wall.

and form a barrier that eventually separates the products of mitosis into two daughter cells.

After cytokinesis, the cell reenters interphase, and if the conditions are favorable, the cell cycle may repeat itself.

4 Cell-Cycle Control and Mutation

When cell division is working properly, it is a tightly controlled process. Cells are given signals for when and when not to divide. The normal cells in Nicole's ovary and the rest of her body were responding properly to the signals telling them when and how fast to divide. However, the cell that started her tumor was not responding properly to these signals.

An Overview: Controls in the Cell Cycle

Instead of proceeding in lockstep through the cell cycle, normal cells halt cell division at a series of **checkpoints.** At each checkpoint, proteins survey the cell to ensure that conditions for a favorable cellular division have been met. Three checkpoints must be passed before cell division can occur; one takes place during G_1, one during G_2, and the last during metaphase (**Figure 9**).

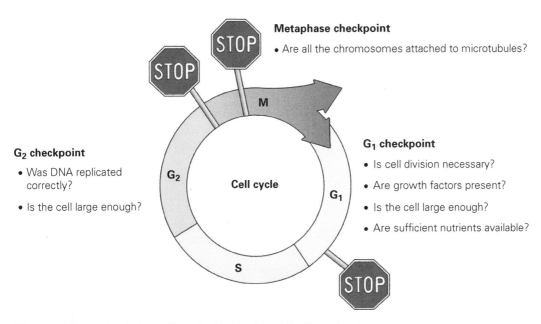

Figure 9 Controls of the cell cycle. Checkpoints at G_1, G_2, and metaphase determine whether a cell will continue to divide.
Visualize This: What would happen if a cell started M phase without having copied all of its chromosomes?

Proteins at the G_1 checkpoint determine whether it is necessary for a cell to divide. To do this, they survey the cell environment for the presence of other proteins called **growth factors** that stimulate cells to divide. Growth factors bind to cell membrane-bound proteins called **receptors** that elicit a response from the cell. If enough growth factors are present to trigger cell division, then other proteins check to see if the cell is large enough to divide and if all the nutrients required for cell division are available. When growth factors are limited in number, cell division does not occur. At the G_2 checkpoint, other proteins ensure that the DNA has replicated properly and double-check the cell size, again making sure that the cell is large enough to divide. The third and final checkpoint occurs during metaphase. Proteins present at metaphase verify that all the chromosomes have attached themselves to microtubules so that cell division can proceed properly.

If proteins surveying the cell at any of these three checkpoints determine that conditions are not favorable for cell division, the process is halted. When this happens, the cell may die.

Proteins that regulate the cell cycle, like all proteins, are coded by genes. When these proteins are normal, cell division is properly regulated. When these cycle-regulating proteins are unable to perform their jobs, unregulated cell division leads to large masses of cells called *tumors*. Mistakes in cell cycle regulation arise when the genes controlling the cell cycle are altered, or mutated, versions of the normal genes. A **mutation** is a change in the sequence of DNA. Changes to DNA can change a gene and in turn can alter the protein that the gene encodes, or provides instructions for. Mutant proteins do not perform their required cell functions in the same way that normal proteins do. If mutations occur to genes that encode the proteins regulating the cell cycle, cells can no longer regulate cell division properly. One or more cells in Nicole's ovary must have accumulated mutations in the cell-cycle control genes, leading to the development of cancer. *See the next section for A Closer Look at mutations to cell-cycle control genes*.

A Closer Look:
At Mutations to Cell-Cycle Control Genes

Those genes that encode the proteins regulating the cell cycle are called **proto-oncogenes** (*proto* means "before," and *onco* means "cancer"). Proto-oncogenes are normal genes located on many different chromosomes that enable organisms to regulate cell division. Cancer can develop when the normal proto-oncogenes undergo mutations and become **oncogenes.** A wide variety of organisms carry proto-oncogenes, which means that many different types of organisms can develop cancer (**Figure 10**).

Many proto-oncogenes provide the cell with instructions for building growth factors. A normal growth factor stimulates cell division only when the cellular environment is favorable and all conditions for division have been met. Oncogenes can overstimulate cell division (**Figure 11a**).

One gene involved in many cases of ovarian cancer is called *HER2*. (Names of genes are italicized, while names of the proteins they produce are not.) The *HER2* gene carries instructions for building a **receptor** protein. When the shape of the receptor on the surface of the cell is normal, it signals the inside of the cell to allow division to occur. Mutations to the gene that encodes this receptor can result in a receptor protein with a different shape from that of the nor-

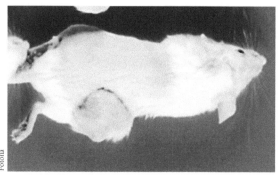

Figure 10 Cancer in nonhuman organisms. Many organisms carry proto-oncogenes, which can mutate into oncogenes and cause the development of tumors or cancer.

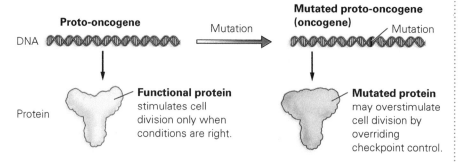

(a) Mutations to proto-oncogenes

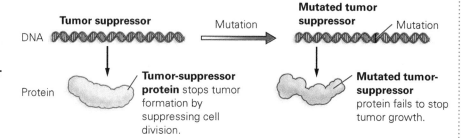

(b) Mutations to tumor-suppressor genes

Figure 11 Mutations to proto-oncogenes and tumor-suppressor genes. (a) Mutations to proto-oncogenes and (b) tumor-suppressor genes can increase the likelihood of cancer developing.

mal receptor protein. When mutated or misshapen, the receptor protein functions as if many growth factors were present, even when there are actually few-to-no growth factors.

Another class of genes involved in cancer are **tumor suppressors.** These genes, also present in all humans and many other organisms, carry the instructions for producing proteins that suppress or stop cell division if conditions are not favorable. These proteins can also detect and repair damage to the DNA. For this reason, normal tumor suppressors serve as backups in case the proto-oncogenes undergo mutation. If a growth factor overstimulates cell division, the normal tumor suppressor impedes tumor formation by preventing the mutant cell from moving through a checkpoint (**Figure 11b**).

When a tumor-suppressor protein is not functioning properly, it does not force the cell to stop dividing even though conditions are not favorable. Mutated tumor suppressors also allow cells to override cell-cycle checkpoints. One well-studied tumor suppressor, named p53, helps to determine whether cells will repair damaged DNA or commit cellular suicide if the damage is too severe. Mutations to the gene that encodes p53 result in damaged DNA being allowed to proceed through mitosis, thereby passing on even more mutations. Over half of all human cancers involve mutations to the gene that encodes p53.

Mutations to a tumor-suppressor gene are common in cells that have become cancerous. Researchers believe that a normal *BRCA2* gene encodes a protein that is involved in helping to repair damaged DNA. The misshapen, mutant version of the protein cannot help to repair damaged DNA. This means that damaged DNA will be allowed to undergo mitosis, thus passing new mutations on to their daughter cells. As more and more mutations occur, the probability that a cell will become cancerous increases. **Figure 12** summarizes the roles of growth factors and tumor suppressors in the development of cancer.

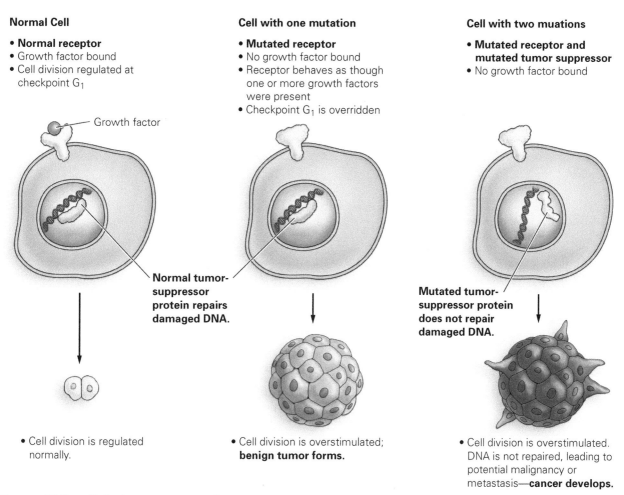

Normal Cell

- **Normal receptor**
- Growth factor bound
- Cell division regulated at checkpoint G_1

Growth factor

Normal tumor-suppressor protein repairs damaged DNA.

- Cell division is regulated normally.

Cell with one mutation

- **Mutated receptor**
- No growth factor bound
- Receptor behaves as though one or more growth factors were present
- Checkpoint G_1 is overridden

- Cell division is overstimulated; **benign tumor forms.**

Cell with two muations

- **Mutated receptor and mutated tumor suppressor**
- No growth factor bound

Mutated tumor-suppressor protein does not repair damaged DNA.

- Cell division is overstimulated. DNA is not repaired, leading to potential malignancy or metastasis—**cancer develops.**

Figure 12 Growth factor receptors and tumor suppressors. When a cell has normal growth factors and tumor suppressors, cell division is properly regulated. Mutations to growth factor receptors can cause cell division to be overstimulated, and a benign tumor can form. Additional mutations to tumor-suppressor genes increase the likelihood of malignancy and metastasis.

Cancer Development Requires Many Mutations

Some mutations that occur as a result of damaged DNA being allowed to undergo mitosis are responsible for the progression of a tumor from a benign state, to a malignant state, to metastasis. For example, some cancer cells can stimulate the growth of surrounding blood vessels through a process called **angiogenesis.** These cancer cells secrete a substance that attracts and reroutes blood vessels so that they supply a developing tumor with oxygen (necessary for cellular respiration) and other nutrients. When a tumor has its own blood supply, it can grow at the expense of other, noncancerous cells. Because the growth of rapidly dividing cancer cells occurs more quickly than the growth of normal cells in this process, entire organs can eventually become filled with cancerous cells. When this occurs, an organ can no longer work properly, leading to compromised functioning or organ failure. Damage to organs also explains some of the pain associated with cancer.

Normal cells also display a property called **contact inhibition,** which prevents them from dividing when doing so would require them to pile up on each other. Cancer cells, conversely, have undergone mutations that allow them to continue to divide and form a tumor (**Figure 13a**). In addition, normal cells do need some contact with an underlayer of cells to stay in place. This phenomenon is the result of a process called **anchorage dependence** (**Figure 13b**). Cancer cells override this requirement for some contact with other cells because cancer cells are dividing too quickly and do not expend enough energy to secrete adhesion molecules that glue the cells together. Once a cell loses its anchorage dependence, it may leave the original tumor and move to the blood, lymph, or surrounding tissues.

Most cells are programmed to divide a certain number of times—usually 50 to 70 times—and then they stop dividing. This limits most developing tumors to a small mole, cyst, or lump, all of which are benign. Cancer cells, however, have undergone mutations that allow them to be immortal. They achieve immortality by activating a gene that is usually turned off after early development. This gene produces an enzyme called **telomerase** that helps prevent the degradation of chromosomes. As chromosomes degrade with age, a cell loses its ability to divide. In cancer cells, telomerase is reactivated, allowing the cells to divide without limit.

Stop & Stretch 4 Telomerase is turned off early in development, causing chromosomes to shorten and eventually lose their ability to replicate. What does this fact imply about the life span of tissue or organ?

Figure 13 Contact inhibition and anchorage dependence. (a) When normal cells are grown on a solid support such as the bottom of a flask, they grow and divide until they cover the bottom of the flask. (b) Cancer cells lose the requirement that they adhere to other cells or a solid support.

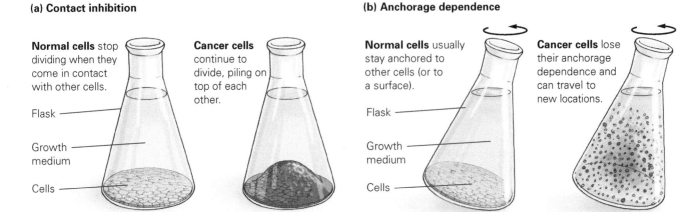

(a) Contact inhibition

Normal cells stop dividing when they come in contact with other cells.

Cancer cells continue to divide, piling on top of each other.

Flask

Growth medium

Cells

(b) Anchorage dependence

Normal cells usually stay anchored to other cells (or to a surface).

Cancer cells lose their anchorage dependence and can travel to new locations.

Flask

Growth medium

Cells

In Nicole's case, the progression from normal ovarian cells to cancerous cells may have occurred as follows: (1) One single cell in her ovary may have acquired a mutation to its *HER2* growth factor receptor gene. (2) The descendants of this cell would have been able to divide faster than neighboring cells, forming a small, benign tumor. (3) Next, a cell within the tumor may have undergone a mutation to its *BRCA2* tumor-suppressor gene, resulting in the inability of the BRCA2 protein to fix damaged DNA in the cancerous cells. (4) Cells produced by the mitosis of these doubly mutant cells would continue to divide even though their DNA is damaged, thereby enlarging the tumor and producing cells with more mutations. (5) Subsequent mutations could result in angiogenesis, lack of contact inhibition, reactivation of the telomerase enzyme, or overriding of anchorage dependence. If Nicole were very unlucky, the end result of these mutations could be that cells carrying many mutations would break away from the original ovarian tumor and set up a cancer at 1 or more new locations in her body.

Multiple-Hit Model. Because multiple mutations are required for the development and progression of cancer, scientists describe the process of cancer development using the phrase **multiple-hit model.** Nicole may have inherited some of these mutations, or they may have been induced by environmental exposures. Even though cancer is a disease caused by malfunctioning genes, most cancers are not caused only by the inheritance of mutant genes. In fact, scientists estimate that close to 70% of cancers are caused by mutations that occur during a person's lifetime.

Most of us will inherit few if any mutant cell-cycle control genes. Our level of exposure to risk factors will determine whether enough mutations will accumulate during our lifetime to cause cancer. Risk factors for ovarian cancer include smoking and uninterrupted ovulation. Ovarian cancer risk is thought to decrease for many years if ovulation is prevented for periods of time, as it is when a woman is pregnant, breastfeeding, or taking the birth control pill. When an egg cell is released from the ovary during ovulation, some tissue damage occurs. In the absence of ovulation, there is no damaged ovarian tissue and hence no need for extra cell divisions to repair damaged cells. Because mutations are most likely to occur when DNA is replicating before division, fewer divisions equal a lower likelihood of the appearance of cancer-causing mutations.

Regardless of its origin, once cancer is suspected, detection and treatment follow.

5 Cancer Detection and Treatment

Early detection and treatment of cancer increase the odds of survival dramatically. Being on the lookout for warning signs (**Figure 14**) can help alert individuals to developing cancers.

Detection Methods: Biopsy

Different cancers are detected using different methods. Some cancers are detected by the excess production of proteins that are normally produced by a particular cell type. Ovarian cancers often show high levels of CA125 protein in the blood. Nicole's level of CA125 led her gynecologist to think that a tumor might be forming on her remaining ovary. Once he suspected a tumor, Nicole's physician scheduled a biopsy. A **biopsy** is the surgical removal of cells, tissue, or fluid that will be analyzed to determine whether they are cancerous.

C hange in bowel or bladder habits

A sore that does not heal

U nusual bleeding or discharge

T hickening or lump

I ndigestion or difficulty swallowing

O bvious change in wart or mole

N agging cough or hoarseness

Figure 14 Warning signs of cancer. Self-screening for cancer can save your life. If you experience 1 or more of these warning signs, see your doctor.

When viewed under a microscope, benign tumors consist of orderly growths of cells that resemble the cells of the tissue from which thy were taken. Malignant or cancerous cells do not resemble other cells found in the same tissue; they are dividing so rapidly that they do not have time to produce all the proteins necessary to build normal cells. This leads to the often abnormal appearance of cancer cells as seen under a microscope.

A needle biopsy is usually performed if the cancer is located on or close to the surface of the patient's body. For example, breast lumps are often biopsied with a needle to determine whether the lump contains fluid and is a noncancerous cyst or whether it contains abnormal cells and is a tumor. When a cancer is diagnosed, surgery is often performed to remove as much of the cancerous growth as possible without damaging neighboring organs and tissues.

In Nicole's case, getting at the ovary to find tissue for a biopsy required the use of a surgical instrument called a **laparoscope.** For this operation, the surgeon inserted a small light and a scalpel-like instrument through a tiny incision above Nicole's navel.

Nicole's surgeon preferred to use the laparoscope because he knew Nicole would have a much easier recovery from laparoscopic surgery than she had from the surgery to remove her other, cystic ovary. Laparoscopy had not been possible when removing Nicole's other ovary—the cystic ovary had grown so large that her surgeon had to make a large abdominal incision to remove it.

A laparoscope has a small camera that projects images from the ovary onto a monitor that the surgeon views during surgery. These images showed that Nicole's tumor was a different shape, color, and texture from the rest of her ovary. They also showed that the tumor was not confined to the surface of the ovary; in fact, it appeared to have spread deeply into her ovary. Nicole's surgeon decided to shave off only the affected portion of the ovary and leave as much intact as possible, with the hope that the remaining ovarian tissue might still be able to produce egg cells. He then sent the tissue to a laboratory so that the pathologist could examine it. Unfortunately, when the pathologist looked through the microscope this time, she saw the disorderly appearance characteristic of cancer cells. Nicole's ovary was cancerous, and further treatment would be necessary.

Treatment Methods: Chemotherapy and Radiation

A treatment that works for one woman with ovarian cancer might not work for another ovarian cancer patient because a different suite of mutations may have led to the cancer in each woman's ovary. Luckily for Nicole, her ovarian cancer was diagnosed very early. Regrettably, this is not the case for most women with ovarian cancer, many of whom are diagnosed after the disease has progressed. The symptoms of ovarian cancer are often subtle and can be overlooked or ignored. They include abdominal swelling, pain, bloating, gas, constipation, indigestion, menstrual disorders, and fatigue. The difficulty of diagnosis is compounded because no routine screening tests are available. For instance, CA125 levels are checked only when ovarian cancer is suspected because (1) ovaries are not the only tissues that secrete this protein; (2) CA125 levels vary from individual to individual; and (3) these levels depend on the phase of the woman's menstrual cycle. Elevated CA125 levels usually mean that the cancer has been developing for a long time. Consequently, by the time the diagnosis is made, the cancer may have grown quite large and metastasized, making it much more difficult to treat.

Nicole's cancer was caught early. However, her physician was concerned that some of her cancerous ovarian cells may have spread through blood vessels or lymph ducts on or near the ovaries or spread into her abdominal cavity, so he started Nicole on chemotherapy after her surgery.

Chemotherapy. During **chemotherapy,** chemicals are injected into the bloodstream. These chemicals selectively kill dividing cells. A variety of chemotherapeutic agents act in different ways to interrupt cell division.

Chemotherapy involves many drugs because most chemotherapeutic agents affect only one type of cellular activity. Cancer cells are rapidly dividing and do not take the time to repair mistakes in replication that lead to mutations. These cells are allowed to proceed through the G_2 checkpoint with many mutations. Therefore, cancer cells can randomly undergo mutations, a few of which might allow them to evade the actions of a particular chemotherapeutic agent. Cells that are resistant to one drug proliferate when the chemotherapeutic agent clears away the other cells that compete for space and nutrients. Cells with a preexisting resistance to the drugs are selected for and produce more daughter cells with the same resistant characteristics, requiring the use of more than one chemotherapeutic agent.

Scientists estimate that cancer cells become resistant at a rate of approximately one cell per million. Because tumors contain about 1 billion cells, the average tumor will have close to 1000 resistant cells. Therefore, treating a cancer patient with a combination of chemotherapeutic agents aimed at different mechanisms increases the chances of destroying all the cancerous cells in a tumor.

Unfortunately, normal cells that divide rapidly are also affected by chemotherapy treatments. Hair follicles, cells that produce red and white blood cells, and cells that line the intestines and stomach are often damaged or destroyed. The effects of chemotherapy therefore include temporary hair loss, anemia (dizziness and fatigue due to decreased numbers of red blood cells), and lowered protection from infection due to decreases in the number of white blood cells. In addition, damage to the cells of the stomach and intestines can lead to nausea, vomiting, and diarrhea.

Several hours after each chemotherapy treatment, Nicole became nauseated; she often had diarrhea and vomited for a day or so after her treatments. Midway through her chemotherapy treatments, Nicole lost most of her hair.

Radiation Therapy. Cancer patients often undergo radiation treatments as well as chemotherapy. **Radiation therapy** uses high-energy particles to injure or destroy cells by damaging their DNA, making it impossible for these cells to continue to grow and divide. Radiation is applied directly to the tumor when possible. A typical course of radiation involves a series of 10 to 20 treatments performed after the surgical removal of the tumor, although sometimes radiation is used before surgery to decrease the size of the tumor. Radiation therapy is typically used only when cancers are located close to the surface of the body because it is difficult to focus a beam of radiation on internal organs such as an ovary. Therefore, Nicole's physician recommended chemotherapy only.

> **Stop & Stretch 5** One risk of radiation therapy is an increased likelihood of secondary cancer emerging 5 to 15 years later. Why might this treatment increase cancer risk?

Nicole's treatments consisted of many different chemotherapeutic agents, spread over many months. The treatments took place at the local hospital on Wednesdays and Fridays. She usually had a friend drive her to the hospital

Figure 15 Chemotherapy. Many chemotherapeutic agents, such as Nicole's Taxol, are administered through an intravenous (IV) needle.

very early in the morning and return later in the day to pick her up. The drugs were administered through an intravenous (IV) needle into a vein in her arm (**Figure 15**). During the hour or so that she was undergoing chemotherapy, Nicole usually studied for her classes. She did not mind the actual chemotherapy treatments that much. The hospital personnel were kind to her, and she got some studying done. It was the aftermath of these treatments that she hated. Most days during her chemotherapy regimen, Nicole was so exhausted that she did not get out of bed until late morning, and on the day after her treatments, she often slept until late afternoon. Then she would get up and try to get some work done or make some phone calls before going back to bed early in the evening. After 6 weeks of chemotherapy, Nicole's CA125 levels started to drop. After another 2 months of chemotherapy, her CA125 levels were back down to their normal, precancerous level. If Nicole has normal CA125 levels for 5 years, she will be considered to be in **remission,** or no longer suffering negative impacts from cancer. After 10 years of normal CA125 levels, she will be considered cured of her cancer. Because Nicole's cancer responded to chemotherapy, she was spared from having to undergo any other, more experimental treatments.

Even though her treatments seemed to be going well, Nicole had other worries. She worried that her remaining ovary would not recover from the surgery and chemotherapy, which meant that she would never be able to have children. Nicole had always assumed that she would have children someday, and although she did not currently have a strong desire to have a child, she wondered if her feelings would change. Even though she was not planning to marry anytime soon, she also wondered how her future husband would feel if she were not able to become pregnant.

In addition to her concerns about being able to become pregnant, Nicole also became worried that she might pass on mutated, cancer-causing genes to her children. For Nicole, or anyone, to pass on genes to his or her children, reproductive cells must be produced by another type of nuclear division called meiosis.

6 Meiosis

Recall that mitosis is the division of a somatic cell's nucleus that ultimately results in two daughter nuclei that are exact copies of their parent. **Meiosis** is a form of cell division that *reduces* the number of chromosomes to produce specialized cells called **gametes** with only one-half the number of chromosomes of the parent cell. Gametes further differ from somatic cells in that gametes are produced only within the **gonads,** or sex organs.

In humans, and in most animals, the male gonads are the testes, and the female gonads are the ovaries. In animals, the male gametes are the sperm cells, while the gametes produced by the female are the egg cells. Because human somatic cells have 46 chromosomes and meiosis reduces the chromosome number by one-half, the gametes produced during meiosis contain 23 chromosomes each. (When an egg cell and a sperm cell combine their 23 chromosomes at fertilization, the developing embryo will then have the required 46 chromosomes.)

The placement of chromosomes into gametes is not random. For example, meiosis in humans does not simply place any 23 of the 46 human chromosomes into a gamete. Instead, meiosis apportions chromosomes in a very specific manner. Chromosomes in somatic cells occur in pairs. For example, the 46 chromosomes in human somatic cells are actually 23 different pairs of chromosomes. Meiosis produces gamete cells that contain one chromosome of every pair.

Autosomes (22 pairs)

Sex chromosomes (1 pair)

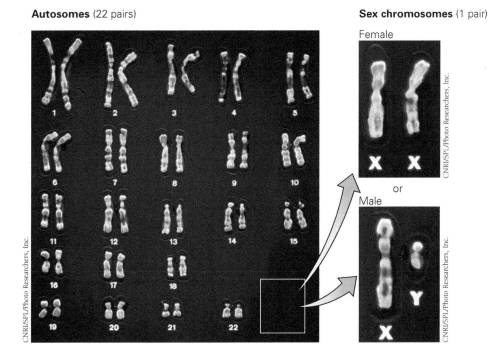

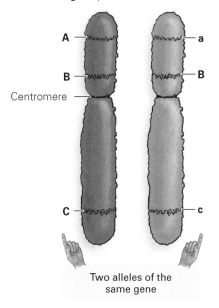

Figure 16 Karyotype. The pairs of chromosomes in this karyotype are arranged in order of decreasing size and numbered from 1 to 22. The X and Y sex chromosomes are the 23rd pair. The sex chromosomes from a female and a male are shown in the insets. **Visualize This:** How do the X and Y chromosomes differ in terms of structure?

Homologous pair of chromosomes

Two alleles of the same gene

Figure 17 Homologous and non-homologous pairs of chromosomes. Homologous pairs of chromosomes have the same genes (shown here as A, B, and C) but may have different alleles. The dominant allele is represented by an uppercase letter, while the recessive allele is shown with the same letter in lowercase. Note that the chromosomes of a homologous pair each have the same size, shape, and positioning of the centromere. One member of each pair is inherited from one's mother (and colored pink), while the other is inherited from one's father (and colored blue).

It is possible to visualize chromosome pairs by preparing a **karyotype,** a highly magnified photograph of the chromosomes arranged in pairs. A human karyotype is usually prepared from chromosomes that have been removed from the nuclei of white blood cells, which have been treated with chemicals to stop mitosis at metaphase (**Figure 16**). Because these chromosomes are at metaphase of mitosis, they are composed of replicated sister chromatids and are shaped like the letter X. The 46 human chromosomes can be arranged into 22 pairs of nonsex chromosomes, or **autosomes,** and one pair of **sex chromosomes** (the X and Y chromosomes) to make a total of 23 pairs. Human males have an X and a Y chromosome, while females have two X chromosomes.

Each chromosome is paired with a mate that is the same size and shape and has its centromere in the same position. These pairs of chromosomes are called **homologous pairs.** Each member of a homologous pair of chromosomes carries the same genes along its length, although not necessarily the same versions of those genes. Different versions of the same gene are called **alleles** of a gene (**Figure 17**). In your cells, one member of each pair was inherited from your mother and the other from your father.

There are normal and mutant alleles of the *BRCA2* gene. Note that there is a difference between the same type of information in the sense that both alleles of this gene code for a cell-cycle control protein, but they happen to code for different versions of the same protein. Alleles are alternate forms of a gene in the same way that chocolate and vanilla are alternate forms of ice cream.

When a chromosome is replicated, during the S phase of the cell cycle, the DNA is duplicated. Replication results in two copies, called *sister chromatids,* that are genetically identical. For this reason, we would find exactly the same

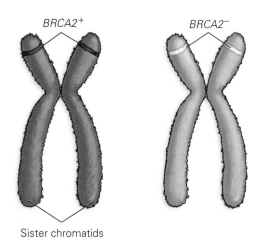

Figure 18 Duplicated chromosomes. This homologous pair of chromosomes has been duplicated. Note that the normal version of the *BRCA2* gene (symbolized *BRCA2*+) is present on both sister chromatids of the chromosome on the left. Its homologue on the right carries the mutant version of this allele (symbolized *BRCA2*−).

information on the sister chromatids that comprise a replicated chromosome (**Figure 18**).

Meiosis separates the members of a homologous pair from each other. Once meiosis is completed, there is one copy of each chromosome (1–23) in every gamete. When only one member of each homologous pair is present in a cell, we say that the cell is **haploid (*n*)**—both egg cells and sperm cells are haploid. All somatic cells in humans contain homologous pairs of chromosomes and are therefore diploid. For a diploid cell in a person's testes or ovary to become a haploid gamete, it must go through meiosis. After the sperm and egg fuse, the fertilized cell, or **zygote,** will contain two sets of chromosomes and is said to be **diploid (2*n*)** (**Figure 19**). Like mitosis, meiosis is preceded by an interphase stage that includes G_1, S, and G_2. Interphase is followed by two phases of meiosis, called meiosis I and meiosis II, in which divisions of the nucleus take place (**Figure 20**). Meiosis I separates the members of a homologous pair from each other. Meiosis II separates the chromatids from each other. Both meiotic divisions are followed by cytokinesis, during which the cytoplasm is divided between the resulting daughter cells.

Interphase

The interphase that precedes meiosis consists of G_1, S, and G_2. This interphase of meiosis is similar in most respects to the interphase that precedes mitosis. The centrioles from which the microtubules will originate are present. The G phases are times of cell growth and preparation for

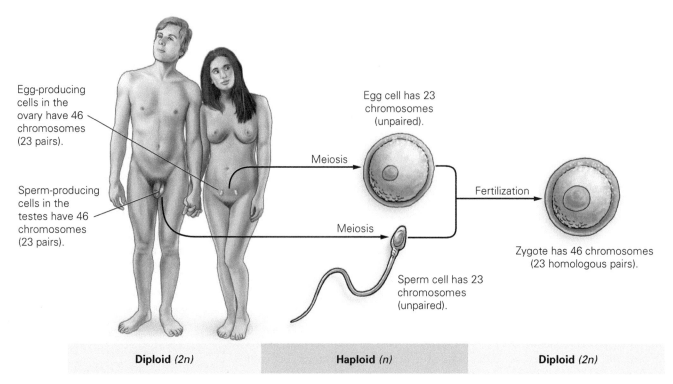

Figure 19 Gamete production. The diploid cells of the ovaries and testes undergo meiosis and produce haploid gametes. At fertilization, the diploid condition is restored.

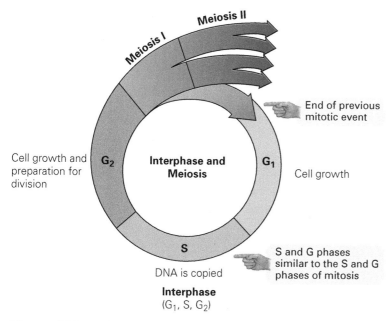

Figure 20 Interphase and meiosis. Interphase consists of G_1, S, and G_2 and is followed by 2 rounds of nuclear division, meiosis I and meiosis II. **Visualize This:** Does DNA duplication occur during the interphase preceding meiosis II?

division. The S phase is when DNA replication occurs. Once the cell's DNA has been replicated, it can enter meiosis I.

Meiosis I

The first meiotic division, meiosis I, consists of prophase I, metaphase I, anaphase I, and telophase I (**Figure 21** on the next page).

During prophase I of meiosis, the nuclear envelope starts to break down, and the microtubules begin to assemble. The previously replicated chromosomes condense so that they can be moved around the cell without becoming entangled. The condensed chromosomes can be seen under a microscope. At this time, the homologous pairs of chromosomes exchange genetic information in a process called *crossing over*, which will be explained in a moment.

At metaphase I, the homologous pairs line up at the cell's equator, or middle of the cell. Microtubules bind to the metaphase chromosomes near the centromere. Homologous pairs are arranged arbitrarily regarding which member faces which pole. This process is called *random alignment*. At the end of this section, you will find detailed descriptions of crossing over and random alignment along with their impact on genetic diversity.

At anaphase I, the homologous pairs are separated from each other by the shortening of the microtubules, and at telophase I, nuclear envelopes re-form around the chromosomes. DNA is then partitioned into each of the two daughter cells by cytokinesis. Because each daughter cell contains only one copy of each member of a homologous pair, at this point the cells are haploid. Now both of these daughter cells are ready to undergo meiosis II.

Stop & Stretch 6 How is meiosis I similar to mitosis? How is it different?

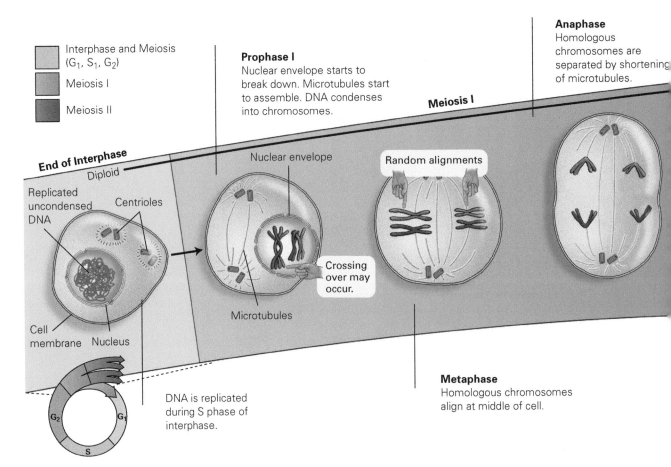

Figure 21 Sexual cell division. This diagram illustrates interphase, meiosis I, meiosis II, and cytokinesis in an animal cell.

Meiosis II

Meiosis II consists of prophase II, metaphase II, anaphase II, and telophase II. This second meiotic division is virtually identical to mitosis and serves to separate the sister chromatids of the replicated chromosome from each other.

At prophase II of meiosis, the cell is readying for another round of division, and the microtubules are lengthening again. At metaphase II, the chromosomes align in single file across the equator in much the same way that they do during mitosis—not as pairs, as was the case with metaphase I. At anaphase II, the sister chromatids separate from each other and move to opposite poles of the cell. At telophase II, the separated chromosomes each become enclosed in their own nucleus. In this fashion, half of a person's genes are physically placed into each gamete; thus, children carry one-half of each parent's genes.

Each parent can produce millions of different types of gametes due to two events that occur during meiosis I—crossing over and random alignment. Both of these processes greatly increase the number of different kinds of gametes that an individual can produce and therefore increase the variation in individuals that can be produced when gametes combine.

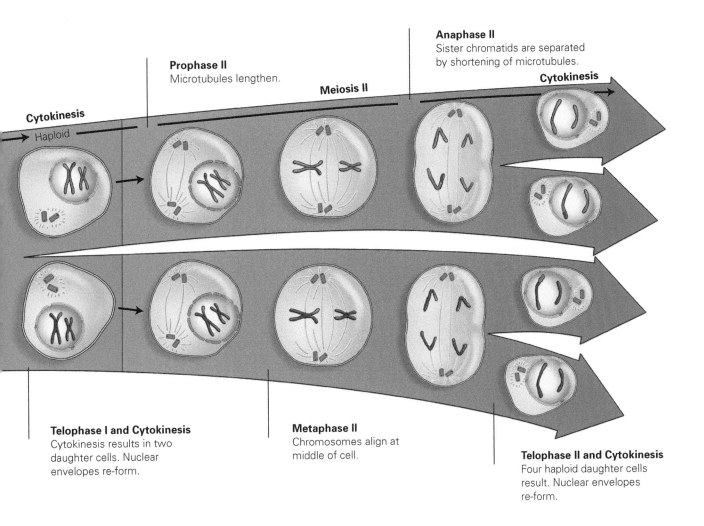

Anaphase II
Sister chromatids are separated by shortening of microtubules.

Prophase II
Microtubules lengthen.

Meiosis II

Cytokinesis

Cytokinesis

Haploid

Telophase I and Cytokinesis
Cytokinesis results in two daughter cells. Nuclear envelopes re-form.

Metaphase II
Chromosomes align at middle of cell.

Telophase II and Cytokinesis
Four haploid daughter cells result. Nuclear envelopes re-form.

Crossing Over and Random Alignment

Crossing over occurs during prophase I of meiosis I. It involves the exchange of portions of chromosomes from one member of a homologous pair to the other member. Crossing over is believed to occur several times on each homologous pair during each occurrence of meiosis.

To illustrate crossing over, consider an example using genes involved in the production of flower color and pollen shape in sweet pea plants. These two genes are on the same chromosome and are called **linked genes.** Linked genes move together on the same chromosome to a gamete, and they may or may not undergo crossing over.

If a pea plant has red flowers and long pollen grains, the chromosomes may appear as shown in **Figure 22** (on the next page). It is possible for this plant to produce four different types of gametes with respect to these two genes. Two types of gametes would result if no crossing over occurred between these genes—the gamete containing the red flower and long pollen chromosome and the gamete containing the white flower and short pollen chromosome. Two additional types of gametes could be produced if crossing over did occur—one type containing the red flower and short pollen grain chromosome and the other type containing the reciprocal white flower and long pollen grain chromosome. Therefore, crossing over increases genetic diversity by increasing the number of distinct combinations of genes that may be present in a gamete.

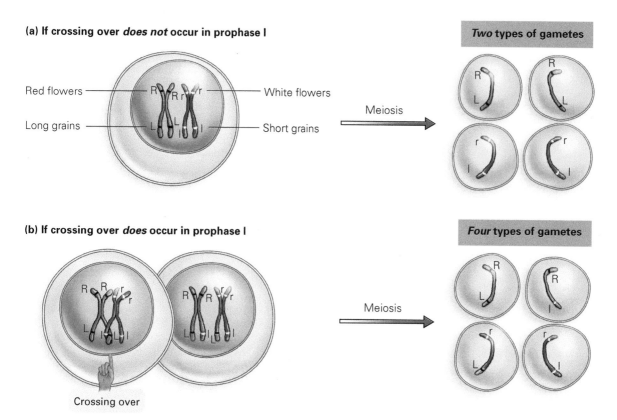

(a) If crossing over *does not* occur in prophase I

Red flowers

White flowers

Long grains

Short grains

Meiosis

Two **types of gametes**

(b) If crossing over *does* occur in prophase I

Crossing over

Meiosis

Four **types of gametes**

Figure 22 Crossing over. If a flower with the above arrangement of alleles undergoes meiosis, it can produce (a) two different types of gametes for these two genes if crossing over does not occur or (b) four different types of gametes for these two genes if crossing over occurs at L.

Random alignment of homologous pairs also increases the number of genetically distinct types of gametes that can be produced. Using Nicole's chromosomes as an example (**Figure 23**), let us assume that she did in fact inherit mutant versions of both the *BRCA2* and *HER2* genes and that these genes are located on different chromosomes. The arrangement of homologous pairs of chromosomes at metaphase I determines which chromosomes will end up together in a gamete. If we consider only these two homologous pairs of chromosomes, then two different alignments are possible, and four different gametes can be produced. For example, when Nicole produces egg cells, the two chromosomes that she inherited from her dad could move together to the gamete, leaving the two chromosomes she inherited from her mom to move to the other gamete. It is equally probable that Nicole could undergo meiosis in which one chromosome from each parent would align randomly together, resulting in two more types of gametes being produced.

Mistakes in Meiosis

Sometimes mistakes occur during meiosis that result in the production of offspring with too many or too few chromosomes. Too many or too few chromosomes can result when there is a failure of the homologues (or sister chromatids) to separate during meiosis. This failure of chromosomes to separate is termed **nondisjunction** (**Figure 24**). The presence of an extra chromosome is termed **trisomy.** The absence of one chromosome of a homologous pair is termed **monosomy.** Nondisjunction can occur on autosomes or sex chromosomes.

Because the X and Y sex chromosomes do not carry the same genes and are not the same size and shape, they are not considered to be a homologous pair.

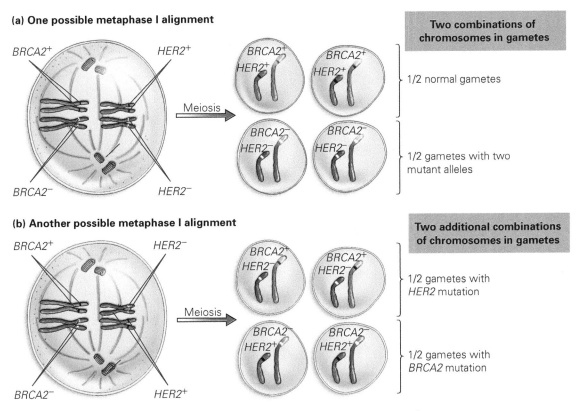

(a) One possible metaphase I alignment

$BRCA2^+$ $HER2^+$

Meiosis

Two combinations of chromosomes in gametes

$BRCA2^+$ $HER2^+$ $BRCA2^+$ $HER2^+$ — 1/2 normal gametes

$BRCA2^-$ $HER2^-$ $BRCA2^-$ $HER2^-$ — 1/2 gametes with two mutant alleles

$BRCA2^-$ $HER2^-$

(b) Another possible metaphase I alignment

$BRCA2^+$ $HER2^-$

Meiosis

Two additional combinations of chromosomes in gametes

$BRCA2^+$ $HER2^-$ $BRCA2^+$ $HER2^-$ — 1/2 gametes with *HER2* mutation

$BRCA2^-$ $HER2^+$ $BRCA2^-$ $HER2^+$ — 1/2 gametes with *BRCA2* mutation

$BRCA2^-$ $HER2^+$

Figure 23 Random alignment. Two possible alignments, (a) and (b), can occur when there are two homologous pairs of chromosomes. These different alignments can lead to novel combinations of genes in the gametes.
Visualize This: How many different alignments are possible with three homologous pairs of chromosomes?

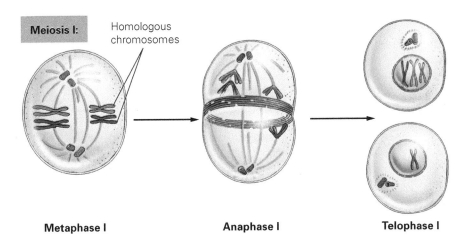

Meiosis I:

Homologous chromosomes

Metaphase I   Anaphase I   Telophase I

Figure 24 Nondisjunction. Nondisjunction during meiosis I produces gametes with too many and too few chromosomes.

There is, however, a region at the tip of each chromosome that is similar enough so that they can pair up during meiosis. Typically, early embryos with too many or too few chromosomes will die because they have too much or too little genetic information. However, in some situations, such as when the extra or missing chromosome is very small (such as in chromosomes 13, 18, and 21) or contains very little genetic information (such as the Y chromosome or an X chromosome that will later be inactivated), the embryo can survive. **Table 2** (on the next page) lists some chromosomal anomalies in humans that are compatible with life.

TABLE 2

Autosomal and sex-linked chromosomal anomalies.

Conditions Caused by Nondisjunction of Autosomes	Comments
Trisomy 21—Down syndrome	Affected individuals are mentally retarded and have abnormal skeletal development and heart defects. The frequency of Down syndrome increases with parental age. Down syndrome among the children of parents over 40 occurs in 6 per 1000 births, which is six times higher than the rate found among the children of couples under 35 years old.
Trisomy 13—Patau syndrome	Affected individuals are mentally retarded and deaf and have a cleft lip and palate. Approximately 1 in 5000 newborns is affected.
Trisomy 18—Edwards syndrome	Affected individuals have malformed organs, ears, mouth, and nose, leading to an elfin appearance. These babies usually die within 6 months of birth. Approximately 1 in 6000 newborns is affected.

Conditions Caused by Nondisjunction of Sex Chromosomes	Comments
XO—Turner Syndrome	Females with one X chromosome can be sterile if their ovaries fail to develop. Webbing of the neck, shorter stature, and hearing impairment are also common. Approximately 1 in 5000 female newborns is born with only one X chromosome. Turner syndrome is the only human monosomy that is viable.
Trisomy X: Meta female	Females with three X chromosomes tend to develop normally. Approximately 1 in 1000 females is born with an extra X chromosome.
XXY—Kleinfelter syndrome	Males with the XXY genotype are less fertile than XY males; have small testes, sparse body hair, some breast enlargement; and may have mental retardation. Testosterone injections can reverse some of the anatomical abnormalities in the approximately 1 in 1000 males with this condition.
XYY condition	Males with two Y chromosomes tend to be taller than average but have an otherwise normal male phenotype. Approximately 1 in 1000 newborn males has an extra Y chromosome.

From the previous discussions, you have learned that cells undergo mitosis for growth and repair and meiosis to produce gametes. **Figure 25** compares the significant features of mitosis and meiosis.

It is now possible to revisit the question of whether Nicole will pass on cancer-causing genes to any children she may have. Because Nicole developed cancer at such a young age, it seems likely that she may have inherited at least one mutant cell-cycle control gene; thus, she may or may not pass that gene on. If Nicole has both a normal and a mutant version of a cell-cycle control gene, then she will be able to make gametes with and without the mutant allele. Therefore, she could pass on the mutant allele if a gamete containing that allele is involved in fertilization. We have also seen that it takes many "hits" or mutations for a cancer to develop. Therefore, even if Nicole does pass

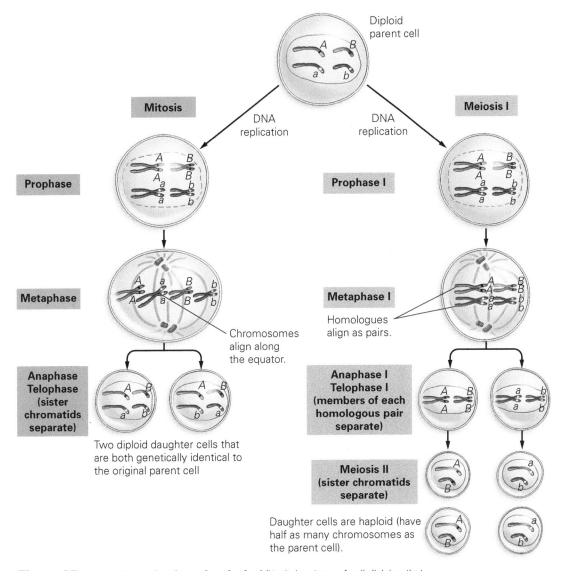

Figure 25 Comparing mitosis and meiosis. Mitosis is a type of cell division that occurs in somatic cells and gives rise to daughter cells that are exact genetic copies of the parent cell. Meiosis occurs in cells that will give rise to gametes and decreases the chromosome number by one-half. To do this and still ensure that each gamete receives one member of each homologous pair, the two members of each homologous pair align across the equator at the metaphase I of meiosis and are separated from each other during anaphase I.

on one or a few mutant versions of cell-cycle control genes to a child, environmental conditions will dictate whether enough other mutations will accumulate to allow a cancer to develop.

Mutations caused by environmental exposures are not passed from parents to children unless the mutation happens to occur in a cell of the gonads that will be used to produce a gamete. Nicole's cancer occurred in the ovary, the site of meiosis, but not all cells in the ovary undergo meiosis. Nicole's cancer originated in the outer covering of the ovary, a tissue that does not undergo meiosis. The cells involved in ovulation are located inside the ovary. A skin cancer that develops from exposure to ultraviolet light will not be passed on, and the same is true for most of the mutations that Nicole obtained from environmental exposures. Therefore, for any children that Nicole (or any of us) might have, it is the combined effects of inherited mutant alleles and any mutations induced by environmental exposures that will determine whether cancers will develop.

SAVVY READER

Alternative Cancer Treatments

One website claims that 80% of cancer therapies are blocked by the patient's emotions and that these blocks can be removed by a technique called tapping. Just buy the CD, follow the tapping instructions, and you will feel better in no time. Another website claims that sharks do not get cancer and that taking shark-cartilage supplements can help treat cancer. In a study of the effectiveness of shark cartilage, the study authors report that 15 of 29 patients diagnosed with terminal cancer were still alive 1 year after beginning to take the supplements, which is "a remarkable result by any measure," according to the study authors.

Websites for alternative cancer treatment centers offer unproven treatments to patients that cost tens of thousands of dollars and are not covered by insurance. These treatments are often supervised by actual medical doctors. These sites are filled with testimonials, but no data, about the effectiveness of such treatments.

1. Is there any guarantee that something written on a website is true?

2. The website that suggested that emotions can block cancer therapies presented no evidence to back up this claim. What would you do if you wanted to know whether that claim had any merit?

3. The study on shark cartilage was published in a non-peer reviewed journal. Does this fact add or subtract from the credibility of this article?

4. What other information do you need to determine whether the one-year survival rate of the shark cartilage study has any real meaning?

5. Would the fact that the author of the shark cartilage study owns a company that sells the product make you more or less skeptical of his findings? What about the fact that sharks actually do get cancer?

6. While most medical doctors have dedicated their lives to helping people in need, a few will promote products and services simply to make money. Should you always believe the word of someone with an advanced degree?

7. Why do you think that so many people fall prey to dubious cancer cures?

Chapter Review

Learning Outcomes

MasteringBIOLOGY

Go to the Study Area at www.masteringbiology.com for practice quizzes, myeBook, BioFlix™ 3-D animations, MP3Tutor sessions, videos, current events, and more.

LO1 Describe the cellular basis of cancer (Section 1).

• Unregulated cell division can lead to the formation of a tumor.

LO2 Compare and contrast benign and malignant tumors (Section 1).

• Benign or noncancerous tumors stay in one place and do not prevent surrounding organs from functioning. Malignant tumors are those that are invasive or those that metastasize to surrounding tissues, starting new cancers.

LO3 List several risk factors for cancer development (Section 1).

• Risk factors for cancer include smoking, a poor diet, lack of exercise, obesity, alcohol use, and aging.

LO4 List the normal functions of cell division (Section 2).

• Cell division is a process required for growth and development.

LO5 Describe the structure and function of chromosomes (Section 2).

• Chromosomes are composed of DNA wrapped around proteins. Chromosomes carry genes.

LO6 Outline the process of DNA replication (Section 2).

• During DNA replication or synthesis, one strand of the double-stranded DNA molecule is used as a template for the synthesis of a new daughter strand of DNA. The newly synthesized DNA strand is complementary to the parent strand. The enzyme DNA polymerase ties together the nucleotides on the daughter strand.

LO7 Describe the events that occur during interphase of the cell cycle (Section 3).

• Interphase consists of two gap phases of the cell cycle (G_1 and G_2), during which the cell grows and prepares to enter mitosis or meiosis, and the S (synthesis) phase, during which time the DNA replicates. The S phase of interphase occurs between G_1 and G_2.

LO8 Diagram two chromosomes as they proceed through mitosis of the cell cycle (Section 3).

• During mitosis, the sister chromatids are separated from each other into daughter cells. During prophase, the replicated DNA condenses into linear chromosomes. At metaphase, these replicated chromosomes align across the middle of the cell. At anaphase, the sister chromatids separate from each other and align at opposite poles of the cells. At telophase, a nuclear envelope re-forms around the chromosomes lying at each pole.

LO9 Describe the process of cytokinesis in animal and plant cells (Section 3).

• Cytokinesis is the last phase of the cell cycle. During cytokinesis, the cytoplasm is divided into two portions, one for each daughter cell.

LO10 Describe how the cell cycle is regulated and how dysregulation can lead to tumor formation (Section 4).

• When cell division is working properly, it is a tightly controlled process. Normal cells divide only when conditions are favorable. Proteins survey the cell and its environment at checkpoints as the cell moves through G_1, G_2, and metaphase, and can halt cell division if conditions are not favorable. Mistakes in regulating the cell cycle arise when genes that control the cell cycle are mutated. Proto-oncogenes regulate the cell cycle. Oncogenes are mutated versions of these genes. Tumor suppressors are normal genes that can encode proteins to stop cell division if conditions are not favorable and can repair damage to the DNA. They serve as backups in case the proto-oncogenes undergo mutation.

LO11 Explain how genes and environment both impact cancer risk (Section 4).

• Mutated genes can be inherited, or mutations can be caused by exposure to carcinogens.

LO12 Discuss the various methods of cancer detection and treatment (Section 5).

• A biopsy is a common method for detecting cancer. It involves removing some cells or tissues suspected of being cancerous and analyzing them. Typical cancer treatments include chemotherapy, which involves injecting chemicals that kill rapidly dividing cells, and radiation, which involves killing tumor cells by exposing them to high-energy particles.

LO13 Explain what types of cells undergo meiosis, the end result of this process, and how meiosis increases genetic diversity (Section 6).

- Meiosis is a type of sexual cell division, occurring in cells, that gives rise to gametes. Gametes contain half as many chromosomes as somatic cells do. The reduction of chromosome number that occurs during meiosis begins with diploid cells and ends with haploid cells.
- Meiosis is preceded by an interphase stage in which the DNA is replicated. During meiosis I, the members of a homologous pair of chromosomes are separated from each other. During meiosis II, the sister chromatids are separated from each other.

LO14 Diagram four chromosomes from a diploid organism undergoing meiosis (Section 6).

- Homologues align in pairs during meiosis I and as individual chromosomes at metaphase II.

LO15 Explain the significance of crossing over and random alignment in terms of genetic diversity (Section 6).

- Homologous pairs of chromosomes exchange genetic information during crossing over at prophase I of meiosis, thereby increasing the number of genetically distinct gametes that an individual can produce. The alignment of members of a homologous pair at metaphase I is random with regard to which member of a pair faces which pole. This random alignment of homologous chromosomes increases the number of different kinds of gametes an individual can produce.

Roots to Remember

The following roots of words come mainly from Latin and Greek and will help you decipher terms:

cyto- and **-cyte** relate to cells. Chapter term: cytoplasm

-kinesis means motion. Chapter term: cytokinesis

meio- means to make smaller. Chapter term: meiosis

mito- means a thread. Chapter term: mitosis

onco- means cancer. Chapter term: oncogene

proto- means before. Chapter term: proto-oncogene

soma- and **-some** mean body. Chapter terms: somatic and chromosome

telo- means end or completion. Chapter term: telophase

Learning the Basics

1. **LO8 LO14** List the ways in which mitosis and meiosis differ.

2. **LO12** What property of cancer cells do chemotherapeutic agents attempt to exploit?

3. **LO8** A cell that begins mitosis with 46 chromosomes produces daughter cells with _____.

   A. 13 chromosomes; **B.** 23 chromosomes;
   C. 26 chromosomes; **D.** 46 chromosomes

4. **LO5** The centromere is a region at which _____.

   A. sister chromatids are attached to each other;
   B. metaphase chromosomes align; **C.** the tips of chromosomes are found; **D.** the nucleus is located

5. **LO4 LO8** Mitosis _____.

   A. occurs in cells that give rise to gametes; **B.** produces haploid cells from diploid cells; **C.** produces daughter cells that are exact genetic copies of the parent cell; **D.** consists of two separate divisions, mitosis I and mitosis II

6. **LO4 LO8** At metaphase of mitosis, _____.

   A. the chromosomes are condensed and found at the poles; **B.** the chromosomes are composed of one sister chromatid; **C.** cytokinesis begins; **D.** the chromosomes are composed of two sister chromatids and are lined up along the equator of the cell

7. **LO5** Sister chromatids _____.

   A. are two different chromosomes attached to each other; **B.** are exact copies of one chromosome that are attached to each other; **C.** arise from the centrioles; **D.** are broken down by mitosis; **E.** are chromosomes that carry different genes

8. **LO6** DNA polymerase _____.

   A. attaches sister chromatids at the centromere;
   B. synthesizes daughter DNA molecules from fats and phospholipids; **C.** is the enzyme that facilitates DNA synthesis; **D.** causes cancer cells to stop dividing

9. **LO13** After telophase I of meiosis, each daughter cell is _____.

   A. diploid, and the chromosomes are composed of one doublestranded DNA molecule; **B.** diploid, and the chromosomes are composed of two sister chromatids; **C.** haploid, and the chromosomes are composed of one double-stranded DNA molecule; **D.** haploid, and the chromosomes are composed of two sister chromatids

10. **LO15** List two things that happen during meiosis that increase genetic diversity.

11. **LO10** Define the terms *proto-oncogene* and *oncogene*.

12. **LO7 LO9** In what ways is the cell cycle similar in plant and animal cells, and in what ways does it differ?

13. **LO14** State whether the chromosomes depicted in parts (a)–(d) of **Figure 26** are haploid or diploid.

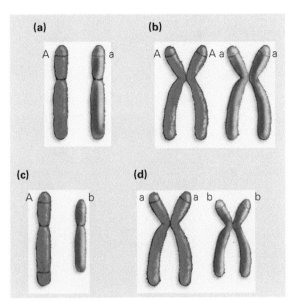

(a) A a
(b) A A a a
(c) A b
(d) a a b b

Figure 26 Haploid or diploid chromosomes?

Analyzing and Applying the Basics

1. **LO3 LO11** Would a skin cell mutation that your father obtained from using tanning beds make you more likely to get cancer? Why or why not?
2. **LO2** Will all tumors progress to cancers?
3. **LO12** Why are some cancers treated with radiation therapy while others are treated with chemotherapy?

Connecting the Science

1. Should members of society be forced to pay the medical bills of smokers when the cancer risk from smoking is so evident and publicized? Explain your reasoning.
2. Would you want to be tested for the presence of cell-cycle control mutations? How would knowing whether you had some mutated proto-oncogenes be of benefit or harm?

ANSWERS

STOP & STRETCH
1. If a cell has many mutations, it is better that it is not allowed to continue to replicate.
2. DNA is semi-conservatively replicated; that is, each strand serves as a template for the synthesis of a new strand. Photocopying is completely conservative. One copy is conserved and the other is new.
3. Descent with modification explains the existence of similar processes in distantly related organisms.
4. Tissues and organs will cease functioning as cells reach their cell division limit.
5. Because it damages DNA.
6. Both meiosis I and mitosis produce two daughter cells. Meiosis I differs from mitosis in that meiosis I separates homologous pairs of chromosomes from each other. Mitosis does not do this.

VISUALIZE THIS
Figure 5: Four DNA molecules would be produced. Two of those would be all purple; two would be half purple, half red.
Figure 10: The cell should be prevented from passing the G2 checkpoint.
Figure 18: The X chromosome is the larger of the two and carries more genetic information.
Figure 22: No
Figure 25: 4

SAVVY READER
1. No
2. Check some highly regarded sources. Ideally peer reviewed literature. Otherwise check reputable websites and see if there is a consensus.
3. Subtract
4. In addition to controlling for type of cancer, age of patient, etc., it is imperative to know what percentage of people not taking the supplement were alive one year after taking the supplement.
5. more skeptical; more skeptical
6. An advanced degree is not a guarantee that a person will act in your best interest.
7. Desperation is one reason.

LEARNING THE BASICS
1. Mitosis occurs in somatic cells, meiosis in cells that give rise to gametes. Mitosis produces daughter cells that are genetically identical to parent cells, while meiosis produces daughter cells with novel combinations of chromosomes and half as many chromosomes as compared to parent cells.
2. Rapid cell division
3. d; **4.** a; **5.** c; **6.** d; **7.** b; **8.** c; **9.** d
   10. a, diploid; b, diploid; c, haploid; d, haploid
   11. Crossing over and random alignment of the homologues
   12. Oncogenes are mutated versions of proto-oncogenes.
   13. Cytokinesis in plant cells requires the building of a cell wall.

ANALYZING AND APPLYING THE BASICS

1. No. Only mutations in cells that produce gametes are passed to offspring.

2. No, but more cell divisions means more opportunities for mutations to occur.

3. Cancers that are thought to be localized (not yet spread) are treated with radiation.